# THE HOUSE
# THAT
# JACK BUILT

# THE HOUSE
# THAT
# JACK BUILT

The True Story
Behind The Marsden Grotto
and the Search for Buried Roman Treasure

by

Michael J. Hallowell

AMBERLEY

*To the memory of my late grandmother
Joan Hallowell*

*This book could not have been written
without her help and inspiration*

First published 2008

Amberley Publishing Plc
Cirencester Road, Chalford,
Stroud, Gloucestershire, GL6 8PE

www.amberley-books.com

British Library Cataloguing in Publication Data.
A catalogue record for this book is available from the British Library.

isbn 978 1 84868 067 8

Typesetting and Origination by Diagraf (www.diagraf.net)
Printed in Great Britain

# CONTENTS

# ACKNOWLEDGEMENTS

*Alan Robinson*, author and local historian, for allowing me to quote from his own work on the history of Marsden Bay and for supplying some of the photographs used in this book. / The staff and experts at *Arbeia Roman Fort*, for helping me understand more clearly what circumstances were like during the Roman occupation of Britain. / The current custodians of *The Marsden Grotto, Bev and Paul Wright-Simpson,* for allowing me to take photographs in the premises and for their assistance in numerous other ways. / Fellow author *Darren W. Ritson,* for his friendship and permission to use photographs of the *Arbeia Roman Fort.* / *David Bell,* author of *Garibaldi in Shields,* for allowing me to quote from the aforementioned work, for the photograph of *Garibaldi in Shields* and for the benefit of his insight. / *The Department of Prehistoric and Romano-British Antiquities* at *The British Museum,* for information regarding the recording of antiquity sales in Victorian England. / *The descendants of Peter Allan,* including *Roy Allan, Archie Allan and Pat Moore,* for anecdotal tales supplied to me several years ago when I began my research, several of which are recounted here. Also thanks to Pat for permission to use a picture of Peter Allan. / *Doreen Monteiro,* of the *Caer Urfa Heritage Association,* for supplying information regarding her ancestor William Yellowly, and for providing other vital leads. / *Eric Morton,* taxidermist, and *the staff of the Hancock Museum* in Newcastle Upon Tyne, for helping me in my [as yet] unsuccessful quest to find Ralphy the Raven, and for information supplied regarding the activites of William Yellowly, naturalist. / The late *Evelyn Waugh-Almond,* archaeologist, for information regarding the history of *Arbeia Roman Fort* and other historical detail, and for permission to use an old photograph of *The Marsden Grotto* and the "Monkwearmouth Monster". / *The Friends of South Tyneside Museum and Art Gallery,* for giving me a public platform from which to air my admittedly controversial ideas. / The numerous *H. M. Revenue & Customs* officials, both in Tyneside and in London, who helped me with my research. / *Jon Downes,* editor, author and researcher, for writing the foreword to this book and casting his seasoned eye over the draft manuscript. I will be forever in his debt for this and much else. / *Hildred Whale, Keith Bardwell, Ann Sharp, Doris Johnson and other present (and former) staff at South Tyneside Central Library* and *Local Studies Library,* for putting me in touch with the relatives of Peter Allan and Sidney Milnes-Hawkes, and for being helpful in so many other ways. Also for permission to quote from Amy Flagg's book, *Notes on the History of Shipbuilding in South Shields, 1746 to 1946* and *The Borough of South Shields* by George B. Hodgson. / *Kathleen Hardy*, descendant of Sidney Milnes-Hawkes, for valuable information regarding one of *The Marsden Grotto's* most enigmatic and interesting characters. / *Ken Fenton* and the staff of *InBiz* at Newcastle Upon Tyne. Your advice and guidance will never be forgotten. / *Natalie Lisbona*, for steering me through a hundred and one professional minefields, and for her incredible support and encouragement. / *Nick and Sue Garvey* and their family, who were pillars of encouragement and support during my quest to find out the truth concerning *The Marsden Grotto.* They inherited a precious mantle and treated it with the reverence it deserves. I will never forget their co-operation, kindness and patience. / *Peter S, "Jonty", Alex Fowlie, Barry Clark* and the other ex-miners who told me everything they knew about those strange tunnels under the South Shields coastline. / *The Public Records Office* at Kew, for detailed information regarding the activities of the "Preventives" during the eighteenth and nineteenth centuries. / The late *Ronnie Ward*, former Hoist Man at *The Marsden Grotto Inn*, and his wife Lorna, for welcoming me into their home and sharing with me the evidence which Ronnie had the wisdom to both remember and record. / *The Shields Gazette*, for allowing me access to their archives and for permission to quote from relevant editions of the paper. / The staff at the *South Tyneside Museum and Art Gallery*, for supplying me with information about the life of William Yellowly. / *Sybil Reeder*, of Whitburn Local History Society, for supplying genealogical information and other details about the Williamson family. / *Vaux Inns, Ltd*, and their parent company the *Swallow Group*, and especially *Hilary Florek*, for allowing me unlimited access to their archives and for allowing me to quote liberally from the several booklets they have released over the decades dealing with the history of *The Marsden Grotto Inn*. / The *many readers* of my *WraithScape* column in the *Shields Gazette* who have written in or e-mailed me with fascinating anecdotes about Peter

Allan and other famous Marsden personages. / *Ivor Muncey*, for supplying other rare photographs of *The Marsden Grotto*. / Last, but most certainly not least, my dear wife *Jackie*. Writing this book has taken several years out of our lives. Never once has she complained or murmured, giving me unstinting support whilst continually making great sacrifices to fund my research. I owe her a debt that I will never be able to repay.

# FOREWORD

I first met Mike Hallowell when I was the editor of a magazine to which he contributed regularly, and I remember being impressed by both his meticulous research and his engaging writing style. When he asked me to write the foreword for this book I was happy – as well as honoured – to accept the offer.

Despite the many fine articles he has written for me during our professional relationship, I must confess to being completely unprepared to discover what a truly remarkable book this is. As a dyed-in-the-wool student of Forteana, it never ceases to amaze me how strange the world is. I have made a career out of travelling to obscure parts of the globe and collating a veritable catalogue of 'high strangeness' stories associated with those near-flung and far-flung regions. I have done it for southern Cornwall, east Devon and even the island of Puerto Rico, amongst others, but now my humble efforts have been totally eclipsed by this remarkable book. Where I have written books about reasonably small geographical areas, Mike Hallowell has managed to take this *modus operandi* to extremes and pen an entire volume about one building.

But what starts off as a relatively simple investigation into the history of a lonely pub near the Tyneside town of South Shields soon turns into something far more peculiar; a tale of political intrigue and a search for a hoard of hidden Roman treasure. In this remarkable book Mike Hallowell weaves a complex web of interlocking stories, which eventually coalesce together to reach a completely stunning conclusion.

Both as a consummate storyteller and as a researcher worthy of note Mike Hallowell has produced a remarkable volume that should be on the bookshelf of every local historian and Fortean investigator alike.

Jon Downes,
Exeter, April 2008

# INTRODUCTION

This book reveals, for the first time, the true facts about one of the most bizarre treasure hunts in recorded history.

The legend of the mysterious character known as Blaster Jack, and his successors, is strange indeed. It really begins with an eighteenth-century quarryman and his wife who were forced, through financial impoverishment, to leave their rented home and find other accommodation. In time they ended up living in a cave by the sea at a strange place called Marsden Bay. Then they stumbled upon a secret which had lain dormant for the better part of 2000 years; a secret which had in part been carefully maintained by a group of strange mystics who's true nature, character and mission we have only recently begun to understand.

I first began to research the history of Marsden from a very particular perspective. Throughout the north east of England there are literally scores of legends concerning sea monsters and dragons, and it is a little-known fact that a dragon-based cult existed in pre-Roman Britain and may actually have survived into the twenty first century. During my research I accumulated many details concerning the lives of numerous mystics, seers and other assorted characters that lived at or frequented Marsden Bay, in South Tyneside, over a period of several centuries. Many of these, indeed most, were either directly or indirectly associated with the aforementioned cult. This dragon-centred 'order' actually believed that a species of leviathan-like aquatic creature – sea monsters, if you will – inhabited a vast complex of underground tunnels and caverns beneath Marsden Bay and much of the North Sea. Two of my colleagues at the Centre for Fortean Zoology, Jonathan Downes and Richard Freeman, are currently working with me on a book about this extremely mysterious religious fraternity.

During our research we initially blundered into a historical cul-de-sac, which, fortunately, we were later able to extricate ourselves from. Had we not made this error, it is unlikely that you would be reading the book that you now hold in your hands. This in itself needs some explanation.

As our investigations progressed we eventually discovered that the strange mystics and dragon-cult adherents saw themselves as guardians, posted to watch over numerous entrances to this subterranean complex. Their function – at least from their own perspective – was two-fold. They were there to protect the 'wyrms' or dragons from the interference of prying humans, but also to protect human beings from the dragons themselves.

Now it just so happened that one of the main entrances to this subterranean tunnel network lay within the large cliff-face at Marsden Bay. Over a period of nearly 1000 years, cult members arrived at and departed from the bay in succession. This is no fantasy; their peculiar lives and strange antics are detailed in contemporary literature of the time. All that escaped the notice of the local populace was the real reason for their presence.

There is another weird legend attached to Marsden Bay, and one which is almost certainly not connected to the first, other than that it is set in the same geographical location. Generations ago, when the Roman armies pulled out of Britain, they deserted a large fort at South Shields known as Arbeia. There have long been legends that, just before the Legionaries departed, they stashed away a huge hoard of treasure in the caves at Marsden and never returned to claim it. Some believe it is still there to this day. Our initial belief was that the hermits and seers at Marsden were simply a loosely connected bunch of treasure seekers, all out to find that elusive hoard of Roman coinage and silverware. We discovered our error, and came to see that their presence had little or nothing to do with the alleged treasure, and everything to do with the *wyrms* or dragons that they believed lived beneath the coastline. Our research did not answer all the questions about the mysterious dragon cult, obviously, but it answered many. But what about the other, probably unrelated tale about buried Roman treasure? During our research into the dragon cult we uncovered a wealth of historical information that was unconnected to the subject matter of our research, but presented us with another mystery that was equally as baffling. It seemed likely that the Romans had indeed secreted away treasure in the cliffs at Marsden, and centuries later; that treasure was stumbled upon almost by accident.

This book concerns a group of persons well known to South Tynesiders in local history and folklore. What is *not* well known is the monumental effort made by those aware of the treasure's existence, to get their hands on it. Their efforts – coloured by intense political intrigue and Machiavellian cunning – even involved the Chancellor of the Exchequer of the day.

In putting to bed one mystery, then, we inadvertently stumbled upon another. The story of the Marsden Bay treasure hunt has not yet ended by any stretch of the imagination. To this day, new characters are being drifted in to play their part in the drama, and others – gracefully or otherwise – exit the stage when their part is done. I do not know if or when the play will end. What I do know is that those who pay their entrance fee and sit through the performance are never disappointed.

Like all good adventure stories, this one contains its own 'Indiana Jones' hero in the shape of a man called Peter Allan. No scriptwriter could have dreamed up such an intriguing character, and I remain amazed that no one has, as yet, made a film of his life or written his biography. By writing this book I hope at least in part to rectify this situation.

Researching this book has changed my entire perception of the world in which I live. There is a powerful presence at Marsden Bay that has the ability to wrench people from the 'real' world and plunge them into a surreal dimension, which is both breathtaking and wonderful. And yet I can assure you that this book is entirely factual. I have spent hundreds of hours accumulating historical evidence and eyewitness testimony to prove my case, unbelievable though my conclusions may seem to many. To those who doubt, I say, "come to Marsden Bay yourself and do your own research. Then you will see".

I am aware, of course, that it may not be the facts that some historians and researchers take issue with, but rather my admittedly shocking interpretation of them. There are good folk who have helped me enormously in my research, and I suspect that the contents of this book may irritate them, particularly when my theories jar sharply with their own, more orthodox perceptions. All I would ask is that they try to refrain from becoming irate simply because I interpret history in a different (and certainly more colourful) way. I have tried to be as conscientious as I can, but, being only human, I may have made the odd mistake here and there. If so, then I welcome constructive correction.

This story has been locked away for far too long, a neglected jewel in the historical crown of the North East of England. It is high time the story was told.

Welcome to the lair of the smuggler. Welcome to the darker watches of the night. *Welcome to the House that Jack Built.*

Michael J. Hallowell
West Boldon, 2008

# CHAPTER 1

# WHISPERED LEGENDS

Ever since childhood I had heard whispered legends about Marsden Bay: Tales about a strange public house – *The Marsden Grotto Inn* – that was supposedly haunted. I had heard rumours of a weird ritual; something about a pint of beer being left on the bar counter every night to quench the thirst of a ghost who resided there. In the morning the beer would be gone.

But it was all very tongue-in-cheek. The landlord really drank the ale when no one else was looking, of course. But it was a ripping yarn, as they say, and probably good for business.

There were other rumours, however. Tales of smugglers who frequented the area centuries ago, for instance. Some spoke of buried treasure left behind by pirates; pirates who sailed off across the North Sea in search of adventure and planned to return one day for their booty. But in reality they sailed off into the uncharted waters of oblivion, never to return. Their treasure, say some, still lies buried at the foot of Marsden's treacherous cliffs.

Talk to any South Tynesider, and the chances are they will have heard about 'The Grotto Ghost'. They will also probably be rather vague on the details. They know it is something to do with a smuggler. Or perhaps a pirate. And that he was murdered there. Or did he murder someone else? And then he – or some other person – buried some treasure. Or took it abroad on a ship. But putting aside the infinite variations on the theme, they *all* know that his ghost haunts *The Marsden Grotto Inn*.

Although the history of Marsden *per se* has been detailed in various tomes, relatively little has been written about what is undoubtedly the most colourful piece of its historical tapestry; namely, *The Marsden Grotto Inn* and the smugglers who lived nearby and plied their nefarious trade around it. A relatively small number of people have bothered to research the truth behind the legend. Local historians have scrutinised Marsden's past from time to time, and the Vaux Company, until relatively recently possessors of the inn in one form or another since 1898, periodically released short booklets on the building's history for promotional purposes. I have three in my possession, and there may well have been more. Unfortunately, these short works did not receive a wide circulation. *The Borough of South Shields* by George B. Hodgson[1] does mention Blaster Jack and one or two other local characters, but in reality furnishes no more detail than the Vaux booklets. Perhaps the best conventional history of Marsden written to date is *The Story of Marsden and Peter Allan*[2] by local historian Alan C. Robinson. Sadly, this excellent work was neither appreciated nor as widely read, as it should have been. Consequently, although South Tynesiders all know about *The Grotto* and its reputation, few can put any meat on the historical bones when pushed. Strangely, this dearth of factual information has helped spawn a wonderful variety of inaccurate but fascinating rumours. Distracting though they may be for serious researchers, even I must admit that they have nevertheless coloured the legend wonderfully and given it an irresistible romantic appeal

All these wonderful tales I heard as a child, but for some reason they did not fascinate me. They should have, for as every schoolboy of my era knows, pirateering legends have a powerful magnetism. But they did not, and that was that.

Until I received a telephone call from my mother...

## References

[1] Hodgson, George B: *The Borough of South Shields* (South Tyneside Libraries, 1996) ISBN: 0906617 25 1
[2] Alan C. Robinson, *The Story of Marsden and Peter Allan* (published privately by the author, 1971).

# CHAPTER 2

# THE HOIST MAN'S TALE

For a decade now I have penned a column in South Tyneside's local newspaper, *The Shields Gazette*. The column, entitled 'WraithScape', deals with all aspects of the paranormal. Readers will send me their tales of ghosts, goblins, UFO sightings and things that go bump in the night, and I will write them up in an unashamedly populist and entertaining manner. But the stories are, as far as I am able to ascertain, all true; or at least, the experiences are sincere, which I readily admit is not exactly the same thing.

Initially the then editor of the *Gazette*, Rob Lawson, had intended to run the column for a few months – perhaps two or three – to gauge its popularity. Rob quite rightly wondered how many stories the column could cover before it ran out of steam. Fortunately, for every one that was published two or three more were generated, and so 'WraithScape' still fills up half a page of the *Shields Gazette* every Thursday evening. My family and friends are good sources of stories too.

It was 11 am on a Sunday morning when the telephone rang. My mother had been talking to my now-deceased stepfather, David Ward, about one of my published articles, and they had hit upon an idea for a story for the column. My stepfather had casually mentioned that his brother, Ronnie, had worked as a lift attendant for many years at *The Marsden Grotto Inn*. *The Marsden Grotto Inn* has not always carried that name. Over the centuries it has been blessed with a number of epithets, including the *Cave Bar*, *The Tam O'Shanter* and, briefly, *Smuggler Jack's*. Most people still refer to the inn as *The Grotto*, however, and so during most of the pages ahead I will speak of it as such.

As will become clear later in this volume, *The Marsden Grotto Inn* is situated in a most unusual location, nestling at the foot of a craggy and treacherous cliff on the northeast coastline. For well over a century it was only accessible by a flight of steep steps that lead from the cliff tops of Marsden to the beach below. These steps will play an interesting part in our story as it unfolds. In 1938, the now defunct Vaux Company bought *The Grotto* outright and began an extensive renovation and refurbishment programme. This included the installation of an elevator – colloquially known as 'The Hoist' – to provide easier accessibility to *The Grotto* from the cliff top. Until recently, provision was always made for a lift attendant to ferry passengers back and forth, or rather up and down. Ronnie Ward was one of many who had that privilege. I had never covered the 'Grotto ghost' in my column, and my mother and stepfather both thought that a chat with Ronnie may unearth some good material for a story. Dave thought that Ronnie may even have had one or two close encounters with the apparition himself, and that was enough to convince me that I should pay him a visit. At 6.30 pm that same evening I knocked on his door.

I had only met Ronnie and his wife Lorna once before, briefly, at my mother and stepfather's wedding. I honestly could not remember him, and would probably not have recognised him had we passed in the street. Nevertheless, both Ronnie and Lorna made us welcome, and I warmed to their openness and humour. Ronnie was more than willing to talk about his time as 'the Hoist Man', a position that he held for some nine years, from April 1989 until his retirement in 1998.

Ronnie said that during his employment at *The Grotto* he had experienced numerous bizarre happenings. He had also spoken to other staff members who had related similar tales, but it will prove helpful, perhaps, if I detail at this stage Ronnie's version of the 'Grotto Ghost' story. This will, I believe, validate my earlier statement that the tale has been repeatedly embellished and reinterpreted. Interestingly, however, it became clear when I was interviewing Ronnie and others that, although the tale had changed from one teller to another, certain core features had remained intact:

MH: Ronnie, tell me what you know about the *Marsden Grotto* Ghost.
RW: Well, part of the pub is actually set into a cave wall at the foot of the cliffs. In the early days it – the cave – was lived in by a smuggler called Blaster Jack.
MH: What do you know about this Blaster Jack?
RW: Like I say, he was a smuggler. He lived in the cave which is now the back bar of the pub.
MH: What happened to him?
RW: Well, they also called him Jibber John. They called him that because he 'jibbed' on his mates to the authorities. But his mates caught him out, and they killed him.

MH: How did they do that?

RW: Well, they got him in the cave where they used to store their stuff. Now at that time there was a shaft leading from the cave roof to the cliff top up above. When the Customs men [1] weren't around Jack and his mates would haul their booty up the shaft to the top. Their mates would then hide it until the coast was clear. Now they knocked Jack – or John – out and stuffed him in this wicker basket – or as some say a barrel. They hauled him up to the top and left him there to rot. They just left him hanging there in the shaft. No one could hear him.

MH: And the ghost that haunts *The Grotto* is Blaster Jack?

RW: As far as I understand it.

After talking to Ronnie, a picture was beginning to coalesce in my mind. A smuggler called Blaster Jack had, for some strange reason, actually lived in a cave within the cliff face at Marsden. Some other smugglers had killed Jack because he had betrayed them to the Customs men. Then, unknown persons had enlarged and refurbished Jack's dwelling and made it into a public house. This public house was now known as *The Grotto*. So far, so good.

But Ronnie had more to say. He eventually went on to tell me something else that would be of great significance to the Marsden Bay enigma.

## References

[1] The Customs Officers were commonly called "Preventives" in the eighteenth and nineteenth centuries.

CHAPTER 3

# THE LANDLORD'S TALE

At the time I interviewed Ronnie Ward, Nick Garvey was actually the licensee and tenant of *The Grotto*, but as pub managers are usually referred to as 'Landlord' I will try not to break with tradition.

I telephoned Nick on Monday, 26th April 1999. He immediately agreed to see me, so I arranged to go on the following Friday morning when things would be relatively quiet. I had never been in *The Grotto* before, and as I stepped through the door several days later it dawned on me that I was now entering the abode of the spectral Blaster Jack. I wasn't sure what to expect.

Physically, Nick Garvey is a giant. He also has searching, intense eyes, which betray an intellect as sharp as any razor shell, which lies upon the nearby beach. He has a well-kept beard, which, in some fitting way, would make him look perfectly at home in *The Grotto* in any era. I had a beard too, then, and as any beardee will tell you, there is an instant commune between those who have chosen to grow facial hair. He had a beard, and I had a beard. "Good start", I thought. When I first approached the table at which he sat he clasped my hand with a vice-like grip and smiled genially. He then asked one of his staff to bring me a coffee.

After introducing myself formally I waited for a response. Quietly, Nick sucked on his pipe and eyed me up. I later told his wife, Sue, that I almost expected him to say, in an intense Devonshire accent, "Oooh-arrrh! So ye want to heeeer about Blasturr Jaaack, dooo-eeee?" He didn't, of course, but *The Grotto* is a place that gently slides both the intellect and the emotions into a bygone era of pirates, doubloons and flintlock pistols, and it does so without the unsuspecting visitor even being aware of it.

I told Nick about my conversation with Ronnie the Hoist Man, and related 'The Grotto Ghost' story as Ronnie had told it to me. It soon became clear that Nick had done his homework since becoming the landlord, and knew infinitely more about *The Grotto* than anyone else I'd met up to that juncture. He also set me straight on several points. What I'd been told by Ronnie was simply one of the variant legends of The Grotto Ghost. The historical reality was slightly more complex.

Blaster Jack and Jibber John were actually two different characters, and neither proved subsequently to be the main player in the Marsden Bay historical drama. Jack had been the first 'tenant' of the cave that later became a pub, certainly. In fact, his name eventually became the platform upon which the Marsden legends were built, but he had been succeeded by another character who was, if anything, equally enigmatic and certainly more influential in shaping the future of *The Marsden Grotto Inn*. This man was known locally as Peter the Hermit. As for Jibber John, he was one of a multitude of smugglers who had frequented the area, and he had indeed died in the manner Ronnie the Hoist Man had described. As our story unfolds the role which each of these characters played will become clear.

As Nick related the factual story concerning Blaster Jack, Peter the Hermit and the others we were joined by Sue. She too had a passion for *The Grotto* legend. As she explained:

> It's no good *just* being a manager or a tenant here. You have to *love* this place. When you provide food for visitors you can't help being conscious of the fact that you're part of a long tradition. We're doing exactly what Blaster Jack and his wife – and Peter Allan and his wife – did all those years ago; serving food and drink to visitors. It's a heritage, really.

And you could tell that Nick and his wife loved *The Grotto*. The food they served was superb, regularly mentioned in the local press and much of it was in keeping with the character of the place. Even bar sandwiches, such as 'The Sailing Club' and 'The Molly Malone', all reflected the intimate connection between *The Marsden Grotto* and the sea.

Strangely, it was whilst eating at *The Grotto* that I had my first 'psychic' experience there. My wife and I turned up at the inn for lunch one Saturday. Jackie plumped for a salad, I for the seafood. My dish consisted of a huge platter of steamed mussels bathed in what tasted like old-fashioned milk-and-onion sauce. It was decorated with parsley, and came with its own crusty cob loaf. I looked at it, and immediately smelt the ocean. This, surely, was a dish that Blaster Jack would have savoured, and Peter the Hermit after him. A thought passed through my mind that I was eating my meal in exactly the same place that they themselves had once eaten in. At the very same moment that I pondered over this I felt what I can only describe as a 'tide of timelessness' washing gently over me. I was also aware that this strange sensation was, in a way almost impossible to articulate, connected with the food in front of me on the table. Bizarre, I know, but there you have it. Something about the 'Grotto Mussels' dish fascinated me, and a week later, after several hours of research, I found out exactly what it was.

Florence White was the daughter of a long line of Sussex innkeepers. She was a veritable mine of information on culinary matters, and spent much of her life researching ancient and traditional recipes. She would go to any length to seek out family recipes and ancient inn-food descriptions that had been passed down from generation to generation, and then preserve them for posterity. She eventually went on to found The English Folk Cookery Association and became a member of the prestigious American Home Economics Association.

Florence was determined that much of the English culinary heritage should not be lost to future generations, and so she eventually compiled the fruits of her research into a volume entitled *Good Things in England* [1]. In her book - described, as "a classic" by no less a culinary expert than Elizabeth David - is a recipe for mussel sauce. This recipe is itself based on earlier ones that can be traced back to the seventeenth century. No mean cook myself when I get started, I recreated the recipe in Florence White's book and was surprised to find that it was almost indistinguishable from the sauce used by the chef at *The Grotto*. Was the chef aware of this strange coincidence? Almost certainly not, so why is this relevant? For this reason only: when one enters *The Grotto*, the past has a way of grasping hold of you, just as it does on the beach below. The fayre of the ancient mariner was part of the character of *The Grotto* from the very beginning, and is still to be found therein. Those who study this strange hostelry and its history soon become aware that the past continually erupts into the present, and I am not the only one who has had this strange sensation of temporal dislocation there.

During my research I came across a retired doctor who told me that he had a very similar experience to myself, only more intense. Whilst eating a bar meal at the inn he was amazed to see that the plate and its contents kept changing for a split second before his very eyes:

One second there was a ham sandwich and salad on a white ceramic plate, the next it was something akin to a ploughman's lunch on an earthenware platter. This happened three times as I was eating. For a split second I could see a different meal on a different plate. I know it sounds stupid. I just cannot explain it.

Having spent month after month exposing myself to *The Grotto* and its paranormally charged history, I can state unequivocally that the good doctor is not stupid. What he experienced was *The Grotto*'s ability to lift its patrons out of the linear time-line and allow them to touch past and present together in one, glorious collage.

Nick Garvey and his wife were determined not to let The Grotto traditions fade away into the mists of history, and hence the pride they took in the food they served. Hence also those 'Grotto Mussels', which, along with much else inside this strange inn, attempted to dislocate you from the present and carry you back to a bygone age.

Nick proceeded to tell me about his own experiences in the building. He, like many others, had seen and heard things that have no conventional explanation. These experiences did not trouble him, however. He harboured a philosophical approach to the apparitions and poltergeist-type phenomena, which manifested themselves in *The Grotto*, and is strongly of the opinion that those who manage the building can stamp their own character upon it just like those who came before them. Certainly, *The Grotto* has a warm and friendly atmosphere, which is noted by its patrons.

I asked Nick about the pint of beer that is left on the bar every evening: a fairy tale to intrigue the punters with, surely? "Not really", he retorted. He surprised me somewhat by telling me that the beer was not left out in any old pint pot. It was poured, with due reverence, into a Georgian pewter tankard which had been in the pub for the better part of two centuries. Sometimes, when the bar was opened in the morning, the tankard would be drained of every last drop. Sometimes it would be half-drunk, or not even touched at all. As Ronnie the Hoist Man had said; "it depends what sort of mood he's in". Common lore suggests that the tankard belonged to Blaster Jack. Nick Garvey wasn't so sure, and tended towards the idea that it belonged to Peter Allan.

"He had more to do with this place," said Nick, correctly. "He really enlarged Blaster Jack's cave and made it more or less what it is today. He was the true architect of *The Grotto*."

After researching the history of the tankard I actually came to a different conclusion; namely that the tankard belonged to neither Blaster Jack *nor* Peter the Hermit, but more about that later.

During my visits to *The Grotto*, on several occasions I observed Nick and sometimes his wife standing on the patio outside looking out to sea. My wife and I once bumped into Nick as he strolled, deep in thought, by Marsden Rock. Like so many others who are aware of the ancient legends regarding Marsden, when Nick and his wife breathed in the sea air they seemed to suck in the very essence of the place. They were not just tenants. They were, as Sue had said, custodians.

## References

[1] White, Florence: *Good Things in England: A Practical Cookery Book for Everyday Use*, (Jonathan Cape Ltd. 1968)

# CHAPTER 4

# SUBTERRANEAN PASSAGES

There have long been rumours circulating in South Tyneside that, underneath the land, which incorporates the borough and its boundaries, there lies a complex network of subterranean passages. Many of these passages are said to lie underneath the coastal region at Marsden Bay.

For example, in the May 1887 edition of the *Monthly Chronicle*, naturalist William Yellowly spoke about 'spacious caverns' which could be penetrated by visitors. That these caverns can no longer be seen or easily accessed does not mean that they never existed. The appearance of the cliff face at Marsden has changed dramatically over the last century. Rock falls and cave collapses have covered up numerous fissures in the cliff, which may have provided access to the "caverns" that Yellowly spoke of. We have good reason to believe that several – or even many – more caverns are to be found within the cliff itself, but without the benefit of an obvious entrance for the convenience of curious explorers.

In the September 1875 edition of *Chamber's Journal*, an article appeared concerning both the history of *The Marsden Grotto Inn* and its most famous personage, Peter Allan. The author took time to mention the numerous caves in the Marsden cliff face, and stated:

> Of caverns there are *very many indeed*, they succeed each other in succession *and are, here and there, connected; often having small channels which tempted us to crawl on hand and knees to see whither they lead.* One of the largest, with a domed roof, has a perfectly cut circular hole in its loftiest portion, through which, by standing immediately underneath, we could detect daylight. [Emphasis mine]

A copy of the *Shields Gazette,* published in July 1969, contained a feature written by one C.A. Smith. Like this author Smith once ran a regular column in that paper, and on one occasion spoke about the alleged subterranean tunnel network said to run under nearby Cleadon Village. Smith had received a letter from a Mr. W. Gibbon-Dowson who stated:

> There are such underground passages. I have seen one myself. This leads from the … [location withheld to protect the anonymity of the current owners of the property] … and under the floor of the Post Office, and many years ago Mr. William Welsh, the sanitary inspector, did traverse this passage for one mile in a south-westerly direction. He had eventually to give up his attempt due to falls and foul air. One wonders who built these passages and why.

During our research, Jonathan Downes, Richard Freeman and I spoke to one retired resident from Whitburn who told us that, as a child, she frequently played on the beach near Marsden Rock. On one occasion she and two friends entered one of the numerous caves that were then accessible – time has obliterated her memory regarding which one – and decided to make a "play house" as she put it. With great determination they carried large rocks from the side of the cave and began to stack them into piles. One pile would serve as a chair, another as a makeshift table, and so on.

Eventually the girls created an entire "room" full of stone furniture and were delighted with the result. At some point one of the youngsters picked up a particularly large boulder and noticed that there was "a hole in the rock", or cliff face behind. Excited at their discovery, they pulled away more of the stones until they had uncovered an aperture large enough to squeeze through.

One by one the youngsters crawled through the hole and were astonished to find themselves in a spacious cavern. Even in the dim light, which entered the cave from the small aperture they had just crawled through, they could see that the space they stood in was absolutely enormous:

> It really went back a long way [she said]. I could see arches and large boulders. It was quite frightening, actually. As far as we could see the cave extended backwards, and there were arches in the walls, which seemed to be leading to other caves. To the right there was also what looked like a tunnel. I only wish there had been more light.

The three girls eventually returned to the first cave and secured the entrance with a large pile of rocks. They were determined that no one else should know of their discovery.

I was intrigued by this story, and it reminded me of a similar tale I'd covered in my 'WraithScape' column on 4 September 1998. In the article I'd suggested that there might be some truth in the legends that these mysterious tunnels did indeed exist. Several days later I received a call from Julie Storey, a journalist at the *Gazette*. That morning another letter had arrived for she and me thought I needed to take a look at it as soon as possible. The letter was from Alex Fowlie, who worked at Whitburn Colliery from 1953 until its closure:

> Regarding your article in the Gazette on Friday 4th Sept: I worked at Whitburn from 1953 until it closed and knew the tunnel very well.  As an electrician I examined a pump in it every week.
>
>  The tunnel was found when water broke into the No.50 Face in the East Drift. It took months to pump the water away so that further excavation found the tunnel [*sic*]. Yes, it was definitely man-made; a beautiful Y shaped brick junction with little brick-arched refuge holes. It was a work of art. It was similar to other brick archways in old roadways near No.1 Shaft. The NCB [National Coal Board] took photographs of it.
>
> There was supposed to be two of these roadways, and they called them 'the Commissioner's Headings'. Those tunnels were the scourges of Whitburn Colliery. They flooded and finished No.50 face, and in later years flooded out another new area about a mile further out just before the colliery closed. The tunnel was discovered about 1958.

Alex further suggested that the tunnels might have been excavated 'for working a small seam of smokeless coal used for ships in the First World War.'

The problem was that no plans or maps of any such workings were known to exist. Alex put forward a possible explanation. He said that the tunnels may have been "dug in extreme haste because of the war effort", and that normal prerequisites like drawing up plans may have gone by the board.

Much of Alex's theories made sense, but there were some things that didn't sit quite right with the overall picture.

Alex had described the tunnels as "a work of art", pointing out that they were all lined with ornamented brickwork. If the authorities had really been so desperate to remove the coal for the war effort, would they have taken the time to decorate the tunnels in this way? It just didn't make sense.

During our research, Jon, Richard and I also interviewed another ex-miner who lived in South Shields. Peter S. had worked at Westoe Colliery, and related to us a most peculiar incident, which, as far as he could recall, occurred around the year 1976.

According to Peter, he and his colleagues had "broken through a face" in the mine and, to their utter amazement, had found themselves staring into a large tunnel. He described the tunnel as "ancient, dirty and damp", and recalled that there were stalactites hanging from the roof. He said that the tunnel "looked old – very old; I'd never see anything like it".

As the miners gingerly entered the tunnel they also noticed what Peter described as "doorways". We asked him to elaborate further, "I'm not sure what they were for … I can only think that they must have been for ventilation. You have to have ventilation, and you have to be careful how you open and close doors so that you don't stop the air from circulating." Peter also recalled that the tunnel contained steps cut into the stone, "These steps would take you up or down to certain levels, and they were definitely man-made. There's no doubt about that in my mind."

According to Peter, the tunnel they first broke into was roughly at a depth of 600 feet below sea level, but it kept descending. "We followed it down to 900 feet. Then it went down to 14,000 feet and we stopped following it at that point. It could have gone deeper for all we knew."

Later, Peter and his fellow miners made enquiries about the tunnel with their superiors and were told that they were simply "monks' workings" and that they'd probably been "connected to a monastery".

Peter admitted to being puzzled as to how the tunnels had been ventilated, "At that depth you would have real problems with ventilation. Those tunnels looked ancient, like from a time before you had pumps and things."

Peter also recalled that they'd discovered one or two artefacts in the tunnel complex, "I remember one thing; there was an old newspaper. It had something on the front page about Hitler. I think it was from World War II."

To Jon, Richard and I it was beginning to look as if the entire coastal area of Marsden contained a large number of these strange tunnels, and it seemed that they were not all of the same type. From the interviews and research we'd carried out we had already concluded that the cliff face behind The Grotto Inn was filled with caves, and that the majority of them were probably unknown to modern historians.

I have a colleague who lives in Sunderland called Alan Tedder. For decades Alan has scoured the British Isles researching ghost stories, myths and legends. Some years ago he wrote a book called *Ghosts, Mysteries and Legends of Sunderland* [1]. This slim volume is a romantic but nonetheless factually accurate jaunt through Wearside history, and contains much folkloric material that is difficult to find elsewhere. It makes for fascinating reading, but its real value lies in the fact that the author has pulled together many obscure threads concerning the underground tunnel network detailed here earlier. Unbeknown to me, Alan had discovered the existence of exactly the same subterranean complex. What made it exciting, however, was that the tunnels discovered by Tedder were *not* the same as the ones that I had discovered. Even more intriguing was the fact that the two complexes were actually one and the same *and linked together.*

## References

[1] Alan Tedder, *Ghosts, Mysteries and Legends of Sunderland* (Black Cat Publications, 1992)

# CHAPTER 5

# THE ROMANS

After the Roman army arrived at South Shields they renamed the town Arbeia, *Arbeia* being a bastardisation of the Latin "Arbeia", which means "The Arab Place" or "Place of the Arabs". This may seem odd, but there was a good reason for the change, at least from the Roman perspective.

The first detachment of soldiers stationed at Arbeia was a cavalry regiment, the 1st Asturians, or *ala I Asturum*. Later, when the fort was enlarged and virtually rebuilt to its present day dimensions, the 1st Asturian Cavalry would be replaced by the *Cohors quinta Gallorum* or 5th Gaulish Cohort. This unit arrived at the fort in 206 AD and remained there until *c.* 316 AD.

Later, the fort played host to the *Barcariorum Tigrisiensium* or Tigris Bargemen. These soldiers were almost exclusively recruited from Arabia (modern-day Iraq), where the *lingua franca* was Aramaic. This language is now almost extinct, but one which was used extensively throughout the Middle East in those times. In Aramaic the word Arabia is pronounced *Arabeeya*, and at this point the similarity to Arbeia becomes all too clear.

Arbeia had a mercurial history. At one juncture it would be crucial to the Roman defensive strategy, then it would degenerate into little more than a backwater until its fortunes revived under new leadership. After 160 AD, Hadrian's Wall to the north underwent a renaissance. As work progressed on fortifying and strengthening the wall, it became clear that a supply depot was needed, and Arbeia was the obvious choice.

To increase the readiness of grain to feed the troops, several new granaries were built at the fort. For a good while Arbeia enjoyed a degree of political and military vibrancy, but then, in the year 310 or thereabouts, there was a fire.

Arbeia was hastily rebuilt; however, it seems that the opportunity was taken to restructure the fort in line with changing needs. The granaries were not rebuilt as granaries, but rather replaced by new barrack blocks to house even more soldiers. Other additions and modifications essentially turned Arbeia into a state-of-the-art complex that was a perfect model of its kind.

During the fourth century AD, there was a noticeable decline at Arbeia. Repairs seem to have been carried out in a slipshod manner, and sometimes not at all. Some buildings became derelict or unused. Even the stone from the precious granaries was utilised to effect repairs at other parts of the fort. The trouble, unfortunately, was not just with Arbeia. The trouble was with Rome, which was slowly but steadily crumbling from within, collapsing under the weight of its own political and social inadequacies. At some point, the soldiers stationed at Arbeia decided to leave, and in all likelihood they simply deserted.

As the Romans prepared to abandon Britain, both the discipline and orderliness of the fort's inhabitants lost their sharpness. The civilian population and the families of the senior officials would have been given a military escort to the nearby docks for transport back to Rome, and a 'skeleton crew' of soldiers would have been left behind to take care of any unfinished business, such as dispatching or selling off the last of the grain.

The Britons, of course, knew full well that the Empire's days were numbered. All they had to do was bide their time and be patient. Sometime – sometime soon – the fort would be theirs.

Whilst the problems on a local level at Arbeia were escalating, things weren't much better elsewhere.

Barbarians were massing on the Rhine and mounting attacks at every opportunity. The province of Gaul was in a state of revolt. Everywhere Caesar looked he saw only darkness.

To some the relatively imminent collapse of Rome was all too obvious, but to others the notion was just too radical to contemplate. Rome the Indestructible. Rome the Eternal. Surely, the greatest empire the world had ever known could *never* come to an end? Most citizens made a psychological compromise. They accepted that Rome was undergoing severe difficulties, but believed that they were transient, temporary problems. Rome would soon get a grip and sort everything out. Rome would rise again, and the troops would be back at Arbeia in no time.

This, of course, left the soldiers stationed in the fort on the horns of a dilemma. They were sitting on a fortune – coins, silverware and other valuables – and didn't quite know the best thing to do with it. Had they truly believed that the Empire was going to disappear forever, then they would have had no choice; they would have had to abandon the fort quickly and take their wealth with them. This would have been risky, as the Britons would harry them every inch of the way. But what if Rome did recover? What if the Legions did return? If the withdrawal were only to be temporary, then a more logical option would have been to hide their booty somewhere safe until they came back.

This is not a wild hypothesis. All over the UK hastily buried valuables have been found on archaeological digs at Roman sites. They bear unmistakable evidence of having been deposited there by citizens who were convinced that, soon enough, they'd be back to dig them up. I believe that this is undoubtedly what happened at Arbeia.

The obvious question, however, is where could such treasure be buried or hidden? It was no good hiding it within the fort. Everyone knew that as soon as the fort was abandoned it would be occupied immediately by the Britons and, in all likelihood, razed to the ground. There was no way of guaranteeing that the local chieftain would not find the hoard no matter how well it had been secreted away. And there was another difficulty. Even if the troops did manage to hide the treasure in such a secure place that the locals couldn't find it, what guarantee was there that, when they returned, the site would not have been built upon?

Burying their hoard in the surrounding countryside was a better option, but even this posed difficulties. Again, the site may have been built upon or otherwise occupied. The ideal solution would be to secure the booty in a place where it would never be found and its location would never become inaccessible.

Before long someone would have worked out that the ideal location in which to store the booty would have been the caves at nearby Marsden Bay.

The Romans knew all about the caves; they had a small quay there, and there was a quarry nearby. Roman coinage and pottery has been found at numerous locations along that particular stretch of coastline.

The height of the cliff at Marsden Bay today varies between 112 and 116 ft. Even now, the cliff is dotted with small caves, some of them at ground level and others, mysteriously, far higher up. The majority of these apertures are very small, and really nothing more than shallow recesses. A few extend for maybe twelve to fifteen feet inside the cliff, and cannot really be explored because their interiors, such as they are, are completely visible from the entrance. But the other niches – particularly those higher up the cliff face – are a different matter. Some of these appear to be natural fissures in the limestone. Others, though, seem to be artificially constructed, or at least show evidence of having been worked upon by human hands.

Several of the more spacious caverns, including the infamous 'Smugglers' Cave', which we will examine presently, are no longer there. Some have collapsed through natural processes, whilst others have been brought down by human demolition because they were unsafe. The cliff face at Marsden is unstable and rock falls are common. In fact, notices have been bolted to the rock in prominent locations warning unwary visitors not to get too close. At this juncture I would like to point out that the caves and the cliff face at Marsden Bay should NEVER be approached or entered as a sudden rock fall could spell injury or even death. Further in this volume the reader will see just how perilous the unstable cliff face can be.

To the casual observer, then, almost all of the caves at Marsden appear to be both small and quite uninteresting. In fact, nothing could be farther from the truth. The cliff face at Marsden is quite capable of holding a multitude of secrets. The Romans were well aware of this, and therefore selected it as the ideal location to hide their hoard of coins and treasure.

CHAPTER 6

# THE WRECKING MEN

The well-known South Tyneside local historian, the late Amy Flagg, compiled a series of volumes on the history of the area before her death. Her notes and writings, some as yet unpublished, are held within South Tyneside Central Library at South Shields. From time to time, researchers will pore through Amy's notes in an effort to resolve whatever puzzle currently taxes them about past events, for she amassed a huge amount of information concerning the legends and history of the locale. A well-known local character, Amy actually has a residential home for the elderly named after her in tribute.

In some ways Amy's notes are frustrating, for she sometimes makes quotations from documents and publications without detailing her sources. Occasionally she will refer to an article in a newspaper or magazine, but only state the year and not the date. Occasionally she will refer to a 'medieval document', but not say which document it is. All of this makes it very difficult indeed for the contemporary researcher to trace her sources. But I am not criticising Amy. It is highly unlikely that she realised just how important her notes would become in unravelling the real story behind the legend of Blaster Jack and *The Marsden Grotto Inn*. Further, she was a lady of impeccable character and no mean intellect, and I have no reason to doubt either her sources or the accuracy of her quotations. Future researchers who wish to follow up the Blaster Jack legend can read Amy Flagg's notes for themselves. We owe her a great debt indeed for her diligent labours.

One of the enduring legends regarding the Marsden area is that of the 'wreckers'. Wreckers were the lowest form of criminal life. They were without conscience, devoid of soul and lacking any sort of humanitarian spirit. One historian I spoke to during my research illustrated this point most crudely but graphically. I asked him if he could describe the character of the wreckers. His answer contained an unpleasant yet chillingly accurate suffix:

The wreckers were simply criminal gangs who would, through their foul expertise, cause ships to run aground on the rocks. They did this by lighting fires on the shore. These fires would confuse incoming vessels because they could be mistaken for harbour lights. Often the ship's captain would only realise the error when it was too late. When the ship hit the rocks and sunk – often with the loss of all hands – the wreckers would set to work. Firstly, any surviving members of the crew would be dispatched on the basis of the old wreckers' adage that 'dead men tell no tales'. Then, with clinically precise organisation, they would set about stripping the ship of its cargo. The wreckers were murderous cut-throats who didn't care a [sic] less whether there were women and children aboard a vessel. They could murder the entire crew of a ship, along with any passengers, and still sleep soundly at night. *I'm telling you – those people would have cut their own grandmother's tits off and sold them from a butcher's stall in the market if the price was right"*.

Quite. Nevertheless, unconscionable though the wreckers may have been, they were well organised. To be successful at their nefarious trade they had to possess an intimate knowledge of the local coastline and the tides. They also needed to have an efficient system for quickly removing their booty from the scene and storing it in a safe place before the Excise men and the soldiers arrived.

The wreckers were, in some respects, similar to modern underworld gangsters and drug dealers. They had a reputation for meting out swift vengeance upon anyone who was suspected of double-crossing them, and few locals would be foolhardy enough to inform on neighbours who they suspected of wrecking without cast-iron guarantees of anonymity.

Wrecking was an unpleasant feature of life in this area for centuries. The earliest recorded report of wreckers operating at Marsden dates back to the thirteenth century. It is likely, however, that the practice existed in far earlier times, possibly even during the Roman occupation of Britain. The evidence for this is scant, but interesting nonetheless.

Many Roman coins have been found in the area of Marsden known as Velvet Beds Island. One possibility we have to consider is that the coins were lost there as the result of a shipwreck. Such shipwrecks may have been accidental, but they may also have been deliberate.

Certainly, the ferocious weather in this area caused the downfall of many a vessel. Tacitus, in *The Life of Agricola* [1], states, 'Of all the islands which have reached the knowledge of the Romans, Britain is the largest... The northern shore, beyond which there is no land, is beaten by a sea vast and boundless.' Another anonymous poet [2] once wrote of Marsden:

> Within the limit of the tidal stream
> A rock arises, bare and tempest riven:
> Such a huge ruin might, as poets dream,
> Be hurled by some proud giant against heaven.
> Its base is scooped in many a rugged seam,
> Through which the waves are by the wild winds driven,
> And hollow arches, crusted o'er with shells,
> Are filled or dry, as the sea ebbs or swells.

McKenzie & Ross, in their history of Durham [3], talk about the 'violence of the sea' around 'Marston Rock' – an old variant of the name Marsden. Later, a promotional booklet designed to attract visitors to *The Marsden Grotto* [4] described the area in the following terms: "It is wild, rugged and picturesque at Marsden, where Britain's most unusual restaurant is set into the 112ft cliffs which have been worn away by the ceaseless pounding of the waves into a variety of grotesque shapes."

In such a tempest-tossed area, it takes little imagination to grasp that shipwrecks must have been a regular occurrence. But the wreckers were at work from an early age too, enhancing the already grim tally of vessels dispatched to a watery grave by Mother Nature. Local historians have little doubt that these murderous bands of criminals have a long and ignominious history. Robinson [5] ventures that, "From *ancient times* Marsden has been the reputed scene of the activities of smugglers and wreckers" [Emphasis mine].

Amy Flagg shared the same belief. The very geographical layout of Marsden *lends itself* to smuggling and wrecking, and it is difficult to imagine that this did not go on in Roman times also. Marsden was then a remote area. This is difficult to picture now, when this strange little stretch of coastline borders a thriving seaside town popular with summer tourists. Now, private dwellings and council estates tightly surround Marsden. Children play on its sands and bathe in its waters by the hundred. Now Marsden is a busy, bustling place. But then it was remote, eerie and silent; the perfect location for a bit of wrecking.

One old history of County Durham [6] describes the coast at Marsden in ancient times as being:

> A wild remote place with no roads leading to it … In any case, few travel-
> lers would dare venture along this rocky coast which was, without doubt, the

'scene of cruel raids by wreckers and dark deeds of smugglers. It was left to the seafowl and the restless waves ever battering out the softer part of the cliffs.

Presumably this would have been a *really* good place for a bit of wrecking, then.

In 1215 "a charge of wrecking" was brought against one of the gangs that effectively governed the area. The suspects are not named, but are described as "certain men of Herton, Wystowe and Whyteberne". These three areas are today known as the villages of Harton, Westoe and Whitburn, all lying within the Borough of South Tyneside. Harton and Westoe are now generally regarded as districts of South Shields, and readers should not imagine quaint villages separated by miles of verdant woodland. However, in the year 1215 it *was* like that, each village being separate and distinct from the other.

The specific charge against the men was that they had, "broken up the King's ship *Falcon*, which had been wrecked near to Whyteberne, and carried off certain good.' [7]

It is interesting to note that the wrecking of the *Falcon* was said to have taken place "near to Whyteberne", and not actually *at* Whyteberne. Whyteberne or Whitburn is the stretch of coastline immediately south of Marsden Bay, and it is therefore likely that Marsden itself was the exact location of the crime.

But it was not only the wreckers who came to grief before the local courts. In 1365 two characters called William Liolf and Thomas Scot, residents of Westoe village, were had up before the Lord Prior to answer the charge that they had found a porpoise at "the Wyringes on the sands near Herton [Harton] from wreck of the sea, which they sold at Newcastle for twelve shillings."   The porpoise was, in those crazy days, regarded as a "royal fish" or "king's fish" – don't ask me why – and as such deemed to be the property of the Prior of Durham. Perhaps they should have stuck to crabbing and winkling.

In later centuries, the coastline of Marsden would literally be littered with the hulls of wrecked ships – those wrecked by nature, and those wrecked by such men as came from "Herton, Wystowe and Whyteberne."

# References

[1] Tacitus. *The Annals of Tacitus* (Walter Scott) p.265.

[2] Anon. *Within the Limits of the Tidal Sea* (q. in *The Monthly Chronicle*, May 1887 p. 128.)

[3] Mackenzie, E. and Ross, M. *An Historical, Topographical and Descriptive View of the County Palatine of Durham*, (Mackenzie & Dent, 1834).

[4] Anon. *The Marine Grotto Marsden, a Short History* (Vaux Breweries, date unknown) p.1.

[5]Robinson, Alan C: *The Story of Marsden and Peter Allan* (published privately by the author, 1971). p.23

[6]Hunter, Christopher; *The Antiquities of the Abbey, or Cathedral Church of Durham* (John Richardson, 1767)

[7]Robinson, Alan C: *The Story of Marsden and Peter Allan* (published privately by the author, 1971). p.1.

# CHAPTER 7

# THE BATTLE OF
# MARSDEN SANDS

The history books are largely silent regarding Marsden from the fourteenth century until the eighteenth. But we can make a better-than-educated guess as to what transpired there; the wreckers would have continued wrecking, and grown in both influence and power. In fact, by the fourteenth century they virtually ruled the Marsden area unchallenged. In reality there is little hard evidence to suggest that the wreckers had such an extensive influence as I have portrayed, but there is a welter of anecdotal tales to be told by the elderly folk of Marsden who were informed about their activities by their parents and grandparents, and so on. One writer spoke about the beach at Marsden being "littered" with the hulls of vessels, which had been "brought in" by the wreckers. Their strength lay both in their manpower and their firepower. As Robinson states, [1] gangs in those days could consist of "many hundreds", and were "well-mounted and armed".

By the 1600's, however, the outlaws had begun to specialise. The wreckers now had to be distinguished from the sea or water smugglers, who themselves had to be differentiated from the land smugglers, and so on. Specialisation was the order of the day. Everyone except the land smugglers, who usually had the firepower to beat them at their own game, feared the wreckers. Sometimes they would co-operate. The wreckers would "bring in" a ship, and the smugglers would help fence the goods quickly – for a cut. But mostly they worked separately, an uneasy truce being the only thing preventing a bloodbath. The wreckers did their thing, the smugglers did theirs, and wherever possible they kept out of each other's way. Trouble only broke out when the wreckers inadvertently "brought in" a ship crewed by sea smugglers who were working with their land-based colleagues. The land smugglers would hardly let the wreckers walk away with tobacco, rum and other valuables, which they themselves had been expecting to take delivery of.

Despite their chilling reputation, the local populace did not, unlike the wreckers, fear the land smugglers. They were in fact regarded as folk-heroes of the Robin Hood *genre*. Most of the locals, a) saw nothing morally wrong with smuggling, and b) believed that it was the only means by which working-class people could afford the occasional luxury. They were obviously wrong regarding the former, but almost certainly right regarding the latter.

But all this smuggling and wrecking made Marsden a dangerous place back then. Only fools and drunkards would dare to tread Marsden sands when so many ne'er-do-wells frequented it. And in 1775 quite a large number of foolish drunkards did exactly that.

In August of that year, a number of young men from North Shields – which lies on the opposite bank of the Tyne to South Shields – decided to have a day trip across the river. Their primary objective was, apparently, to amuse themselves by shooting sea birds, which are not exactly an endangered species at Marsden. This was not a good idea. The birds play a crucial role in the tapestry of the Marsden legend, and the Bay does not take kindly to wanton attacks on its flora or fauna.

Fuelled one presumes by copious quantities of alcohol, these laddish day-trippers soon bored of shooting the birds, most of which had flown away to a safer distance anyhow. One of their number suggested having a mock battle to liven up the afternoon. The crowd agreed, and divided into two "armies"; one calling themselves the Royalists and the other the Rebels.

At first it was just a bit of harmless fun. A few pistols were discharged into the air, a few pebbles thrown, that sort of thing. And then it got a bit serious. The pebbles turned into boulders, and the trajectory of the pistol lead became distinctly horizontal. Then the inevitable happened, and a "Royalist" injected a ball of hot metal into the arm of one of the "Rebels". Not to be outdone, the injured Rebel then fired back and presumably put a hole in his attacker. At this point mayhem ensued, and what began as a prank ended up as a Civil War re-enactment – with live ammunition. Before long the beach was littered with persons bleeding from newly formed orifices. Eventually they went home, their faces blackened with gunpowder, according to a contemporary account, to "repent of their consummate [*sic*] folly". Strange things happen at Marsden Bay.

# References

[1] Robinson, Alan C: *The Story of Marsden and Peter Allan* (published privately by the author, 1971). p.23.

# CHAPTER 8

# THE ARRIVAL OF BLASTER JACK

The facts about Blaster Jack are not hard to uncover. Putting them into a logical sequence, and then harmonising that sequence with a matching time frame, is more difficult. After carrying out extensive research, I believe that the following narrative is as close to the truth, if not closer, than any which has preceded it.

In 1749 there was employed, at the lead mine at Allenheads, in the county of Northumberland, a miner. His surname is generally thought to be unknown, although I have it on good authority from two sources (a living descendant of one of the main characters involved with The Grotto Inn, Peter Allan, being one of them) that it was Bates. His first name was John (or possibly James), although he was commonly known as Jack, and he was born *circa* 1702. At some point before 1753, Jack married a lady of similar age to himself, and her first name was Jessica. (Curiously, a later character in our narrative owned two "prized Russian pigs" which he named "Jack and Jessie", in honour of the couple).

Either Jack or his wife may have originally been from South Shields, which then lay within the boundaries of County Durham. There is no historical proof of this, but if he had roots there it could explain why the man moved to South Shields, in the summer of 1752, at the relatively late age of fifty. It is also possible that they still had relatives in the area. There is no mention of any children being born to the couple.

There is, just possibly, another reason why Jack and his wife may have moved to South Shields. Only a few years had passed since the Scottish Jacobite rebellion. The Jacobites had pledged their allegiance to the Royal House of Stewart. To confuse matters, a former supporter of the Union, the Earl of Mar, tried to raise the country for the Old Pretender James Edward, the son of James II. There was no confusion as to why he did this, however.

He had had his political ambitions blocked in the most cynical way by his former friends, and saw the Rebellion as a means to exact revenge, pure and simple.

By 1715 the Earl had managed to raise most of the Highlanders in support of the Rebellion, but in November of that year the Battle of Sheriffmuir took place. The result was not an outright victory for one side or the other, but it marked the beginning of a decline in support for the rebels.

In 1714 Charles Edward Stuart, the Young Pretender (r1720–1788), made a second grab for the throne. In August he landed at Invernesshire, being taken there by a French vessel. His first move was to declare his father "the rightful King of both Scotland and England", but he was unable to secure the support of the clans save for a few. But he did have some initial successes. He engaged a Hanoverian army at Prestonpans and beat them roundly. Confident of support from both the French and the English Jacobites, Charles then turned his attention south. He had London firmly in his sights.

By November Charles had reached Derby, but by that time his support was faltering. He faced stiff opposition indeed from the Duke of Cumberland, and eventually began to retreat. In April 1746 Cumberland finally caught up with the Young Pretender at Culloden. The Jacobites fought bravely but were tired and poorly armed. Charles fled to France, and the Rebellion was totally crushed.

There was no clear-cut geographical division between the Unionists and the Jacobites. The closer to the border one travelled, the less certain one could be about which way this or that town or village swayed politically. There is a possibility that Jack may have played a part in the war in some way, possibly fighting in it. If so, then his life may have been in danger because of his allegiances. This may have caused Jack and his wife to move to the north-east coast, less susceptible to further uprisings by the Scots and a better hiding place for a man who now wanted to keep his political sympathies to himself.

There is another consideration, too. After the Battle of Sheriffmuir many Rebel prisoners were taken south for trial. This was done in response to a feeling in Parliament, and throughout England at large, that there would be too much sympathy for them north of the border. Perhaps Jack was a Jacobite sympathiser who had managed to escape the clutches of the authorities, or even escape from custody, and moved to South Shields to make his capture or recapture more difficult. It is also possible that Jack was not his real name, but instead a pseudonym which cheekily pointed to his political leanings. But it is all conjecture. All we really know for certain is that Jack and Jessie decided, for some reason, to move to South Shields.

Jack the Miner (as he was known), and his wife took up residence in the town, although no one knows where. What is known is that it was a considerable distance from his place of employment; namely, Marsden quarry. (This quarry had been worked on and off for centuries and is still in use today, but it should not be confused with the original Roman quarry at Marsden some distance away.)

Jack had been fortunate enough to find employment as soon as he arrived in the South Shields area. Initially he walked to work every day, but as time wore on he began to look for a more suitable dwelling closer to the quarry. He found none – at least none that he could afford on his meagre quarryman's wages.

Eventually Jack retired, both his wife and himself living at 'subsistence level'. Despite their poverty, they both seem to have enjoyed good health. This was fortunate, as later events would confirm. Without warning their landlord suddenly increased the rent on their home to an exorbitant degree and, at the age of 80, both Jack and his wife found themselves facing homelessness. He tramped the streets of South Shields, Whitburn, Cleadon and surrounding areas desperately looking for a dwelling. He found none, and as there were no "Bide-A-Wee Homes For Retired Gentlefolk" back then in 1782, the aged but sprightly Jack had to use his initiative. He did this in a most remarkable way.

At the foot of Marsden cliffs there was a large cave. Jack had undoubtedly seen this during his time of employment at the nearby quarry. He quickly realised that it could be transformed into an unusual but reasonably comfortable home. The problem was that there was no direct access to the cave from the cliff top, other than engaging in a precarious climb down an almost sheer cliff face or by entering the Bay from the northerly end at Velvet Beds. Jack remedied this by using his skills as a quarryman, and blasted a set of steps into the cliff face. These steps allowed Jack, his wife and any visitors to reach the cave with relative ease, although the climb back up would certainly challenge the unfit. This feat caused something of a sensation amongst the locals, and thus gave this elderly gentleman an epithet which has characterised him ever since; that of *Blaster Jack*.

The cave itself was divided into two "rooms" which I have named C1 and C2 for future reference (See Fig. 1) and each was reasonably spacious. We cannot be exactly sure *how* spacious, for the original cavern was later expanded beyond all recognition and its original dimensions are therefore not available for study, but a photograph of the outside of the original dwelling, obviously taken much later, suggests a width of thirty-five feet or thereabouts.

As an historical aside, the earliest photograph known to exist is of a latticed window taken at Lacock Abbey, Wiltshire, in the year 1835. We know then, that any photographs taken of the caves at Marsden Bay must have been taken at some time after that date. There is in existence a photograph of the cave originally inhabited by Jack and Jessie Bates before subsequent inhabitants had undertaken too much work on either the exterior or interior. The picture shows an entrance flanked by two windows, and a study of the photograph enables us to determine much about the natural architecture of the cave when Jack lived there. The door to the cave stretches from ground level upwards to a height of approximately six feet. The two windows have their lower proximity situated approximately two-to-three feet from the ground. These windows were not made from natural apertures, and must therefore have been created by Jack to allow light into the premises.

Fig. 2 is a digitally enhanced photographic simulation of the cave as it would have looked in Blaster Jack's day after the door and windows were added. The original door to the dwelling, which Jack made from an old ship's rudder, is now on display in the interior of the pub. I have superimposed a picture of the door in its original location. All other aspects of the photograph, including the windows, remain unchanged and are exactly as they appear in the original.

It appears that the entrance to the cave was originally quite small, but quite large enough for a human to walk through comfortably. Jack set about enlarging the entrance, squaring off the sides and lintel and fitting the enlarged aperture with the aforementioned stout oak door. The door was studded and possessed what would now be considered a wonderful 'olde worlde' charm. Jack then created two further holes in the rock (see Fig. 3), one at each side of the door, to fashion the windows. These were duly fitted with window frames – again made with wreckage – and glazed.

Jack and his wife would have had little in the way of furnishings, and the few items they did possess would have been difficult to carry to the cave because of its location. Again, using his apparently boundless creativity, Jack remedied the situation. He set about building furniture from driftwood and ship wreckage collected from the beach. Cooking utensils, furniture and ornaments were all either made or salvaged from the ships that decorated the sands outside. Before long Jack and his wife had made for themselves an eccentric but delightful home.

It wasn't long before various local dignitaries had their curiosity aroused by this "queer couple", and they would visit Jack and his wife to see for themselves the strange dwelling they inhabited. In the May 1887 edition of *The Monthly Chronicle*, the naturalist and writer William Yellowly commented that:

> To the singular abode of this couple, in one of the caverns under Marsden cliffs, ladies and gentlemen from Shields and Sunderland used to drive in their carriages so long ago as 1782 ... The romantic situation of the place, and the singularity of the old couple, drew, as we have said, numbers of people to visit them; and Marsden thus became one of the sights of the neighbourhood ... But the spot to which they had given notoriety never from their time lost its local distinction...

The wily Jack saw a golden opportunity to make money here, and charged the toffs a small fee to look around their home. But there is a puzzle. It seems unlikely to me that people would have paid simply to have a look around a single room, quaint and charming though it may have been. Indeed, a quick peek through one of the windows would probably have been enough to satisfy the curiosity of most. During my research I came to suspect that Blaster Jack must have altered and enlarged the cave, adding curiosities and whimsies as he went along to engage the attentions of his visitors. The problem is that there is a popular conception about this part of Marsden history; namely that Jack and his wife merely lived in the cave without altering its dimensions, that task being left to the next 'tenant' of the cave, one Peter Allan. But could those who favour this view be mistaken? Although I have been unable to find any direct evidence to prove that Blaster Jack enlarged the cave, I did stumble upon something that added support to the theory.

Vaux Ltd, who later became owners of *The Grotto*, once published a promotional booklet regarding the inn to attract custom. The undated booklet, *The Marine Grotto Marsden – A Short History* [1], states that Jack, "enlarged the cavern, supplied intrigued visitors with refreshment, and died comparatively wealthy about ten years later."

The author of the booklet seemed to have had access to information from some source unavailable to me, which indicated that Blaster Jack did indeed *enlarge* the cavern inhabited by both his wife and himself. Further research led me to *The Borough of South Shields*, by George B. Hodgson [2]. This book, first published in 1903, was I suspect the source used by the author of the Vaux booklet.

Hodgson - a reliable historian - says that Jack "took up residence, with his wife, in a limestone cave, which he *enlarged* and made habitable" [emphasis mine].

The evidence, I think, suggests that the cave was enlarged some time after they first moved in, but we do not need to labour that particular point, as it is not really relevant. What *is* important is the fact that the cave was indeed made bigger, as we shall see.

That Jack enlarged the cave is really not surprising. He had already altered the front wall of the cave by adding a door and windows. He had also blasted a huge stairway into the 112ft. cliff face. Why should a man who had such a penchant for DIY not make his home more spacious? Whether or not Jack did enlarge the original dwelling may not *seem* to possess much significance, but it does. In fact, his decision to make his quaint home in a cave a little larger would forever change the destiny of Marsden Bay.

We must digress momentarily. One local researcher I spoke to queried why Jack and his wife would move into a cave, which was too small. Why did they not choose a larger cave to start with? There are, in fact, several answers to this objection. Firstly, many caves along the coast flooded automatically at high tide. Secondly, local smugglers as we will come to see, used a number of the caves. They would not take kindly to one of their "warehouses" being inhabited by two octogenarians who drew visitors to them like a magnet! Blaster Jack chose a cave that was open and easily accessible – qualities which made it distinctly unattractive to the smugglers. Thirdly, it must be remembered that when Jack and his wife moved into the cave they had no intention initially of running a business from there. *They just wanted somewhere to live.* However, when curiosity-seekers began to call on the couple, and Jack realised the potential to make some money, he *then* began to consider the notion of making the cave bigger. Perhaps he and his wife installed a table or two near the entrance, carved from driftwood and wreckage by Jack in his own unique style. Here, visitors would sit and partake of Jessie's home-made scones, spice-cakes and other dainties along with a cup of tea or a glass of ale. Her spice-cakes were, apparently, the best to be had in the region.

Yet another undated Vaux publication, *The History of Marsden Grotto*[3], suggests a further source of income for the couple; "Jack also found the local smugglers good custom, for he was in an ideal place to assist them!"

So Jack and his wife ended up running what was, essentially, a café in a cave. They catered for the local curiosity seekers, but only in the summer. In the winter the bay was bitterly cold due to the ferocious "north-easters",

and on more than one occasion was cut off from the rest of Marsden due to
heavy snow, making the area totally inaccessible. And they catered for the
smugglers, too, but not very much. Too many smugglers hanging around
would have drawn the attention of the Preventive Officers, and inevitably
precipitated a raid.

So then, are we to believe that Jack and his wife, who, according to contemporary commentators, died "wealthy", made their money simply by
selling scones? I think not.

Jack was, of course, too old to be a smuggler, but he still proved useful to
them. His constant presence on the beach meant that he was in a perfect
position to monitor the comings and goings of the Preventives who were
now starting to make their presence felt. The "good old days" when the
smugglers were undisputed "kings of the manor" were fast disappearing,
and Parliament was coming down heavily on those who avoided paying
excise duty. Before long, Jack was making a few pennies – or maybe even
the odd shilling – here and there by acting as a lookout for his new and
rather dubious companions.

Jack may also have helped the smugglers store their contraband, although
this is merely conjecture. *The Marine Grotto Today*[4], another Vaux publication, carries no publication date but was almost certainly released between
1948 and 1955. The author says of Jack, "he took a chance of living among
the smugglers who were doing a good business in the bay." Jack was *in with*
the smugglers but not *of* the smugglers, if you get the picture.

For ten years Jack and his wife lived in their quaint cave dwelling. They
died peacefully within a short time of each other in or around the year 1792.

We know very little about the character of Jack, although we can deduce
some things. We know that he was exceptionally fit, even in his old age.
We know that he was extremely creative and determined. How many other
octogenarians could have coped so resourcefully with homelessness, and even
turned the situation to their advantage? In addition to this there is one interesting snippet of information, which has come down to us. The nineteenth
century taxidermist William Yellowly relates a story[5] that Blaster Jack himself
told to Yellowly's grandfather. This is, as far as I know, the only authentic rec-
ollection of Blaster Jack's thoughts, feelings or observations on any matter:

Jack the Blaster told my grandfather a curious incident in connection with
Reynard [a collective noun for foxes]. While walking along the sands between
Whitburn and Marsden, accompanied by two greyhounds, he started a fox
from beneath some large boulder stones. The greyhounds immediately gave

chase. The fox, finding he could not reach his den, the dogs being close to his heels, took to the sea nearly opposite to Marsden Rock. After swimming out a considerable distance, he lay upon the surface of the water as if dead. Jack, on coming up to the hounds, waded into the water, and, getting a firm hold of Reynard, who still feigned death, brought him safely to shore, and ultimately had him fastened up with collar and chain.

Chaining up a wild fox is both cruel and unnecessary. This tells us that although Blaster Jack may have been a keen observer of nature, he had no great empathy with it. His successor to the strange dwelling in the cliff, Peter Allan, would never have treated a wild animal so badly. Nevertheless we must not judge Blaster Jack too harshly. People in the eighteenth century were not as sensitive to environmental concerns and the rights of animals as we are today.

The story is interesting from another aspect. We are told by Yellowly that Jack had been walking along the shore between Whitburn and Marsden, and yet the incident with the fox happened near Marsden Rock itself, which was directly in front of Jack's cave-home. From this we can deduce that Jack must have been returning from Whitburn, his walk with the dogs being almost over. It is also likely that he was walking at night. Foxes are still seen on the sands at Marsden, although rarely now, and nearly always at night when it is quiet and the cover of darkness is good.

What was Jack doing returning from Whitburn via the shore, late at night, with only his dogs for company? We may never know, although we cannot rule out that he may have been engaged in meeting his smuggler friends for some illicit purpose.

So then, could the revenue of Jack's 'café in the cave', coupled with the odd back-hander from the local smugglers, be enough to account for the wealth which he and his wife enjoyed? Again, I think not. But if they died reasonably wealthy, where did their wealth come from? And why, once having made that wealth, did they not then move out of the cave to spend the rest of their retirement in more comfortable and more accessible surroundings?

I have a theory.

## References

[1] Anon. *The Marine Grotto Marsden, a Short History* (Vaux Breweries, date unknown) p 2.
[2] George B. Hodgson, *The Borough of South Shields*, (Andrew Reid & Co, Ltd, 1903) p 490

[3] Anon. *The History of Marsden Grotto*, (Vaux Breweries, date unknown) p 6.

[4] Anon. *The Marine Grotto Today* (Vaux Breweries, date unknown) p 4.

[5] Yellowly, William; *North Country Lore & Legend*, (*The Monthly Chronicle*, May 1887 p 131.)

# CHAPTER 9

# THE COMING OF PETER ALLAN SR.

For thirty-six years Jack the Blaster's cave stood vacant, inhabited only occasionally by the odd vagrant, hermit or social misfit. Slowly but surely, the quaint driftwood furniture Jack had lovingly built with his own hands disappeared. Some of it, perhaps, was taken by impoverished souls who could make use of it. Other bits and pieces would have been washed out by the sudden flash tides, which would occasionally engulf the cave. These flash tides were the only thing that would have caused a problem for Jack and his wife, and yet, curiously, he seems to have made no effort to protect the cave from their occasional but nonetheless devastating entries into the dwelling. One by one the glazed windows were broken. An atmosphere of damp and decay now inhabited the cave which once had played host to curiosity seekers from near and far.

Jack's sudden financial upturn in the decade before his death is only explainable, to my way of thinking, if we concede that he had some other source of income apart from the pennies made by selling scones and tea to the gentry during the summer. The modest enhancement of this income by the odd back-hander from the local smugglers does nothing to remove the mystery either.

I think that Jack found something shortly after he moved into the cliff-face. I do not know exactly what it was, but it was probably a portion – and a relatively small portion at that – of treasure that legend says was salted away in the caves by the Romans in the final days before their hasty departure from their local fort Arbeia. In all probability he found it when he enlarged the cave to accommodate tourists seeking refreshments. Perhaps he found coins, perhaps jewellery. But whatever it was, it was something that he was able to translate into hard cash. It is possible that, as he enlarged the cave, he may have broken through into a small cave adjacent to the first.

Here he may have hit paydirt, as they say, and stumbled on part of a fortune that had lain there, undisturbed, for centuries. The treasure may have been placed in this cave via another entrance, perhaps by means of one of the multitude of "connecting channels" mentioned earlier.

This is all hypothesis, of course; but it would explain not only Jack's sudden increase in fortunes, but also one other mystery which locals have argued over – why, after becoming wealthy did Jack and his wife stay in the cave? They were both in their mid-eighties; living in a cavern by the sea – a cavern, which was accessible only by a steep and dangerous flight of steps, which Jack himself, had been forced to create. Why, after making their money, did they not then move out and back to the centre of South Shields where life would have been infinitely more comfortable?

There is only one answer that makes sense. Jack did not want to leave the cave because, having found one small treasure trove, he became convinced that there could very well be others. At some point it must have dawned on him that the cliffs, which were currently affording them shelter, could contain *more than one* hoard of coins or box of jewellery. For this reason only did Jack and his wife continue to battle against the ferocious winds and the temperamental tides, even though they were both nearing the end of their lives. They lived in the hope that they would once again stumble upon something incredibly precious.


## PETER ALLAN SENIOR

Peter Allan was a colourful personage. He was well known in his native town of Tranent, East Lothian, as a mild eccentric. And yet he was respected. He was known to be an extremely principled person with the highest of moral standards. His wife Jane (wrongly called Patricia in some accounts) was by all reports, no less well thought of. In later years, writers such as William Yellowly would describe him as "a character" [1] – a phrase that tells you nothing, and yet everything, at the same time.

Whilst living in Tranent, a local landowner employed Allan as a gamekeeper. It was during this time that he developed a deep and abiding love for wildlife. Revelling in the beauty of the Scottish countryside, Peter sensed that he had an almost spiritual relationship with the local animals. He would feed the birds, tickle the chins of sheep and stroke the horses. Peter Allan loved his work, and what made him leave Tranent we will never know. But he did, and his departure was likely to have been between the years 1799–1803, just a few short years after the death of Jack the Blaster and his wife.

Dating the time of the Allan family's departure from Tranent is not difficult. It is known that Peter Allan and his wife had children, one of whom was Peter Allan Jnr. Peter Jnr. was born in 1798, at Tranent, and the family's departure took place, according to most commentators, when he was "a young child", "a small boy" or a "little child". These descriptions would suit a toddler, but not a newborn baby. At any rate, we can confidently estimate a window of 1798 – 1803, during which Peter Allan, his wife and his children left their native home and travelled to Whitburn, which was then in the County of Durham.

It is simply impossible to imagine that Peter Allan would have travelled all the way to Whitburn without the security of a job to go to. From this we can deduce that he must have successfully applied for the post, which he took up as soon as he arrived. Peter Allan was now gamekeeper for Sir Hedworth Williamson, the Lord of Whitburn Hall.

One thing that becomes abundantly clear to anyone who researches the life of the Allan family is that Peter Allan was a valued employee. This may be due in no short measure to the character of the man. Allan was a devoutly religious person, although there is some confusion about exactly which denomination he belonged to. Certainly he was not a Roman Catholic, for he on more than one occasion denounced the Pope as "Anti-Christ, Man of Sin, Son of Perdition." (The Pope at this time was Pius VII who presided over an extremely turbulent period of Church history. One of his most important decisions was to institute the Jesuit Order in 1814.) Some of Peter's descendants have told me that they believe he was a Presbyterian.

Peter Allan was also an avid Bible reader, and could quote chapter and verse spontaneously – and with such accuracy – that it amazed his listeners. His favourite books were those of Daniel and the Apocalypse, and he would often give an impromptu sermon on the folly of Solomon and his multitude of wives. A person of strong moral rectitude, imbued with the work ethic, Peter Allan proved himself a faithful and loyal servant to Sir Hedworth.

Peter Allan and his wife lived rent-free on the Whitburn estate, and it wasn't long before his astounding rapport with animals once again drew the attention of the locals, just as it had in Tranent. Peter Allan kept bees. The bees were kept in hives, and the hives were kept in the living room of Peter Allan's cottage. By leaving the window ajar the bees had constant access to both their hive and to the world outside. The bees never stung Peter Allan, and seemed to have an extraordinary affection for him. He would happily let them crawl on him, gently stroking them, according to one story. Peter loved to watch the bees at work, and constructed the hives from glass so that he could, in his private hours, observe them as they went about their business.

Another talent that Peter Allan possessed was for shooting. Even at the age of eighty-five, he could hit a bulls-eye on a target one hundred yards away with consummate ease. When pigeons were required for supper he would simply leave his cottage, wait for some to pass and then shoot them. He would hit each one at the first attempt.

Peter and his wife seemed to have had a happy and contented marriage, some suggesting that their close ages – they were born within three months of each other – meant that "the gude Lord meant for thaem to be togither". Behind his apparently Calvinistic leanings, Peter was a tender person who cared deeply for his wife and children. He also seems to have possessed a dry sense of humour. He once commented, "I sometimes tell the gude wife she's weariet o' me, an wants me awa that she may get anither.". To this his wife fondly replied, "Troth, Pate, ye're clean mistaken, I can tell ye. I'd no fash my thoom wi' ony mair; I've enough to de wi' you."

Never consciously having had my own thoom fashed – working on the presumption that I actually possess one, of course, and that it is not an appurtenance wholly peculiar to the female of our species – I will refrain from speculating on the meaning of Mrs. Allan's words. But she clearly adored Peter, who was known locally, and fondly, as "the canny owld man of Tranent". This is significant, for Peter never forgot his place of birth, and yearned for bygone days when, as a child, he had adventured "amang the heathery hills."

Peter was also a great lover of Burns, and was acquainted intimately with some of the poet's family. Contrasting starkly with his Presbyterian spirituality was a warm and romantic nature that could melt the stoniest heart. After his death, his wife would quote fondly the poetic words:

> When he was a callant, young, feckless, and braw,
> Unheeding what storm-brewing breezes might blaw:
> When he felt as if sorrow was naething to thole,
> For it seldom e'er bound his glad heart in controul:
> We had heard how, a wooer to Patie, he sang
> The auld ballants o' Ramsay the simmer day lang.
> And at nicht by the ingle, wi' Pate by his side,
> How he'd kiss'd her, weel kennin' she'd sune be his bride.

We do not know exactly how many children Peter and his wife raised However, we know that Peter Jr. had both brothers and sisters. These were Jane (DOB unknown), Archibald (04 05 1803), a third son (name and DOB unknown), John (16 09 1804), a fifth son (name and DOB unknown), a sixth son (name unknown, 13 08 1807), a second daughter (name and DOB unknown), Margaret (03 12 1811) Jane (sic) (03 12 1811), and George Cowey (March 1815).

There are several interesting things for us to note here. Firstly, two daughters born to the Allans were named Jane. This may well be because the first child died and the second was named after her in her honour – not an uncommon practice in some parts. Secondly, we can see that Margaret and the second Jane were twins.

One little-known fact about the family was the existence of John Allan. Even experienced local historians were surprised when I pointed this out to them. John Allan is only discussed once in two surviving documents in my possession. However, he will play a significant role in one aspect of this story, as we will discover.

## References

[1] Yellowly, William; *North Country Lore & Legend*, (*The Monthly Chronicle*, May 1887 p. 130.)

# CHAPTER 10

# PETER ALLAN, MAN OF MYSTERY

Peter Allan Jr. was a remarkable person in many ways, not least of which was the uncanny way that he mirrored many of his father's unique talents. Like his father, Peter Jr. had an affinity for animals, which has variously been described as "psychic" and "paranormal". Indeed, one of Peter Jr.'s pets was a tame raven called Ralphy (more of him later), which was itself said to possess "supernatural" abilities [1].

When researching the history of the Allan clan one hits several knotty problems. Firstly, the births of the children are registered in a variety of parishes. Secondly, the parish records for Whitburn show that the variant spellings Allan and Allen were used interchangeably. Peter and Elizabeth's daughter Jane is listed as Jane Allan, whilst their son Thomas is registered as Thomas Colley Allen. This variation in spellings has caused some researchers to overlook members of the Allan family because their name was spelt as Allen. This is why Peter's older brother John is ignored by all but two researchers, to my knowledge, for the simple reason that they are unaware of his existence.

We know precious little about John Allan/Allen, except that in May 1815 he married one Margaret Blair. Thereafter they seem to have taken it upon themselves to increase the population of Whitburn significantly. Their children – at least those we know of – included Ann Allan (April 1816), Margaret Allan (August 1818), Joseph Allen (July 1821), Mary Allen (May 1824), Dorothy Allen (October 1827), William Allen (May 1831) and John Allen (November 1833). Again, notice the variant spellings.

As young Peter grew, his father taught him all the secrets of the gamekeeper's profession. An incredibly fast learner, it was not long before he would be as skilled as Peter Sr. at most aspects of the job. His father also taught him how to shoot, and he soon developed a degree of accuracy with the pistol that even seems to have put Peter Snr's legendary abilities in the shade.

In his mid teens, young Peter was approached by Sir William Williamson – brother of Sir Hedworth – who had heard favourable reports about the young man. He was offered the position of Sir William's valet, an opportunity that he seized readily. He seems to have held this job for several years, and there is, to my knowledge, no suggestion that when he left it there had been any sort of dispute with Sir William. More than likely Peter yearned to be out in the fresh air amongst the animals. Communing with the flora and the fauna would have been infinitely preferable, to such a free spirit, than making sure his master's shirts were ironed on time.

Following his instincts, Peter successfully applied for the post of gamekeeper on the estate of the Marquis of Londonderry at Seaham, Co. Durham. This does not seem to have been to Peter's liking, however, for before too long he was back living in Whitburn with his parents. At this point it seems that he developed a restlessness that would stay with him for most of his natural life. Peter was hard working and industrious. He also seems to have developed a reputation as a Jack-of-all-trades and master of quite a few. Continually frustrated, however, and unsure about what direction he wished his life to take, he drifted from job to job, even trying his hand at cobbling for a while. A degree of stability only re-entered his life when he began courting his future wife, Elizabeth.

It began to dawn upon Peter that he needed a regular trade or profession, as he now wanted to marry and have children. (He accomplished the former, and succeeded most admirably in the latter, establishing, as we shall see, that his virility was as unquestionable as his ability to hit a fly on a barn door at a hundred paces.) For reasons unknown he decided to try his hand at being a publican. Shortly thereafter Peter married his sweetheart Elizabeth, and purchased a public house in Whitburn at the young age of twenty-four. The establishment was called *The Highlander*, but I have been unable to discover whether Peter himself gave this name to it – an obvious choice given his country of birth – or whether the place already bore that name before Peter Allan secured it. At any rate, Peter became the owner and gained his first experience of retailing alcoholic beverages. What Peter Snr. thought about this is now lost to us, but it is not beyond the bounds of possibility, taking into account his religious convictions, that he was less than pleased. We know that Peter Jnr's parents both lived into their nineties, and attended the marriage of their son and his bride. We also know that they had saved much of their income to offset poverty in their old age. These savings, coupled with a private pension paid by a mutual benefit society and the revenue from sales of honey produced by his bees, ensured that Peter Allan Sr. and his wife had a good income until their death.

The burning question at this juncture is how Peter Jnr. secured the finances, at such a young age, to *buy* a public house. His father was reasonably wealthy, as we have discovered, but I think it unlikely that he would have bankrolled his son to buy an inn. From what we know of his spiritual convictions he would at best have felt uneasy about it, although we know from other accounts that he was not opposed to visiting licensed premises. To tell the truth we just can't be sure. But if Peter Allan didn't bankroll his son's purchase of *The Highlander*, how may Peter Jnr. have secured the finances to do it? I would like to make a suggestion. At this stage it will appear to be nothing more than wild speculation, but I believe that later events will bear out my theory.

On October 27 1999 the *Daily Express* contained an interesting feature in its *Money* section entitled 'The Fabled Riches That May Still Lie In Wait'. The article detailed several legendary accounts of buried/lost/hidden treasures that have, over the centuries, fuelled numerous searches. Almost all of them, I have to say, have been unsuccessful. Do the crown jewels that belonged to King John really lie at the bottom of the Wash? Did the Catholic Bishop John Veysey really bury a huge treasure trove in or near the vicarage at Colyton, Devon, when Catholics were being persecuted during the Reformation? Such tales have caused many seekers-after-riches to spend whole lifetimes questing for that which is lost or hidden away in secret.

Peter Allan Jr. possessed, as William Yellowly and the anonymous author of *The Marine Grotto Today*[2] admitted, "a fascination for rocks" and a "passion for excavating" even as a youngster. What exactly they meant by "excavating" is never elaborated upon, but my dictionary defines it as, 'hollowing out, to form a cavity'. It seems that he must have been in the habit of caving, that is, exploring the caves at Marsden Bay and perhaps even creating new interconnecting passages in the soft, marly rock between one cavern and another. It is well known that young Peter often frequented the beach at Marsden Bay, studying the ravens, and other birds that nested in the cliffs. His fascination with wildlife would have made the place a magnet for an inquisitive soul such as his. I believe that, at some point, perhaps whilst exploring the numerous "spacious caverns" and "interconnecting passages", Peter Allan found something. I believe that it was of significant value, and that, when sold and converted into hard currency, it provided him with the money he needed to purchase *The Highlander* outright. Whatever the truth, he could *not* have afforded to purchase *The Highlander* on the paltry savings he would have made whilst game-keeping and cobbling. Whatever Peter found, he kept it a secret, perhaps only sharing that secret with his beloved wife Elizabeth.

At this point in his life, having married and carved out a career for himself, the future looked bright indeed for Peter Jnr. On July 4 1824 Elizabeth gave birth to their first child and daughter, whom they named Jane.

Peter had, at this juncture, a happy marriage and a young child. He was a most likeable character and a phenomenally hard worker. He owned a thriving public house and supplemented his income with other work of varying types, later including occasional employment as a foreman at nearby Marsden quarry. To all appearances he now possessed the contentment and stability that he had lacked in previous years. Peter Allan Jnr. should have been happy with the hand that life had dealt him. This, more than anything else, makes the decision he was to take three years later outwardly all the more extraordinary. Peter Allan decided that, before long, he would take up residence in the derelict cave, which had once belonged to Blaster Jack.

Due to his "fascination with rocks" Peter must have frequently wandered down to the shore, perhaps to examine the richly textured cliffs that make the area so geologically interesting. Many times must Peter have looked around Jack's cave. He must have heard the tales about old Blaster. Staring at the derelict and decrepit hole in front of him he must have marvelled at the way the old man and his wife had managed to live there, in relative comfort, despite their advanced years.

There is a generally accepted story regarding Peter Allan Jnr's decision to move into the cave, and it is described eloquently by William Yellowly[3]:

It was while working in the latter capacity [as a quarryman] that the idea of taking up his abode on the shores of Marsden Bay first occurred to him. To a mind so acute and speculative as his, it was apparent that, if proper means of accommodation and refreshment were on the spot, those picnic parties might be indefinitely multiplied whom the amenity of the neighbourhood brought thither, almost every day, from the adjacent towns, to ramble along the shore, camp on the Velvet Beds, penetrate into the spacious caverns, walk at dead low water through the fretted arches of Marsden Rock, wash their hands and face in the Fairy's Kettle, or try to climb to the top of one or other of those singular stacks or isolated rocks, such as Pompey's Pillar or Lot's Wife, which abound all along the coast between Frenchman's Bay and Byers's Quarry. Peter Allan, cogitating these matters with a practical purpose, came to the conclusion that a good thing might be made, at small risk, out of the holiday-makers or pleasure-seekers whom he saw frequenting the place.

Mr. Yellowly was obviously never one to use just a single word when 183 would do. Nevertheless, he makes the point clear. Peter Allan apparently concluded that what Marsden Bay needed was a public house-come-café-come-hotel-come-restaurant. To it would flock tourists by the score, drinkers by the dozen and picnickers in their droves. Peter Allan would make a fortune.

Well, that's the accepted story. In fact, it is one that Peter Allan may have actually devised and would have been all too eager to promote. But that doesn't mean that it's true. In fact, there are more holes in this theory than there are grains of sand on Marsden beach.

Let us examine the facts. Peter Allan was running a thriving business in busy Whitburn. He lived on the premises in spacious, comfortable surroundings. To move his tender young family into a cave would have been unthinkable, and would undoubtedly have caused outrage in the tightly knit community. Of course, researchers will point out that Peter Allan didn't actually move his family into the cave until it was fully habitable, and that he lived in it alone until he made it so. But this idea is problematical in itself. Peter Allan was a strong family man. He was very protective of his wife and children, and would never have dreamt of moving out of the family home above *The Highlander* to live in a cave, leaving them to live alone above licensed premises. Not unless he had a very compelling reason to do so – a reason which was so compelling that even Elizabeth was happy to endure any imaginable hardship during its outworking.

But there are other reasons for doubting the traditional story. Why leave one thriving inn, which had already proved itself, to set up another on a remote and inaccessible part of the shoreline which would at worst be frequented by a motley band of smugglers and wreckers, and at best by a handful of holiday-makers during a few short weeks in the summer? Would a caring husband and father really be happy at the thought of his family living amongst a bunch of murderous cutthroats? Would a businessman with Peter's talent for making money really have thought that such a plan was a good investment? Impossible. Peter Allan would only have considered these two options if he believed that their habitation of the cave was to be of a short duration only. In other words, they would live in the cave until they found what they were looking for, and then move out in an instant.

Even contemporary writers were staggered at Peter's plan, and could see no sense in what he intended to do. One observer wrote, 'As you examine this singular abode you are anxious to know the motive which induced our hero to fix on such an outlandish a locality, and thus revert, in the boastful nineteenth century, to the obsolete architecture of the Edomites.'[4]

I couldn't have put it better myself. Why indeed? Whatever Peter Allan's *main* motives were for moving into the cave, they had nothing to do with setting up a business – at least, not the sort of business which most people associate him with; the running of a public house. Regarding the theory that Peter got the idea for living in the cave whilst employed at the Marsden quarry, we need only point out that he did not begin working at the quarry until sometime after 1837, a full decade after he began to work on the Marsden cavern. The evidence for this will be given presently. Astonishingly, however, Peter Allan himself *made the very same claim* about his motives for relocating to the Marsden Bay sands.

In 1848, not long before he died, Peter Allan Jnr. read an article about his family and their habitation at Marsden in the *Sunderland and Durham County Herald*. So impressed was he by this biography, apparently, that he contacted the editor of the paper and commissioned him to publish the article in booklet form at Peter's own expense. On September 16 of that year, the booklet, compiled by a journalist known only to us as "Mr. Smith", was released under the title, 'Marsden Rock; or the Story of Peter Allan, and Marsden Marine Grotto'.[5]

On page sixteen the author discusses Allan's employment at the quarry and states that it was there that "the idea of colonizing [*sic*] Marsden Bay first occurred to him." This is patently untrue, and Peter Allan had every opportunity of pointing out to the editor of the *Herald* this factual error. But he did not. The only possible reason for this is that Peter Allan was happy for this mistake to be perpetuated, *as it masked his real reason for moving into the cave.*

How can we date Allan's employment at the quarry so conclusively? Quite simply because the facts point to it.

In the booklet 'A Ramble to Marsden Rocks'[6], which was published the year after Peter's death, the writer, who knew Allan personally, wrote:

We next find him married and settled as a publican in Whitburn, where he bought some property. He also went out, as occasion offered, to execute work by contract. In this manner he obtained employment at the North Dock, Monkwearmouth, during its construction in the years 1835–37. He likewise acted as foreman for some time, to Mr. Mordey, of Wallsend, over some eight or ten men employed in quarrying stone for the limekiln from the rocks about Marsden.

This contemporary account, accepted as factual by Peter Allan's children, places his varying employments in their chronological order. This shows that Allan did *not* work in the quarry before moving to Marsden Bay, as he was, at that time, busy running *The Highlander*! Alan Robinson also dates Peter's employment between 1835–37 and states, "Peter *later* worked as a foreman for a Mr. Mordey of Wallsend."[7] (Emphasis mine). Thus, a complete study of the records available, tempered by the researches of local historians, authors and other investigators, irresistibly draws one to the conclusion that Peter Allan was happy for an untruth – let us say a 'white lie' – to be perpetuated regarding his motives for originally moving to the Marsden Bay area.

So then, why did Peter Allan decide to move into the cave? If Peter had found something in the caves at Marsden Bay, he may well have concluded – correctly – that there were still other valuables salted away amongst the rocks. Perhaps he even found a second, smaller trove – just a few coins, say – but enough to make him think. At some point the truth must have dawned upon him that the cliffs at Marsden might well be playing host to a treasure trove of unimaginable proportions. For this reason alone did Peter Allan Jnr. take the decision – boggling though it must have been to all around him – to move into Blaster Jack's cave. If there was treasure to be found, then he wanted to be the one to find it.

Of course, to announce his real intentions would have been foolhardy. The last thing Peter wanted was for every resident from miles around frantically digging at the cliff face with a pick in the search for buried treasure. No, he would have to keep this quiet. What he needed was a cover story. He also needed a plan.

To find whatever it was that might have been secreted away in the caves, Peter knew that he would need to spend a great deal of time looking for it. However, suspicions might grow if he was constantly seen rummaging around the caverns. What Peter needed was a valid reason to be 'on site'. Then the idea came to him: what if he was to do what Blaster Jack had done, and actually *live* in the large cave opposite Marsden Rock? He could work under the pretence of setting up a small business there – again, just like Jack and his wife had done. Old Blaster had made a few coppers selling tea, scones and beer to the locals, so it wouldn't look so strange if someone else did it. Under the cover of running a small business Peter would be able to make a systematic exploration of the cliff face, and – if there was treasure there – claim it as his own.

Peter's plans were put on hold for a while after Lizzie became pregnant with their second child. In 1826 she gave birth to a son, William, whom Peter doted on. Then, he threw himself into his new passion with vigour.

Of course, to set up such a business required capital, and Peter did not have enough. He had developed a moderate gambling habit, and money that at one time would have been banked was now ending up in the book-maker's pocket. But Peter Allan had Lady Luck sitting on his shoulder.

Allan managed to scrape together enough money for one, last, audacious flutter on the horses. According to all surviving accounts he travelled "to the Shields Races" and put his money on a nag. The animal romped past the post ahead of all the others, and Peter came away with a small fortune. But it was still not enough. Peter was going to need help excavating the caves, and hired labour did not come cheap. He would also need tools, equipment, and money to set up the business, which would act as a front for his activities. Peter reasoned that he would, in some way, have to use his money gained at the races to generate even more capital.

One day during May or June of 1827, Peter travelled to Newcastle[8] in a large cart. Once there, he purchased a huge marquee tent – from whom we do not know – and a supply of food and drink. Within days, whilst leaving the running of *The Highlander* to Elizabeth and other employees, Peter opened a new business.

There was at one time a singular road leading from Cleadon to Marsden. It is now covered by two golf courses, although dozens of alternative routes currently provide the same access. Over the previous few seasons Peter had noticed a steady increase of tourists coming into the area. Relatively few ventured down onto the sands, of course, for access was still difficult and dangerous. But they would stop at beautiful Marsden for a while, enjoying the breathtaking countryside and the inspiring view of both the sea and its eternal guardian, Marsden Rock. Then they would travel on, perhaps to Seaburn, perhaps to South Shields.

Peter opened his marquee tent at the end of the lane that linked Cleadon to Marsden[9]. An assortment of tables and chairs graced the grass outside, whilst inside Peter provided tea, scones, singing hinnies, crumpets and spice cakes. The provender was uncannily similar to that which Blaster Jack's wife had supplied years earlier, but if you were discreet Peter would also supply you with beer, porter or even gin. The alcoholic beverages were kept strictly 'under the counter', however, for he had no license to sell them from that location.

It seems that Peter did a roaring trade, and before long he had accumulated enough money to begin excavating the cliff face. But first he had to open up his 'business' in Blaster Jack's old haunt.

# References

[1] Yellowly, William; *At Marsden Rock* (published privately, date unknown).

[2] Anon. *The Marine Grotto Today* (Vaux Breweries, date unknown) p 5.

[3] Yellowly, William; *North Country Lore & Legend*, (*The Monthly Chronicle*, May 1887 p. 126.)

[4] Smith, Mr; *Marsden Rock; or the Story of Peter Allan, and Marsden Marine Grotto* (The Sunderland & Durham County Herald, 1848) p. 12.

[5] Ibid.

[6] Anon. *A Ramble to Marsden Rocks,* (publisher unknown).

[7] Robinson, Alan C: *The Story of Marsden and Peter Allan* (published privately by the author, 1971). p. 7

[8] Anon. *A Ramble to Marsden Rocks,* (publisher unknown) p. 8.

[9] *Ibid.*

# CHAPTER 11

# THE DOCKS OF CANNY SUNDERLAND

The docks of canny Sunderland,
How beautiful are they;
Secure from wave and rocky strand,
From tempest and dismay.
The ships lie there in peaceful rest,
Nor heed the tempest shocks;
Oh, may the hands and hearts be blest,
That raised our canny docks!

The docks of canny Sunderland,
The sailor's hope shall be,
To cheer his heart and nerve his hand,
Amid the raging sea.
And he will speak in grateful strain,
When he has cleared the rocks;
For well he knows he'll lie again,
Safe in his canny docks!

The docks of canny Sunderland –
The glory of the town,
Shall, like the works of Egypt, stand,
Long storied in renown.
As long as Wear shall roll her flood
Amid the hoary rocks,
The tongues of men shall bless the good,
That raised these noble docks!

The above poem was written on the spur of the moment by a friend of Robert Ward, the publisher of *A Ramble to Marsden Rocks*, during an excursion.

CHAPTER 12

# PHASE 1: THE EXCAVATION BEGINS

Peter began by cleaning out the derelict dwelling himself and possibly enlarging it slightly. He then toured the area and assembled a gang of labourers to help him with the more complex and arduous work. Some were unemployed miners. Others were unemployed quarrymen. One or two were retired friends who were still fit and not averse to making a bit of money to supplement their pensions. It is also likely that Peter's brother John helped out, although what he could do would be limited. (He had, several years previously, lost one of his hands in a shooting accident [1] and found it difficult to obtain work.) Having assembled his team, Peter then needed materials. To cut costs he scoured the sands of South Shields, Marsden, Whitburn and Seaburn and stripped all the timber he needed from the wrecks that littered the shore.

We have a good idea what Peter's original establishment looked like, and it is possible to reconstruct, with a fair degree of accuracy, how his excavations proceeded. It will help if we divide the work into phases, each one covering an additional excavation or building project, and each one being examined in a specially dedicated chapter. For clarity, the caves will be referred to by the prefix 'C'. Jack's original abode consisted of what we will hitherto refer to as C1 and C2 (See Fig. 1).

The first modernisation to the cave excavated by Peter Allen was an extension of the cave C2 (See Fig. 4) which he accomplished by blasting away the southerly cave wall until he had enlarged the room to the size he required. He also added three further apertures to serve as windows.

After excavating C2, Peter would then have had to spend time making the premises hospitable once again. The floor in C1 may have still been in a reasonable condition, but the floor in C2 would have had to be levelled, and then the surface of the two floors again covered with joists and boarded.

Whilst some of Allan's employees were working on the cave interior, others would have begun to construct the wooden frontage to the premises. The original stone frontage which had been there in Jack's day – part of the natural cliff face – was almost entirely covered by a porch which protruded approximately eight feet from the cliff itself. The flat roof of this entrance or porch, was supported by ten stout wooden pillars. The entrance was entirely open, but would have severely curtailed the light entering the interior had not Peter enlarged the original opening into the cave wall that, in old Blaster's day, had been the doorway. This allowed a reasonable amount of light in, but would be intolerable in the colder months. To compensate, Peter seems to have added a series of glazed interior windows and doors. These are just visible on an extremely old photograph of the dwelling in my possession.

The pillars that supported the roof of the porch rested upon a level stone platform, and there is some evidence that the platform itself may have been covered in planking for some reason. The entire effect was, bizarrely, uncannily similar to a nineteenth century American saloon bar.

It is commonly believed that the sea wall, which now fronts the building, was a much later addition, and that previously there was no defence against the occasionally violent tide. However, some early photographs of the dwelling show clearly that a crude sea wall was actually in place much earlier, and must have undoubtedly been there from the first days of Peter Allan's excavation of the cliff.

Having completed what I have labelled Phase 1 of the building and excavation work, Peter began to furnish his new apartment. He did this, again, by utilising everything he could find within the wrecks upon the shore. This followed firmly the tradition begun by Blaster Jack decades earlier, and caused one writer to state [2], "Its furniture is comprised of odds and ends, – old sea chests and drawers, cabinet stools of diverse patterns and forms, all and each unquestionably of the flotsam and jetsam class."

Phase One of the work in its entirety is unlikely to have taken more than two months to complete. During this time Peter Allan would have only slept on the premises occasionally, perhaps after working late and being wary of travelling back to Whitburn after dark when the smugglers were about their business.

Having hastily created this crude but charming building, Peter began to sell essentially the same refreshments as he was retailing from the marquee tent, which was still doing a thriving business up above on the cliff face; tea, scones, pies, muffins, singing hinnies, spice cakes and – on the quiet, of course

– the demon drink. Peter Allan, still a Scot at heart even though he was also a naturalised Geordie – named his strange but attractive establishment *The Tam O'Shanter* after his father's favourite Robbie Burns composition. Peter Allan was now open for business.

But of course, he didn't hope to make much. His cliff-face venture was being largely subsidised by his profits from *The Highlander* – now growing by the day – and from the marquee tent. Still, it all *looked* perfectly respectable.

It may help at this juncture if we take a mental tour of The Tam O' Shanter as it would have appeared in 1827. Approaching from the shoreline, the visitor would walk across the sand and boulders. Eventually you would reach a crude sea wall, which had been roughly made from large rocks. This sea wall would have been between three and four feet in height. Having climbed the sea wall to the higher ground, you would then walk in a northerly direction, to your right, for a distance of twenty feet or so. At this point you would step under the stout porch roof, which fronted the entrance to the inn. Then, stepping through an inner entrance, which sported a glazed door, you would find yourself in Peter Allan's bar. To the right of you would be a cave (C1), which Peter Allan was using as his living quarters. To your left would be a doorway cut into the rock. Through this doorway lay the second cave (C2) containing a roughly constructed counter from which the 'landlord' sold his wares. Scattered around would be an odd assortment of tables and chairs. Later, C1 would become known as the cellar, and later still it would be renamed the Engine Room.

Welcome to *The Tam O' Shanter*, the forerunner of *The Grotto Inn*.

## References

[1] Yellowly, William; *North Country Lore & Legend*, (*The Monthly Chronicle*, May 1887 p. 131.)
[2] *Chambers Journal*, September 1875.

## CHAPTER 13

# PHASE TWO: THE DEVIL'S ROOM & THE GAOL

Just north of C1 there was another cave, unconnected to those already excavated by Blaster Jack and Peter Allan. The entrance to this cave was as wide and as tall as the interior, meaning that the interior – all of it – was immediately visible to anyone standing on the sands outside and looking towards the cliff face. This cave was essentially the size of C1, but to our knowledge was never used by Jack and Jessie Bates. As the cave – we'll call it C3 – was entirely open to the elements it would have been no use as a shelter, and, in fact, it was not so much a cave as a large indentation in the cliff itself.

For reasons that are not entirely clear, Peter became aware that there was yet another cave, hereinafter referred to as C4, to the north (see Fig. 5). C4 was immediately adjacent to C3, and we can only speculate as to how Peter stumbled upon its existence. It is possible that as the cliff face eroded over the millennia part of the cave, perhaps only a small aperture, became exposed to the astute observer walking past on the sands. Whatever the truth, Peter Allan knew of its existence and determined that it would have to be explored. Of course, the problem was that because the mouth of C3 was so large, anyone passing would have been able to see him digging northwards and wondered what he was up to. One option would have been to extend the porch covering the entrance to C1 and C2 northwards to cover the entrance to C3. However, this also would have looked suspicious. Why would Peter want to cover the entrance to an exposed, shallow cave that was no use to anyone?

We do not know exactly what Peter's overall plan was for concealing his endeavours, but we can say with certainty that he would only want his trusted associates to know of the existence of C4. It seems that he took two steps to accomplish this.

First, Peter erected a marquee tent in front of C3 and essentially made sure that an outdoor party was held in it every week or so. This didn't look out of place, because for a number of years Peter and his brother John managed a similar tent on the cliff top up above. Undoubtedly, the back of the marquee would have been jammed up against the cliff face so that curious visitors couldn't just wonder in to C3 and start to investigate. Nevertheless, it must have been possible to gain access – just not easily. Snoopers would have been conspicuous.

Peter, of course, had no idea what may (or may not) have lain in the as-yet unexcavated C4. His second strategy was not to tunnel directly into C4 from the northerly wall of C3, but to first excavate around it. The first part of the operation began when Peter tunnelled in a westerly direction from the back of C3. He then turned 90° and excavated due north, effectively creating a tunnel *behind* C4. This took him out of the line of sight of curiosity seekers, and enabled him to turn another 90° and tunnel east into C4 from behind.

There is an interesting point to be made here about Peter's strategy. He seems to have known *exactly* when to stop tunnelling west and start tunnelling north to ensure that the tunnel ran parallel with the westerly wall of C4 and that both were just within a few feet of each other. This means that Peter *must* have been able to see into C4 before it was excavated so that he could judge the depth of the cave. This reinforces the proposition made earlier that there may have been a small aperture visible from outside the cave that enabled him to peek inside.

Once Peter had excavated the tunnel behind C4 he could then attempt to gain entrance to it. This would not have taken long, as the marly, sandstone rock is extremely soft. Peter first created a small entrance into C4 at the south westerly aspect of the cave. He then created a larger entrance at the north westerly aspect. What, if anything he found when exploring the interior of C4 for the first time we do not know. However, he made a number of curious trips to London subsequently, and there is some circumstantial evidence that he may have been trying to sell antiquities there, to the British Museum and other places. If he did discover such items in the cave, then there is a strong probability that they may have been part of the Roman hoard left there when the legionnaires finally departed from Arbeia.

Of course, once the cave had been explored it would make no sense simply to abandon it. We know that in Peter's day C3 was nicknamed the Devil's Room and C4 was known as the Gaol. Was C4 actually used as a gaol? We cannot say, but there were peculiarities about it that we will return to in a subsequent chapter. Why was C3 named the Devil's Room? We do not know the answer to that question either, although the epithet may simply have been a sinister-sounding artifice to deter people from prying inside.

# CHAPTER 14

# PHASE THREE: THE STAIRWAY

To imply that Peter Allan Jr. was a greedy man would be unfair. He did not love money for its own sake, but merely its potential to bring happiness into the lives of his family members and friends. Everyone who ever knew Peter Allan testified that he was one of the kindest individuals you could ever hope to meet. But Peter Allan was also an adventurer of *Indiana Jones* proportions. The concept of finding more treasure salted away in the caves would have thrilled Peter – and that is exactly my point. It is the *finding* that would have appealed to him almost as much as the value of the hoard. Hence, Peter quickly became consumed with his search of the cliff, and thus fulfilled his role in the legend of Marsden Bay admirably.

By November 1827, *The Tam O' Shanter* was fully furnished, decorated and actually beginning to attract a few customers, much to the surprise of Peter and his family. Fishermen, smugglers and even wreckers – although the latter profession was almost extinct by this time – began to use the establishment as a convenient watering hole and eatery. There were more fishermen in the area now as compared to the days of old Blaster, and the number of farms on the cliff top had increased too. These factors, coupled with the expanding population of Whitburn and a slow but steady increase in the number of summer tourists, convened to give *The Tam O' Shanter* a potential that it would, years later, recognise and fulfil. Until then, however, it would run at a loss that Peter could only cover by means of his other businesses.

At night Peter would secure the premises and begin the long walk up the steps laid by Blaster Jack. Then he would head south towards Whitburn and his beloved Lizzie and the two weans. Occasionally he would allow some of the labourers whom he had hired to help him sleep over. It was good security.

Before Peter could begin the next phase of his excavations, he had an extremely unpleasant altercation. This was not – surprisingly – with the local smugglers, but with officialdom.

By any standards, the idea of moving into a cave to either live or run a business is bizarre. When Blaster Jack and his wife had done this in the previous century, the Excise men had been a little suspicious. However, as they were both octogenarians the officers knew that they could not be smugglers in the fullest sense. Whether they realised or suspected that Jack was actually receiving back-handers from the smugglers to 'keep look-out' we cannot say, but it is unlikely that they considered the couple to be a serious threat. There were bigger fish they wished to fry: the smugglers themselves.

But when Peter Allan began excavating the cave and erecting his 'shop front' from driftwood and wreckage, things were different. The Excise could see no legitimate reason whatsoever why a sane person would want to engage himself in such an activity in such a sparsely populated and inhospitable place. There were, however, two *illegitimate* reasons; smuggling and dealing in contraband. Not realising Peter's true motives for being at Marsden Bay, the Excise quickly convinced themselves that he had to be engaging in one or both of these pursuits, and the Supervisor from the Excise Office in South Shields decided to pay Mr. Allan a visit.

The meeting, by all accounts, was an acrimonious one. Peter had been a law-abiding citizen, if one sets apart his selling of a small amount of alcoholic beverages 'on the side'. But it was this, unfortunately, which got him into trouble. The Supervisor had launched himself aggressively at Peter and threatened to report him for selling "ale and porter without a license." Peter, taken aback by this sudden confrontation, admitted later to being "frightened until I was nigh into a shake." For reasons now lost to us, the Supervisor did not prosecute Peter. Perhaps he was a genuine man whose bark was worse than his bite. Or perhaps he had other motives, such as allowing Peter to continue his business for a while and having the place put under surveillance. Valuable information could be gained about the smugglers' tactics by such a ruse if their comings and goings could be noted.

To keep himself right and to avoid further brushes with the authorities, Peter immediately applied for a license to sell liquor from the Magistrates of the East Chester ward at South Shields. His application was rejected outright. Peter continued to sell alcohol illegally, but now only to those he knew and trusted. He knew that the Excise would not be so gracious as to give him a second warning.

On 22 June 1828, Lizzie gave birth to their third child, Thomas Colley, in their home above *The Highlander*. Whilst Peter continued to traverse between Whitburn and *The Tam O' Shanter*, his wife and other family members maintained *The Highlander* as a vibrant business. Peter was desperate to continue his excavations, but needed to maintain *The Tam O' Shanter* as a legitimate front. Without a license to sell alcohol he knew that the Excise would be always sniffing around in the hope that they could catch him out. So, in 1829 he applied again. And, again, he was rejected. Bitter and angry, Peter pressed ahead with his excavations regardless.

This time, Peter decided to excavate south again, but on another level. Firstly, he needed to incorporate the newly excavated $C3$ and $C4$ into the main complex of caves, basically consisting of $C1$ and $C2$. He achieved this by tunnelling from the south westerly corner of $C3$ in a southerly direction until he broke through into $C1$. He then cut a stairwell from the floor of $C3$ (south-west corner, next to the stairwell) up over (See Fig. 6). This does not seem to have been coincidental, for, at the top of the stairwell; Peter continued excavating and broke through into a small, circular cave, hereinafter referred to as $C5$. Again we must ask how Peter knew of its existence.

Later in this book we'll see how Peter's brother John, with Peter's assistance, surreptitiously excavated the cliff face from the outside. I think it is highly likely that John hacked through the cliff face and broke into $C5$. Once the brothers were aware of its location, it would be a relatively simple matter for Peter to excavate upwards from $C3$ until he also broke through into $C5$ from a different direction.

Peter and his team then cut two apertures into the rock which were, in effect, windows looking out of the cliff face. These two openings can be seen on early photographs of *The Tam O'Shanter*.

There is a further question that needs to be addressed at this juncture. We have seen copious evidence to suggest that the limestone around the Marsden area is literally riddled with caverns large and small, and that most of these are hidden from view. What we do not know is what percentage of Peter Allan's excavations were a) the enlargement and exploration of natural caves already present in the cliff face, or b) totally new caves blasted out of solid rock. In fact, both hypotheses are correct.

Through a process of logical deduction, Peter Allan must have realised that Blaster Jack had stumbled upon something in the caves. Indeed, had it not been for this assumption Peter would not have moved into the cliff face himself. From this he would have deduced that whatever the old quarryman had found must have been in relatively close proximity to the original dwelling, C1. The question was, *where?* We know that Peter spent some time looking for concealed entrances and apertures leading into the cliff face. This is most likely how his brother John stumbled across C5. At some point, having realised that further searching was futile, Peter may have decided that the only way to find and expose additional hidden caverns in the cliff face was by excavation. In short, he would simply blast his way through the rock like a worm tunnelling through earth until he achieved his objective. If this were his conclusion, Peter would then have to decide which direction to head in. The logical direction, for several reasons, would be south. Firstly, the further south you head along this stretch of coastline the more cavernous the rock appears to be. Secondly, when Blaster Jack had enlarged his cave he had blasted to the south. Maybe the old man knew something that Peter didn't. If Blaster had enlarged the original C2 dwelling in a southerly direction then he must have had a reason, so it would be sensible to follow his lead. However, whatever Peter's motivation may have been he was now excavating on two levels, which we will henceforth refer to as L1 and L2.

At the same time as he was continuing his excavations south, Peter began building a permanent dwelling for his family to the north of C4. This dwelling – often referred to in popular literature as 'the cottage' – was not so much set into the cliff face as set against it. Allan hired local bricklayers and labourers, and within a few months the two-storey house was complete. Then Peter excavated a tunnel in the cliff face to connect the house to his expanding network of caves, giving direct access to The Tam O' Shanter. It thus became possible to visit between *The Tam O'Shanter* and the house without walking outside.

In January 1830, Peter once again applied to the magistrates sitting at East Chester for a license to sell alcoholic beverages, and again he was rejected. He immediately hired an attorney and had his case heard at a Vestry in Whitburn. Here too, Peter was rebuffed. He appealed, and a second Vestry was called. Here, Peter Allan made an impassioned plea based on the principles of natural justice. He won by just one vote. Now he could sell alcohol legitimately from the *Tam O' Shanter*.

CHAPTER 15

# PHASE FOUR: OF BALLROOMS, TUNNELS AND SECRET APARTMENTS

It is likely, I think, that the largest excavation Peter carried out was the artificial creation of a cavern within the cliff.

First, Peter created a small tunnel in the southerly wall of C5. The tunnel obviously led in a southerly direction, and would have taken Peter and his helpers directly above C2. His plan was to excavate a room equal in size to the enlarged C2 below, but it seems that no natural caverns existed in the rock that could simply be enlarged. This forced Peter to employ a tactic used by Blaster Jack when he created the stairwell which led from the top of the cliff to the bottom and, later, when he enlarged his modest dwelling; the use of explosives. Jack had been something of an expert at blasting due to his long years of employment at the quarry. Peter's abilities in this regard were only moderate, and his lack of expertise would eventually precipitate a minor disaster.

Working south, Peter began to excavate a large cavity hereinafter referred to as C6. This excavation eventually formed a spacious cavern, which became known, as the Upper Room. In some ways this was the most peculiar room in the entire complex, and as we shall see, held many secrets.

To the outside world, this was how the *Tam O' Shanter* appeared in those days: Four rooms on the ground floor, and two on the first floor. A quaint – not to say eccentric – inn built into a cliff face. If anyone studies floor plans of *The Marsden Grotto Inn* today, those six, original caverns can still be seen, although the building has now been extended outwards from the cliff face so that what were once external walls are now internal walls.

But there is something wrong here. Peter's original excavations can be seen clearly on the plans; four main rooms – C1, C2, C5 and C6 – plus two smaller rooms, C3 and C4. But contemporary writers and visitors to the *Tam O' Shanter* do not speak of four rooms. They speak of at least nine, and normally *fifteen*.

In the book *Marsden Rock; Or the True Story of Peter Allan, and Marsden Marine Grotto,* published, as we have shown, at Peter Allan's behest, the writer states that, 'on entering the Grotto' one can see that it 'comprises eight dwelling apartments, besides the ball-room.'[1]

Here we have our first problem. Let us assume that the writer, as he clearly indicates, is speaking purely of the rooms within the cliff face and is not including the rooms within the 'cottage' built adjacent to the cliff further north. Peter, as we know, excavated only six rooms, but the writer speaks of 'eight dwelling apartments, besides the ball-room', or, in other words, nine. There is clearly a discrepancy here. But what if the writer *was* including the rooms in the cottage? We know that this dwelling had four rooms. Add these to the six that Peter excavated in the cliff and we arrive at a total of ten. Whether one adds the rooms in the cottage to the inventory or not, it is impossible to arrive at a figure of nine. So, where was the ninth room?

If you visit the premises today, and enter C2, now called the 'Back Bar', you are actually standing in what was called the Ballroom in Peter Allan's day. The Ballroom today is twenty feet in height, culminating in an arched roof. As you cast your eyes around the walls you will occasionally see small, protruding ledges at an approximate height of ten feet. These ledges were actually the supports for a wooden floor, which at one time divided the upper part of the cave from the lower. There was at one time a direct entrance from C5 to the to the "Upper Room", C6; indeed, it was through this entrance that Peter actually excavated C6 into the cliff face. The floor is no longer there, and C2 and C6 have now merged into one, high-vaulted room. What happened to the floor?

During my research I was told on two separate occasions that, during the days of Peter Allan, there had been a disaster of some sorts. There had been a "collapse of a cave" within the complex, which had caused Peter, all sorts of problems, and that a cat had died when it was crushed under tons of falling rock. One researcher told me that the disaster had been caused when part of the cliff face collapsed and nearly demolished the cottage. True, there was an incident like that but it did not take place until 1865, and Peter Allan had died well over a decade earlier in 1849. This "disaster" was obviously a different one to that which I had been told occurred earlier.

My belief is that when Peter Allan was excavating C6 – the first in which he seems to have used explosives – he made an error in judgement and over-did it with the blasting powder. This error caused the stone floor, which separated C6 from C2 to collapse, effectively making the two separate cavities into the one room we see in the premises today. Not to be deterred, Peter substituted the stone floor with a wooden one, again separating the cave into two separate rooms. This wooden floor was later removed and has never been replaced. We know that the wooden floor did actually exist at some point, and during Peter Allan's lifetime, for contemporary records speak of an incident when, whilst sitting in C2, he was forced to jump up and cling on to the supporting beams which underpinned it as we shall see later. Also, the contemporary author of a poem, which we shall refer to presently, spoke of '*rooms* upstairs' at the complex. Had C6 not existed as an independent room, then only the cave C5 would have existed on Level 2. This would have prevented the author speaking of *rooms* upstairs in the plural. The fact that he *did* speak of there being more than one room upstairs indicates that C6 was at that time separated from C2 below and classed as a distinct room in its own right.

If the journalist who penned *Marsden Rock; or the True Story of Peter Allan, and Marsden Marine Grotto* happened to visit the premises *after* the collapse of the stone floor but *before* it was replaced with a wooden one then he may have counted C2 and C6 as one room. This could explain why he speaks of nine rooms and not ten. Unfortunately, though, even this explanation is not adequate. The writer does indeed describe entering the cave complex 'on the ground floor, so to speak' [2]. He then turns left and enters C2, the Ballroom, which he describes as 'a very spacious apartment with vaulted roof'. We can determine from this statement that the writer had visited the complex after Peter had extended the size of C2. However, as he could also see the 'vaulted roof', we know that his visit must also have taken place *after* the collapse of the stone floor and before it was replaced with a wooden one. The trouble is that the writer Smith makes it absolutely clear in his article that the nine rooms he espied were *within the cliff* and did not include those in the cottage. Whichever room you enter 'the rock meets you on all sides', he declares, and refers to the rooms he visited as 'the entire excavation'. Neither of these descriptions could include the cottage, which was not hewn from the cliff face but built adjacent to it from bricks and mortar.

A careful review of this eyewitness testimony inevitably leads us to a rather startling conclusion; when Smith was given his impromptu tour of the cave complex by Peter Allan, it contained far more than the six rooms we have hitherto identified. Wherever these rooms were situated in the complex, *they do not appear on any current plans of the property.*

Later, when the wooden floor of the Upper Room was removed, thus making the Ballroom into a spacious cavern twenty feet in height, the door leading from C5 to the former Upper Room was filled in and plastered over. This would have been done for safety reasons, as the aperture, which formerly led from C5 into C6 now only presented a sheer drop into C2 below. Today, if one stands in C2 and faces north, looking upwards, the plaster covering the doorway, which led from C5 into C6, can still be seen. Curiously though, it is not so easy to see the blocked-up aperture when standing in C5. There is an intriguing explanation for this.

There are actually several hidden rooms in the cave complex. I am confident I know where three of them are, for I have seen evidence to suggest their existence. I also believe that I know the location of several others, although I have not been able to uncover their entrances and thereby prove their existence as yet. How many of these rooms were natural caverns in the cliff simply discovered by Peter Allan and how many were created by him through excavation I cannot say. I also cannot say with any certainty whether Peter made further discoveries of hidden Roman treasure during his explorations. Nevertheless, the rooms are there, but as with C3 and C4, we simply do not know what purpose they were put to after Peter explored them. What we do know is that, unlike C3 and C4, these rooms were not left permanently uncovered and utilised. At some point they were sealed up. Intriguingly, they were sealed up in such a way that their existence would only become apparent to the most astute of observers. Two questions pose themselves at this juncture: How were the rooms 'invisibly' sealed, and why?

When Peter began his excavation of the cave complex he was left with one commodity in abundance; huge quantities of sand-coloured limestone. Initially this was simply thrown through the apertures, which served as windows onto the beach below. However, some of the rock was later put to very good use. When the 'secret' rooms in the complex needed to be hidden from view and 'sealed', the doorways were simply filled up with boulders produced by the excavation. The sealed apertures were then covered over with cement made from pulverised stone of the same source. Because the stone was chemically identical to that around the entrance, and a perfect match in colour, it was possible to render the former entrances virtually invisible. My theory regarding the method Peter and his compatriots used to seal the 'secret' rooms was confirmed as correct when, during my research, I examined what appeared to be a solid wall in one of the caves. The former tenant of the inn, Nick Garvey, was with me at the time, and to our astonishment we found that one particular doorway had indeed been rendered invisible exactly as described. A long-time patron of the pub also confirmed my suspicions. He told me that someone else connected with the inn had admitted to him that the entrances were indeed cemented over in such a way that they could no longer be detected.

Just two years later, shortly after Peter's death, the author of *A Ramble To Marsden Rocks*[3] states, 'Here then, are fifteen rooms *hewn out of the massy cliff* ... '. This statement alone scotches any idea that the rooms of the cottage were included in any inventory of apartments. These rooms were those that had been *hewn* from the very rock! Now, though, there are not nine rooms, but fifteen! This number is also confirmed by other sources.

The author of *The Marine Grotto, Marsden – a Short History*[4] also talks of Peter's '15-room house'. *The Marine Grotto Today*[5] speaks of 'fifteen commodious rooms'.

By 1851 the number of rooms had increased yet again. In that year the poet J. P. Robson wrote, 'Here fifteen apartments by magic arise, *and* Gaol, Ball and Dining room await our surprise'[6]. It is obvious from Robson's words that by 1851 the complex contained 'fifteen apartments' *plus* 'the Gaol, Ball and Dining room'. This would make an incredible *eighteen* apartments or rooms.

The discrepancy is compounded when we consider that Peter's son, William, *added more* rooms to the establishment after Peter's death. A later tenant, Sidney Milnes-Hawkes, *also* enlarged the complex and expanded the number of rooms. Even if William Allan and Sidney Milnes-Hawkes had added only *one* room each then we would still be talking of an absolute minimum of seventeen rooms. Anyone who studies early plans of the building will see that there was, ostensibly, nowhere near this number. A former National Trust employee told me, "I've been in *The Grotto* many times, and if there are fifteen rooms in there I'd love to know where they're situated!"

We must keep in mind that the *Tam O' Shanter* was simply a front – a legitimate business which masked Peter Allan's real activity; the excavation of the cliff face for hidden treasure. Once Peter had excavated enough rooms to make a decent-sized inn, there would be no need to open any more rooms to the public. The 'official' *Tam O' Shanter* had six rooms – including the Upper Room (C6) above the Ballroom (C2), but of these only four, C1, C2, C5 and C6 were generally open to the public. Even C6 could only be visited on Peter's personal invitation. C3 and C4 were 'restricted' rooms and not open to anyone but Peter and his associates.

In *A Ramble to Marsden Rocks*[7], the author details a guided tour he partook of at the cave complex. Fortunately, the narrative enables us to determine quite accurately not only the rooms he visited, but also the sequence he visited them in.

On arriving at the complex, the writer states that he was 'ushered into the front bar' In Peter's day there were two caves in the complex that were referred to as 'bars'. C2 was, as well as being called the Ballroom, often referred to as 'the Back Bar'. It is still called this today because it now sits behind a modern frontage, which was added to the building in the twentieth century. This addition, essentially a huge conservatory, is now 'the front bar', so calling the Ballroom behind it in the cliff the 'back bar' makes sense. However, in the nineteenth century the modern frontage did not exist. The Ballroom was then called 'the back bar' simply because it was recessed much father into the cliff than the shallower and smaller C1, then also often referred to as 'the front bar'. Hence, we know that the author entered the cave complex by the door and was immediately shown into C1. Further evidence of this can be gleaned from the fact that he describes this bar as 'cosy'; a description that could well fit the small C1, but could hardly be applied to the huge Ballroom C2.

## "The Same Room, Upstairs"

Whilst many clues exist in *A Ramble To Marsden Rocks* regarding the 'hidden' rooms within the cave complex, the text also contains mysterious phrases and statements, which initially make no sense. One of these can be found early on in the narrative, where the writer describes being in the 'front bar'. As we have seen, this can only have referred to C1. But if the writer was referring to C1 then we have a problem, for he goes on to say, 'In the same room, upstairs, are several cases of stuffed animals and birds'. The author states clearly that he left 'the bar' and went to inspect this room and its contents.

The first difficulty is that there is no room directly above C1 (at least, none that we are aware of), and the second difficulty is the description itself. What on earth can the writer mean when he says, 'In the same room, upstairs'? If one goes upstairs, how can one still be 'in the same room'?

There is only one 'rational' explanation that I can conceive of, and that is that, contrary to the internal evidence in the text and the clear words of the writer, he was sitting in C2 (the Ballroom) after all, and that when he mentioned 'the same room, upstairs' he was talking about C6, the Upper Room, which was, if we stretch a point, 'the same room' as the Ballroom although separated from it by a wooden ceiling/floor. This explanation is further supported by the writer's description of what 'the room upstairs' contained;

namely, stuffed animals in display cases. We know from historical records that the Upper Room did indeed contain such items, so the mystery would appear to be solved.

So then, was 'the room upstairs' really C6, the Upper Room? It is tempting to say yes, and yet the fact of the matter is that the writer of *A Ramble to Marsden Rocks* claimed to be in the *front* bar and not the back bar when he began his whirlwind tour of the inn. This anomaly simply compounds the mystery of *The Grotto*'s hidden rooms, and we will return to it presently.

The writer then describes how he 'returned to the cosy bar we had left'. We now know, then, that the writer went back to his essential starting point, C1, after visiting the as yet unidentifiable 'same room upstairs'. Eagerly, he then resumes his tour, but curiously he is no longer alone with his companion.

The author makes a point of mentioning that a 'guide' joined him at this point. This guide, who had hitherto not deemed it necessary to act as a chaperone, was described as 'a gentleman who is well acquainted with the family, and who knows every hole and corner of the excavated structure'. Who this 'gentleman' was we are not told, but it seems that the visitors suddenly now needed his expertise and knowledge of the cave complex if they were to continue their tour successfully. This suggests that they were about to visit somewhere that was *not* part of the visible cave complex and where guests were not to stray unaccompanied.

The author continues, 'Leaving the bar, we penetrated a side-door to an inner room … '. Ascertaining the location of this 'Inner Room' proved to be truly problematical. It cannot have been C2, the Ballroom, which was the main room in the complex and can hardly have been described as an Inner Room in any circumstance. There seem to be only two possibilities. One is that C1 was, in those days, actually *two* rooms and that the partitioning wall was removed at a later date and that is why it does not feature on any modern floor plans of the complex. The other possibility is that the Inner Room was actually C3. The problem with this theory is that there is a feature of the mysterious Inner Room, which does not match up at all with what we know about C3 today.

Wherever the mysterious Inner Room was, it apparently contained:

A large, limestone slab … measuring, as we supposed, about five feet long by three feet broad, and five inches thick. The upper surface has been polished, and exhibits wavy lines like watered silk. The under part is in its native state, and very smooth; the edges being cellular, and resembling open lace work. As a

thick pillar interrupts the light from the outer room, you should examine this
curious production of nature by a candle.

This frustrates researchers even more, for there is seemingly only one place
on Level 1 or the ground floor, which could possibly fit this description, and
this is the tunnel part of C3 behind C4.

The author states that a 'thick pillar' interrupted the light, thus causing him
to examine the limestone plaque with a candle. There is apparently only one
'thick pillar' on Level 1 that directly obscures sunlight, and that is the large,
natural pillar of rock that separates the two doorways that lead into C4
from the Tunnel. This would mean that the 'large, limestone slab' must have
been located directly behind the pillar on the westerly wall of the Tunnel.

As the sun rose in the east during the day, the pillar between the two doors
of C4 would have directly impeded the rays of light as they shone towards
the west through the windows of C4 and hence made it difficult to see the
slab with natural light.

I believe that 'the slab' was a cover for the entrance to a series of secret
rooms hidden even deeper in the cliff. Unfortunately, not only is there no
slab to be seen in the Tunnel, but also no visible entrance into deeper parts
of the cave complex. Either the entrance had been expertly covered up, as
was done elsewhere in the complex, or this was not the location of the slab
in the first place.

Try as I might, I could find nowhere within the cave complex at that time
anywhere that matched the description given by the writer regarding the location of the 'slab', the 'Inner Room' and the 'pillar'. Then, a chat with one of
the bar staff at the inn gave me a clue that cleared the mystery up within the
space of twenty minutes – and generated another of far greater consequence.

As I read *A Ramble to Marsden Rocks*, I had been guilty of taking everything the author said too literally. Here was a man not engaged in an
archaeological survey, but a magical mystery tour. He writes precisely, but
not clinically. I therefore concluded that he may not have written down every
doorway he passed through, every room he entered and left in the space of
a few, brief seconds. The writer was relating to his readers the *important*
things he saw on his tour of the cave complex, and may not, therefore, have
bothered to mention inconsequential details. Bearing this in mind, let us
metaphorically rewind the tape and begin anew our tour of the cave complex with the writer of *A Ramble to Marsden Rocks*.

Firstly, we know that he entered the complex through the door that led
directly into C1. This was the 'bar' that he described as 'cosy'. We know also

that he first inspected 'a room upstairs', which, wherever it was located, was unlikely to be the Upper Room, C6. He then returned to C1 before resuming his tour. 'Leaving the bar, we penetrated a side door to an inner-room', he tells us.

I had assumed by this that the writer had literally stepped from the bar, C1, directly into an 'Inner Room' by a 'side door'. But what if this is too easy, too literal an understanding of the words? What if there was *another* room that the writer and his guide had to pass through to go from C1 to get to the mysterious Inner Room? Again this seemed problematical and raised as many difficulties as it solved; until one of the bar staff led me, metaphorically if not literally, into the light.

If one stands in the modern Front Bar and looks due west, one is actually looking at the former front of the cave complex. The four visible interior archways were once doors and windows, which linked the interior of the cave system to the sandy beach outside. They essentially formed apertures in the cliff face. Now that the modern frontage has been added, however, this natural exterior wall has become an interior one which separates the Back Bar, C1, from the modern Front Bar. The distal apertures to the far left and far right now serve as doorways, which lead, from the modern part of the building through into C2. However, the two *central* apertures now sit behind the bar counter and cannot be accessed by the public. These gave easy access to staff behind the counter who wished to walk through from the Back Bar to the Front Bar to serve customers, or vice-versa. The northerly aperture, to the right, is quite thick and I was astonished to find that it actually had a doorway fitted on the right-hand wall of the arch. I went back to the plans and, sure enough, there was the door. How had I missed it? I don't know, but I did. To the right of the arch was what looked like a huge, natural pillar of solid rock, but looks can be deceiving. This pillar was actually hollow, and the door led inside to a room, which was to all intents and purposes hidden from the public, or at least not accessible to them. This large stone pillar was like a colossal hollow tree trunk and actually contained a room; a 'room within a room', one might say, or an inner room.

Now the picture was becoming clearer. The writer of *A Ramble to Marsden Rocks* had started his tour in C1. After visiting the curious 'same room upstairs' he had then returned to C1. From here he walked directly into C2, where his guide took him to the 'inner room' located within the natural stone arch. A room within a room! The title Inner Room fitted it perfectly.

It was in here, then, that he must have seen the strange 'slab' mentioned earlier. If the slab really did conceal an entrance to another, secret part of the cave complex, then that entrance must have been concealed in that small, Inner Room. We will return to the significance of this 'slab' later, but first there is one final mystery over the location of the room that needs to be overcome. The writer describes a 'thick pillar' that obscured the sunlight and made it difficult for him to examine the slab closely without the aid of a candle. The only pillar adjacent to the entrance to the Inner Room lies due south; a natural pillar of rock that forms the left-hand side of the arch that one has to walk through to get to the Inner Room entrance itself on the right. The problem is that the sunlight streams into the cave complex apertures from the east, and this pillar would not have hindered it at all. So then, what pillar could the writer of *A Ramble to Marsden Rocks* have been talking about? We will return to this puzzle later, as it is intrinsically linked to one of the most curious enigmas regarding the cave complex at Marsden Bay. First, though, we need to resume our tour of the complex.

The writer states that after he left the enigmatic Inner Room he was shown 'the Gaol Room', which we know to be C4. He then returned to C3, 'The Devil's Chamber', before being shown the 'circular dining room'. This we know to be C5, and as the stairwell to C5 leads directly from C3 it is plainly C5 that the author is referring to. The author then describes being shown one of the 'ball rooms'. This can only have been C6, or the Upper Room, as it is the only one that can be accessed from C5 without returning down the stairs. Here we have another puzzle, however, for if the 'same room upstairs' was, as usually postulated, C6 or the Upper Room, the visitor had already inspected it earlier in his tour! Why on earth would his guide show him the same room twice? This strengthens my hypothesis that 'the same room upstairs' was *not* C6, the Upper Room, and was in fact another room entirely, which has since been 'sealed' and its location made unknown.

Finally, the writer and his guide return to Level 1 and inspect the most impressive room in the complex; C2, or the Ballroom, not to be confused with the Upper Room C6, which the writer also refers to as a ballroom earlier. To access C2, it would not be necessary for the writer to retrace his steps from C6, through C5, down the stairwell and then through C3 and C2 successively. At that time there was a stairwell, which led from C6 down to C2 directly below. Here the visitor makes an observation, which would help me to clear up the final mystery of the Inner Room and the thick pillar that obscured light getting into its interior:

> In the ballroom, which is very spacious and well adapted for the purpose, we
> discovered some attempts at grotesque carving; but we cannot say that any

praise can be awarded to the sculptor, whoever he may be. Our candid advice to Mrs. Allan is not to allow any one to try his maiden chisel on these pillars; there are many amateur artists who would gladly undertake to finish the work, in a manner creditable to Mrs. Allan and themselves.

What on earth are these 'attempts at grotesque carving' that the writer obviously finds so distasteful? We need not speculate, for they are there to this very day for all to see.

## References

[1] Smith, Mr; *Marsden Rock; or the Story of Peter Allan, and Marsden Marine Grotto* (*The Sunderland & Durham County Herald*, 1848) p. 12.

[2] *Ibid.*

[3] Anon. *A Ramble to Marsden Rocks*, (publisher unknown) p. 7.

[4] Anon. *The Marine Grotto Marsden, a Short History* (Vaux Breweries, date unknown) p.3.

[5] Anon. *The Marine Grotto Today* (Vaux Breweries, date unknown) p 5.

[6] Anon. *A Ramble to Marsden Rocks*, (publisher unknown) p. 1.

[7] *Ibid*, p. 6.

# CHAPTER 16

# THE LAMBTON PILLARS

In C6, or what is now commonly known as the Back Bar, the cave wall is lined with a series of ten stone pillars. There is a conventional history attached to them, which, to my knowledge, is accepted by most if not all local historians who have studied them.

According to legend, Peter Allan carved the stone pillars *in situ* when he enlarged the original cave C2 inhabited by Blaster Jack. Every now and then he would simply allow his hammer and chisel to form a pillar here and there as he worked the cliff face. He then decorated these pillars in an effort to add a little character to the bar. In short, Peter Allan was merely creating a few, whimsical curiosity pieces.

Alas, we now know that this theory is absolutely false. However, the true story of the pillars' origins is far more curious. To understand the significance of their presence in the cave complex we need to take a trip back in history.

During our research, Jonathan, Richard and I drew together a considerable amount of evidence to suggest that for many hundreds of years a dragon-centred religious fraternity had existed in the north east of England and elsewhere. This fraternity believed that there was a huge network of tunnels underground which essentially formed the abode or lair of these dragons. At several locations this subterranean tunnel complex 'erupted' into the upper world, forming several gateways between the world of the dragon and the world of mankind. By now, the reader will not be surprised to learn that the site of the cave complex at Marsden was one such 'eruption'.

The Order was in the habit of stationing specially selected members at each of these points. As stated previously, they essentially acted as guardians, and their function was two-fold. They were there to protect the subterranean dragon world from human interference, but they were also there to protect the world of mankind from the dragon. There are many dragon legends in the north east of England, and perhaps the most famous is that of the Lambton Worm.

The tale of the Lambton Worm begins back in the fourteenth century, when young Sir John Lambton bunked off church one Sunday and went fishing at a secluded spot on the River Wear. For most of the morning he caught little or nothing, but then he suddenly felt a pull on his line and he reeled in a large, worm-like creature the likes of which he'd never seen before. According to legend, it had a head similar to that of a salamander, a series of nine holes on each side of its torso and a pair of prominent fin-like appendages protruding from its neck.

The overall appearance of the 'wyrm' filled young John with revulsion and he promptly threw it down a nearby well and forgot about it. Some time later, John "went off to fight in foreign wars", and during his absence the Worm grew to an absolutely colossal size. It then crawled out of the well and began to terrorise the neighbourhood. At some point John returned and decided to do battle with the creature. He killed it and promptly became a local hero. However, because he had ignored some advice given to him by a local hag, a curse was placed upon his family. Nine generations of the Lambton Lords would "not die in their beds", he was told. Whatever one thinks of the Lambton Worm story, the curse seems to have been activated with a fair degree of success. Most if not all of the next nine Lords of Lambton died by tragic accidents, in combat or by foul play, apparently.

The tale of the Lambton Worm was immortalised in song by one C. M. Leumane in 1867, and is still sung often to this day. Now it happened that the Lambton family owned lands and a castle on the banks of the River Wear to the north of Lumley. Old Lambton Castle, which had existed since at least the thirteenth century, was sadly demolished in 1797 and replaced by a mansion house.

There is no evidence to our knowledge that Peter Allan was a member of the dragon-centred fraternity, but he certainly seemed to be sympathetic to some of their aims. Visitors to the inn were always made most welcome, but were discouraged in equal measure from prying into the cave or tunnel complex. Peter would frighten youngsters and adults alike by telling them that faeries, sprites and other elemental spirits protected the area.

One of the curious things about the pillars in C2 is that they serve no obvious purpose. They are set against the wall and offer no support to the vaulted roof overhead. One could be forgiven for thinking that they were merely decorative or ornamental, except that the author of *A Ramble to*

*Marsden Rocks* renders such an idea impossible when he says that the pillars were 'an attempt at grotesque carving'. Notice he does not say that they were a 'grotesque attempt' at carving, but 'an attempt at grotesque carving'. The difference may seem minor, but it is telling. The writer is making it clear that the attempt at carving the pillars had been made with the deliberate intention of making them *appear grotesque*. This is puzzling, for, as we shall see, the pillars may not be the work of a Michelangelo, but they can hardly be called 'grotesque'.

Walk through the southerly portal into C6 and look slightly to your right. The first pillar to meet the eye bears a remarkable motif; a striking image of a dragon-like creature, which bears every resemblance to the Lambton Worm. Spouting from the beast's neck are two appendages like fins, and a strange head that bears a flat, almost beak-like mouth and a prominent brow ridge. The tail of the Worm points sharply towards the ground, whilst its muscular, snake-like torso reaches upwards towards the skies. Then, suddenly, it arches 180° so that the head plummets towards the earth in a powerful symbol of defeat.

As the Worm was the centre of gravity in the whole Lambton saga, it is logical that its image should appear on the first pillar in the series. Above the Worm is a youthful face staring straight ahead, almost arrogantly. This is undoubtedly the face of Sir John Lambton, and below, metaphorically at his feet, the cowed Worm.

The next nine pillars all bear heads; some old, some young, some handsome some ugly. These are almost certainly the Nine Lords of Lambton who did not die in their beds.

But why would Peter Allan have wanted to carve such a series of images in an inn, which had the reputation of being a friendly and welcoming place? Quite simply, they were meant to be a warning. The Nine Lords of Lambton stare down at you from on high wherever you sit in the Back Bar, C2. They provide a powerful psychological barrier to those who may wish to pry too deeply into either the dragon or its lair. The pillars are grotesque and unsettling not because of the physical carvings they bear, but because of what they represent; war with the Dragon, and a curse upon those who make mistakes when engaging the creature in battle. The pillars were, in effect, the nineteenth century equivalent of a STOP sign. Stay on the right side of the cave complex and enjoy yourself, or go beyond it and suffer the consequences.

Some years ago my wife and I had lunch at the Grotto with two fellow journalists: a newspaper reporter and a news editor from the BBC.

Afterwards we examined the pillars in C2 and one of my friends noticed that the colour of the stone was different to that of the cave wall. This piqued my curiosity; if the pillars had been carved from the rock itself, *in situ*, how could they be different in colour? On closer examination we found that several of the pillars were not carved from the rock at all, but were free-standing. They had, in fact, been cemented in place. Further, several of the pillars were in slices, as if they had been cut up before being reassembled. Before long we unanimously concluded that the pillars – or at least, most of them – had been carved elsewhere and then transported to the cave complex for installation. So, where had they come from?

Sadly, the original Lambton Castle was demolished in the year 1797, just five short years after Blaster Jack and his dear wife Jessie passed away. For a good number of years much of the original stonework could still be found lying around in the ruins. Some of it was cannibalised by local farmers to be used in the building of barns. Other pieces were stolen or sold. I am convinced that the pillars now found in C2 were originally from Lambton Castle, but were transported from there to the Marsden Bay cave complex during the days of Peter Allan's tenancy. In short, I am convinced that they were taken from the site of one tunnel complex 'eruption' to another, and incorporated into the architecture of the Marsden cave complex as a dire warning.

The fact that the pillars were transported to the Marsden cave complex and not carved *in situ* also helps us to answer the final enigma surrounding the Inner Room. The writer of *A Ramble to Marsden Rocks* says that a thick pillar hindered the sunlight from entering the Inner Room and illuminating the polished stone slab it contained. As there are currently no thick pillars in a position to cause such a difficulty we are faced with a seemingly insurmountable problem. However, I have in my possession an old photograph of the Grotto, which provides a powerful solution to the enigma. The photograph in question is undated, but there are features within it that help us ascertain when it was taken with a reasonable degree of certainty.

In 1865 there was an accident at the Grotto. A sudden rock fall demolished half of the family's 'cottage' and they were lucky to escape with their lives. Peter Allen had been dead for well over a decade when this accident occurred, but Lizzie and their children were still living there. After the accident a large section of the cliff wall was covered with a facing to prevent similar falls occurring again. On the photo in question, it is clear that no such facing has yet been erected so we know that the picture must have been taken before the year 1865. There is another curious feature to the picture.

Immediately adjacent to the porch, which fronted the entrance to the inn and the cave complex, one can see two huge stone pillars. They appear to be standing on the patio, but are not attached to anything. They are freestanding, as if they had simply been *dumped* there. My belief is that these pillars had been transported to Marsden from Lambton and placed outside before being eventually situated inside the complex itself. The photograph must have been taken whilst the pillars were still standing outside, and it is clear that both of them are standing immediately adjacent to the porch and, I believe, would have considerably diminished the sunlight streaming in from the east. The thick pillar that obscured the light in the Inner Room was not to be found inside C2, but was actually standing *outside* on the patio!

Can it be ascertained with any degree of certainty that the pillars in the photograph are indeed those now found in C2? To be honest, the pillars do look larger than those inside the complex, but there are several explanations for this. Remember, several of the pillars now inside C2 were cut into slices before being reassembled. It is possible that the reassembled pillars in the Back Bar may not be complete, but only partial restorations of the originals. If the pillars in the photograph are not those now within C2, this still does not mean that one of them wasn't the thick pillar that obscured the light in the Inner Room. If these are different pillars, where are they? It is possible that they may have been taken into the complex and installed in one of the rooms that are now 'sealed' and of unknown location. The author of *A Ramble to Marsden Rocks* ends his description by saying, 'Here, then, are fifteen rooms hewn out of the massy cliff…'.

Fifteen? At best, the author describes visiting only *seven* on his guided tour. Why, in such a methodical and carefully narrated description, does he not at least give a fleeting mention to either the location or contents of the rest? I can only conclude that such details have been deliberately omitted so that the rooms remain, as they were intended to be: hidden and secret.

The author goes on to state that it is 'truly astonishing how all this labour has been effected, even by the indomitable spirit of one man, Peter Allan.' His amazement surely did not come from a quick wander round the basic cave complex of the *Tam O' Shanter*. His amazement could only have been generated by a *full* tour of the complex – including the hidden rooms and caverns. Including 'every hole and corner', we might say.

But if Peter Allan excavated these rooms in secret, how were this writer and other visitors allowed to see them? Remember, the first mention of fifteen rooms came *after* Peter's death. Perhaps his wife, sons and daughters – who inherited the business after him – were not as secretive or cautious as

Peter. Perhaps there was now a realisation that some of the 'secret rooms' were dead-ends and unlikely to yield any treasure. In this case there would have been no value in keeping them hidden, and they would have simply been opened up and added to the list of 'official' rooms, which formed part of the Grotto complex. To complicate matters further, it seems that most, if not all, of the secret rooms that were opened up were, at a later date, hidden again and *not* registered on plans of the building.

On 11 April 1830, Elizabeth gave birth to their fourth child, also called Peter, after what was obviously a family tradition. It was, as we have discussed, Peter's intention to move his family into the *Tam O' Shanter* after it had been made fully habitable. The big problem that Peter had to overcome in this regard was the cold. He had added two fireplaces to the inn – one in the Ballroom, C2, and one in C3, but in the autumn and winter months the bitter north-east winds still made the complex an inhospitable place for a family which included toddlers and a new-born baby. Peter shelved the idea of moving his family into the *Tam O' Shanter* indefinitely. In fact, it would be another five years before they moved in permanently. However, In 1830 Peter, Elizabeth and the four children moved in to the *Tam O' Shanter* for the summer months when the weather was pleasant, moving out again in the autumn when the cold winds once again started to bite at the bone. This tradition of spending the summer months at Marsden and the winter months at *The Highlander* continued until 1835, when the family moved into the *Tam O' Shanter* for good.

But what of the Inner Room and the mysterious polished stone slab? What secrets, we may ask, lie behind?

# CHAPTER 17

# THE WORLD BELOW

There is no doubt that the cave complex behind the Grotto frontage, in the cliff, and the tunnel complex below ground, are connected. Together they form a vast network of caves and tunnels the extent of which we can only guess at. If the dragon fraternity believed that there was an 'eruption' of the complex at Marsden Bay then logic would dictate that they had some facts to substantiate the notion. At some point they must have discovered a link between the cave complex in the cliff and the tunnel complex below. The question we must now address is just where that connection was. The complex of caves at Marsden utilised by Peter Allan comprised of both rooms to which the public had almost open access and others to which access was severely restricted. Our attention is immediately drawn to the Inner Room, which contained a heavy, stone slab that could not be moved except by the efforts of several men. The slab was obviously hiding something that Peter did not want anyone to see.

Famous northern author Dame Catherine Cookson, herself born and bred in South Tyneside, made reference to one of the mysterious tunnels in her book *The Harrogate Secret* [1]:

> "I hate that fellow, you know. I hate meanness, but I'll fix him before he's finished. He's got enough stored away to fill Jingling Geordie's Hole. You know the hole?"
>
> "Yes, the one above the short sands, near the castle. They say the Romans made it."
>
> "They say more than their prayers and they whistle them; they've got no authority for that, no more than they have for the subterranean passage that was supposed to run from there under the Tyne all the way to Jarrow so that the monks could trot through to visit their kin on the other side. But anyway, who knows?"

This is not the only reference Catherine Cookson makes to the subterranean passages in her novels. In *Mrs. Flannagan's Trumpet* [2] she tells a story of smugglers and criminals set in the coastal area of South Shields, and, amazingly, a network of tunnels inside the cliff face,

> And down. And down. And down. Eddie knew that they must be somewhere inside the actual cliff, yet he had the weird feeling that they were descending into the bowels of the earth.

But Cookson goes further. Not only does she mention the 'fictitious' caves within the cliff, but she also gives details concerning how they were hidden:

> A rough plan, but a clever one nevertheless. For if you measure the inside of the house you'll find it all of eight feet short of the outside, and if you measure the width you'll find it two foot less in the inside from where my bedroom begins to where it ends ... As I've said me grandfather was a stonemason, he could make two pieces of stone meet as if they'd never been split. He could make a stone swivel like an oiled hinge. They worked every spare minute they had on the house for three years. People came out and had a look at it. "What thick walls you are building!" they said, "but you'll need them with the sea at your door.", "What's those long narrow rooms on the end for?" they said. "Oh, they're going to be a couple of storerooms and a water closet."

To say the least, the fictional account in *Mrs. Flannagan's Trumpet* bears an extraordinary resemblance to what *really* occurred when Peter Allan excavated the 'fifteen rooms', which comprised *The Grotto* inn. We have secret tunnels. We have rooms in a cliff face. We have secret rooms being excavated under a pretext. We have hidden entrances. We have swivelling slabs of stone. We even have discrepancies in the measurements of the rooms. All of this in a 'fictional' house called Rock End built at *exactly* the same small stretch of coastline, which plays host to *The Marsden Grotto* today!

There is absolutely no doubt in my mind that Dame Catherine Cookson based parts of her novel on true-life incidents and occurrences, and that she had the tunnels and secret rooms of *The Grotto* in mind when she penned her tale. Cookson did a lot of research for her novels, and it is plain to me that she knew more than she ever let on. In short, Catherine Cookson had, somehow, stumbled upon facts, which led her to the conclusion that there were secret rooms and tunnels both behind and beneath *The Grotto*.

Catherine Cookson knew *exactly* what was going on at that enigmatic little alehouse by the sea.

One of the criticisms, which was levelled against my theory regarding the hidden tunnel system is that, if such a system existed, surely portions of it would have been exposed by now as the cliff face slowly erodes. In fact, this may indeed have happened in past times. In her *Notes on Marsden* [3], Amy Flagg quotes an anonymous source as saying:

> Since [previous times] there have been more and more falls and the many caves referred to in preceding accounts have almost disappeared, although there are still one or two 'corridors' which are still traversable at low tide. One of the columns [sic] of the Wishing Chair has gone and the remaining two are now but a few inches thick.

It is curious that in the above-mentioned novels Catherine Cookson mentions a 'grandfather' who was a stonemason. This 'stonemason' could, 'make two pieces of stone meet as if they'd never been split. He could make a stone swivel like an oiled hinge'.

It cannot be beyond coincidence that this fictional character utilises two separate techniques for concealing hidden chambers. Firstly, it is said that he can 'make two pieces of stone meet as if they'd never been split.' This is indeed reminiscent of the aforementioned technique employed at the Grotto by Peter Allan; when doorways would be filled in with stone and then covered with limestone cement so artfully that the result would look like a perfectly solid stonewall.

Secondly, Cookson says that 'grandfather' could 'make a stone swivel like an oiled hinge'. This clearly implies the use of a slab of stone to fashion a swivelling doorway of some kind – *exactly* the type of device we know to have been situated in the Inner Room!

But if there *was* a slab of stone employed as a barrier in the Inner Room, what was it hiding? In past times, the Inner Room – now bricked up and inaccessible – was used by bar staff at the Grotto as a small office. However, at the northern end of this small room there was a hole in the ground – sometimes referred to by staff as "the trapdoor" – which led down into a subterranean cavern known as the Old Cellar. This epithet was obviously given to the chamber to distinguish it from C1, which in later years also became known as the Cellar.

Few people have descended the narrow stone steps into the Old Cellar, but descriptions of it do exist. One former tenant of the Grotto told me that it was "just a cave, like the rest", implying that there was nothing unusual about it. A former barman told me that he had once ventured into the cave and that it made him "feel weird":

> I didn't like it. There was something strange about it. Every time you looked at a wall…well, if you turned away and then looked back at it, it didn't look the same as the first time you looked at it, if you get my drift.

But it was Ronnie Ward, former 'Hoist Man' or lift attendant at the Grotto, who supplied some real detail. When I interviewed Ronnie at the very beginning of my research he made mention several times of an 'underground cave' which was occasionally used for storage. Not having any idea at the time how important this was, I did not think to ask him exactly where this 'underground cave' was situated. It seemed sufficient to me that it was somewhere underneath the inn, and in my mind I pictured a cellar pretty much like any other pub cellar:

> Once I was asked to take some boxes down to the cave. I felt a bit uncomfortable down there I must admit. At one end of the cave there was a large sheet of plywood up against the wall. I noticed that it was wobbling. I laughed to myself and thought, 'Oh, it must be the Grotto Ghost!' Anyway, I went over to the wood and could see that it was attached to the wall with screws, or maybe nails, I can't remember. The top left-hand corner of the wood had come away, and it was there where it was wobbling. I put my hand up and steadied it, and that's when I felt the draught.
>
> I tried to pull the wood away from the rock to see what was behind, but I couldn't move it enough. I figured that there must have been a hole behind it though, otherwise, where was the draft coming from?
>
> I mentioned this to another barman working there at the time. He told me that he had once managed to get the wood away and found a tunnel behind it in the rock. He got a torch from upstairs and walked up the tunnel. He said it seemed to go on for ages. He reckoned it came out at the caravan site across the road.

It wasn't till I learned about the 'Old Cellar' beneath the Inner Room that I realised that this must have been the chamber that Ronnie had described as the "underground cave".

I managed to track down another barman who had worked at the Grotto, John, and I asked him if he had ever been down in the Old Cellar:

No, I never did. I'd heard too many stories about ghosts, and things. But my mate went down there. He never said how, but he reckoned that there was a hidden place you could crawl through into these other caves. He said he'd been down there loads of times and never noticed it. You had to look at it in the right way before you could see that you could go through it. Another thing he said was that you had to be careful, as there was a steep tunnel that went a long way down. He didn't say how far, but he reckoned that if you fell down it you'd be dead.

## References

[1] Cookson, Catherine; *The Harrogate Secret*
[2] Cookson, Catherine; *Mrs Flannagan's Trumpet*
[3] Flagg, Amy; Notes on Marsden (Manuscript prepared by the author, held at South Tyneside Local Studies Library)

# CHAPTER 18

# PETER ALLAN'S DOOR

*It was upon a gallery, that overhangs the shore,*
*I sat and viewed the scenery round Peter Allan's door;*
*The ships were passing near the spot like vessels at the Nore;*
*I smoked my pipe and quaff'd my pot at Peter Allan's door.*

*There running comes a Russian pig, at the well known name of Jack.*
*He with his snout the sand doth plough, two ravens on his back;*
*In yonder cave poor Jessie lies, her litter half a score,*
*With sleep oppressed they close their eyes at Peter Allan's door.*

*To view this rock each stranger hastes, its pillars rudely hewn,*
*Apartments fitted to each taste, with rooms upstairs and down;*
*If you're inclined to shake a foot, there's music in great store,*
*Besides a stall of spice and fruit at Peter Allan's door.*

*The wooden clock fast to the rock the fleeting moments tells,*
*The laden bees return in flocks into their waxen cells;*
*The very pigeons have a cot, their numbers full a score,*
*And wash themselves when th' weather's hot at Peter Allan's door.*

*The merry groups on Velvet Bed with pleasure I did see,*
*The smoke went curling o'er their heads as they enjoyed their tea.*
*The gulls, ne'er dreading Peter's gun, did hover near the shore,*
*Nor yet the murdered skeleton at Peter Allan's door.*

*Teetotal Moses struck the rock, and water gushed therefrom,*
*But Peter yields John Barleycorn, and good old English Tom;*
*So you can sit and drink your fill till you can drink no more,*
*Then find your way as best you can from Peter Allan's door.*

Taken from *The Shields Garland,* published in 1839 by T. F. Brockie and Co. The poem was supposedly written by local chemist James Byram, who later emigrated to New Zealand. However, other sources ascribe it to the Newcastle poet William Mitford, who was a friend of Peter's. Personally I think Byram to be the likely author, but it is impossible to be sure. The poem could be sung to the tune of a popular Victorian ballad entitled 'The Days When We Went Gypsying'.

# CHAPTER 19

# THE ROCK

In the summer of 1830 Peter devised a new and ambitious project. Like everything else at Marsden Bay, it was also strange and enigmatic. The rock at Marsden is, if one accepts the current scientific wisdom, 250 million years old or thereabouts. Technically it is classed as Permian Magnesian Limestone, and has attracted the attention of geologists from all over the globe because of its unique qualities.

Aeons ago, mainland Britain was not an island. Rather, it was part of a huge continent, which straddled a large part of the northern hemisphere. Then, the area, which now comprises the British Isles, was actually much farther south. (In fact, had it been any further south it would have been in the southern hemisphere). Nearby there was a huge tropical ocean, which, through geological turmoil, had layer upon layer of silt and mud laid down on its seabed.

Much later, these hardened layers were thrown up in a series of cataclysms, and now form the cliffs, which surround Marsden Bay. Above them are the remains of a layer of soft anhydrite, which at one time may have been as thick as 500 feet. This has largely eroded, and what is left of it has been covered with a thick layer of broken and collapsed rock – much harder – itself a product of earlier times. Indeed, the rock at Marsden is largely composed of many alternating layers of hard and soft rock. Now, after suffering the ravages of rainfall and sea action for untold ages, the rock has in many places a serrated look. This is due to the soft rock eroding and washing away whilst the harder layers remain intact.

Directly in front of *The Marsden Grotto* is a huge rock. People from other parts of the Borough know it as Marsden Rock. To the locals it is simply *the Rock*, for there is nothing even vaguely similar nearby to confuse it with. To stand in front of Marsden Rock is to stand in awe.

Marsden Rock used to have a singular, eye-catching feature: a large hole or archway that separated it into two halves with a sturdy connecting bridge of rock straddling the two. The central arch of the rock collapsed just a few years ago. This left the larger northern aspect now separated from the southern aspect, which stood like a tall, tenuous pillar next to its stouter compatriot. In the interests of safety, the southern pillar was blown up on the basis that it would inevitably collapse anyway.

In Peter Allan's day, the rock was still intact, and even more breathtaking than it is now. As Peter's spiritual nature was developing, and his affinity – even *oneness* – with the Bay was growing stronger by the day, he undoubtedly came to see the significance of his own name, *Peter.* In *koiné* or common Greek – the *lingua franca* of Judea when Jesus was alive, and the language in which most, if not all, of the New Testament was written – *petra* means *rock.* Peter is the anglicised version of *petra*, and hence also means rock. This, as we know, has a profound significance for Roman Catholics, who place great stock on the words of Jesus to Peter the Apostle, when he said, "And I say unto you, you are Peter, the Rock, and on this rock I will build my assembly [church], and the powers of death shall never conquer it." (Matthew 16;18) As this realisation dawned on Peter, the rock began to assume a powerful symbolic significance in his mind.

For those unacquainted with Marsden Rock there is no better description than that which is found within *Chambers' Journal* [1]:

> On the coast of Durham, about midway between the mouth of the Tyne and the town of Sunderland, stands detached from the shore, a curious, craggy mass termed Marsden Rock: – a huge instalment of rock, through which the perpetual action of the waves has affected many passages, leaving here or there supports which form lofty arches and permit, at certain times of the tide, the intrusion of visitors … [On the summit] rabbits have been colonised, breed and often fall over the edge to meet certain death.

The rock has also been a home, for millennia, to seabirds of various kinds. However, the type of bird that nests on the rock has changed many times during its history, latterly in the twentieth century. Peter decided to build a stairway to the top of the rock. This stairway would enable visitors to climb to the pinnacle of this landmark and enjoy a spectacular view of both the ocean and the bay. Once his mind was set, he lost no time in purchasing the materials.

But Peter also needed help. A small team of labourers was still excavating steadily into the cliff face, but Peter diverted two of them to his new project with the promise of paying them eleven pounds each.

To digress for a moment, we need to add a historical footnote here to the effect that, just before Peter began work on the stairway to the top of the rock, it is likely that one of the two prized Russian pigs that he owned, Jack, probably died. I have in my possession a clipping (undated) from *The Monthly Chronicle*, which may have been printed around 1857. The clipping contains a letter from an unnamed correspondent. The writer recalls how, at the time that the stairway was under construction, Peter 'had a Russian pig, a dark, grizzly animal named Jessie.' Curiously no mention is made of Jack here, which leads me to believe that he may have died previous to the commencement of Peter's project.

The construction of the stairway was completed in a most extraordinary manner. On the first day, one of the men made his way precariously to the top of the rock with a rope and some tools attached to his waist. Once he had reached the plateau he secured the rope and then hauled up various pieces of equipment. These included a tent, more tools, food and large number of branches cut from the trees, which lay in between the fields on the cliff top. Once on top of the rock, the workman erected the tent, pegged it down and interlaced the green boughs around it to give extra protection from the elements. Curiously, a flag was flown from the top of the tent, although we have no idea what was on it. Likely it would have borne a symbol or slogan reflecting Peter's dry sense of humour.

For two weeks the man lived and worked on the top of this barren, stark rock – braving the elements whilst chipping away at the limestone. Meanwhile, Peter and the second labourer were constructing the stairway down below, which steadily grew towards the rock. The steps first connected with the rock at a height of fifty feet, where they met an outcrop of limestone extending horizontally from the main body of the rock itself. In some old photographs of the stairway it is possible to see in some detail a small gantry or 'observation deck', which Peter built at this level. Here, visitors could rest for a while before completing the second stage of their ascent to the top of the rock. After ascending another thirty-five feet or so, the stairway actually bedded into a recess in the rock, which had been cut by the first labourer who worked down over towards his two companions.

Some later accounts claim that all three men ascended to the top of the rock and excavated their way down towards what would become the gantry level. We can discount this theory for several reasons. Firstly, the narrow recess, which was excavated, only allowed for one worker to labour at a time. Secondly, it would be necessary for at least one worker to operate at ground level to make the necessary adjustments to the stairway as it was under construction, to ensure that it dovetailed perfectly with the spot they had chosen to build the Observation Deck above. Once Peter had finished the stairway up to the Observation Deck, he and his companion then erected a smaller ladder, which led to the point where the stairs would actually be recessed into the rock. Here, Peter and his companions could take it in turns to chisel away at the limestone, working upwards towards the other labourer who was cutting his way downwards towards his companions.

Within two weeks the project was finished, and a stairway now existed which would take visitors directly to the top of Marsden Rock. Undoubtedly this would have increased the number of tourists who were just beginning to frequent the bay, and – never one to miss an opportunity – Peter erected yet another tent on the plateau so that tea and refreshments could be served to those hardy souls who made it to the top. Bizarrely, he also took a litter of white rabbits and two goats up to the top of the rock. What became of the goats we shall never know, and although the rabbits bred for many years they are now no longer to be found on that inhospitable summit.

The stairway was an instant hit, and attracted the attention of the locals. It also attracted the attention of the small number of tourists who were starting to frequent the bay, drawn by the magnificent view of the North Sea and the surrounding coastline which could be gained from the plateau. As word got round, people came from far and wide to ascend this colossal monument to Mother Nature's handiwork.

*A Ramble to Marsden Rocks*[2] makes reference to the first woman to climb to the top of Marsden Rock; 'The first of Eve's daughters, in fact, who set foot on the summit of Marsden Rock, since it was violently severed from the mainland some centuries since, was miss Julia Collinson of Gateshead, afterwards Mrs. De Winter.'

It has been suggested that the author is stating here that Julia Collinson later married and became Mrs. De Winter. However, the writer's words could possibly be interpreted to mean that a second lady named Mrs. De Winter ascended to the top of the rock after Miss Collinson, This is in fact the case, for my research has uncovered that Julia Collinson actually married one of Peter's sons. (The Collinson family still runs a thriving watchmakers business in Sunderland.)

Almost overnight the rock became a Mecca for evangelical Christians, writers' guilds, poetry groups and a strange assortment of spiritually minded philosophers. It was as if, by creating the stairway, Peter had fashioned a ladder leading to another level of reality. There is a curious symbolism here, and a parallel with the steps created by Blaster Jack. One set of steps led down to a world of smugglers, wreckers and contraband. The other led away from it, towards a spiritual understanding, which the character and personality of the bay enhanced in its own peculiar fashion.

Even the Society of Friends – better known as the Quakers – began to frequent the Rock. Before long, queues were forming – particularly on Sundays – and Lizzie Allan was working flat-out in an effort to produce enough scones and singin' hinnies for the customers.

Peter was amazed at the attention his project had attracted. Like a divine magnet, the Rock began to draw thinkers from a multiplicity of religious and philosophical backgrounds. After a group of young Quaker-ladies had visited the Rock, Peter commented:

> They first looked up at the Rock and said a lot of poetry and stuff; and then they went through under it, and said some more poetry and stuff. And then they mounted up the ladder, and walked about on the top, and said some more poetry and stuff. And then they came down, and turned around, and looked up at it again, and said some more poetry and stuff. And then they bade me goodday, and went away, all the while reciting more poetry and stuff [3].

Seizing the opportunity, Peter stationed his oldest son at the bottom of the stairway to collect pennies and halfpennies from the visitors, although these were never solicited. Peter had a strict rule that all contributions should be voluntary. (Alan Robinson told me that he remembers his father telling him of how he collected pennies at the bottom of the stairway when he was a boy, which I presume was during the tenancy of his grandfather, Segar Robinson, a later manager of *The Grotto*.) However, as the Rock impressed itself upon Peter's psyche even further, the financial recompense became almost immaterial. The Rock became its *own* reward. Perhaps this is best summed up in the words of the poet John Peacock, who said of Marsden Rock:

> *So mortals flourish and decline*
> *Whilst thou, bold rock, still mocks at Time!*
> *Unchanged – thou still remains to me,*
> *An emblem of eternity.* [4]

# References

[1] *Chambers Journal*, September 1875.
[2] Anon. *A Ramble to Marsden Rocks,* (publisher unknown) p. 3.
[3] Peacock, John; *On Marsden Rock.* 1813.
[4] *The Monthly Chronicle*, May 1887, p. 128.

# CHAPTER 20

# STAND! 'TIS THE EXCISE!

As the wicked art of wrecking lost its foothold in the black economy, the smugglers gained a new lease of life. Even today, people do not realise the enormous power and influence that these contrabanders enjoyed. There is a quaint, stereotypical image of smugglers fixed in the minds of most people, largely the product of a surfeit of Hollywood movies. The stereotype portrays a gang of six people or so, a motley collection of ne'er-do-wells, footpads, pirates and other curmudgeons. The leader of the clique will be a menacing figure of great girth, sporting a fierce beard, an earring, a tri-cornered hat and a penchant for saying "Ah-harrrrr me mateys!" with monotonous regularity. Typically, he will be called Old Ned, Hook-hand Jack, Blackbeard or Trader Jim. His followers will all wear bandannas, have a patch over one eye – or a wooden leg – and drink rum. Fed on the Hollywood image, few people have any conception of what the real smuggling gangs were like.

Unlike the wreckers, the smugglers had, in the main, a conscience of sorts. They were normally well liked by the local populace, as they afforded protection and were a source of both cheap alcohol and cheap tobacco. These were the only two pleasures that the poor could hope to indulge in from time to time, and then only if the smugglers made them available. It paid the smugglers to let the locals have rum and tobacco at cost price or less, thereby buying their silence. An Achilles heel in the smuggling game was the ever-present possibility that locals would become 'jibbers' - that is, informers, snouts or grasses in modern parlance. (The word jibber is actually the linguistic ancestor of the modern Geordie term *dobber*; an epithet still used by northeast schoolchildren to describe classmates who tell tales to the teacher.) The Excise men would pay well for valuable information, but those who supplied it ran a terrible risk. Should their duplicity come to the attention of the smugglers themselves, assassination in cold blood would be the final reward of the jibber.

It is important to differentiate between the sea smugglers and the land smugglers. The sea smugglers were responsible for transporting the goods from their point of origin to the coast. Once off-loaded, the land smugglers would take over the responsibility of hiding the goods and fencing them out. This was a complicated operation that required great skill, and was far beyond the abilities of just a handful of common thieves. Far from being small coteries of half-a-dozen people, many smuggling gangs were veritable armies. As mentioned previously, Alan Robinson states that the land smugglers operated in gangs 'consisting of many hundreds'[1]. They were well mounted, well armed and ferociously defensive of their 'patch'.

In an article in *Chambers Journal,* one writer described[2] how, 'There are old men who still remember having seen as many as thirty pack horses laden with spirits and ridden or attended by as many armed smugglers, conveying whiskey over the moors.'

Robinson quite rightly states that the smugglers 'reigned uncontrolled' until 1784. They answered to no one, and had the firepower to stand up to all but a heavily armed battalion of soldiers. From the mid-1780s onwards, however, the smugglers saw their power slowly wane.

But although past their zenith, the smugglers were still influential and powerful. Always casting a vigilant eye, the Excise authorities continually monitored the Marsden/Whitburn coastline, as they knew that a large and sophisticated contrabanding operation was taking place there.

Early in 1831 a new Supervisor arrived at South Shields, and immediately became suspicious of Peter Allan. Like his predecessor, he concluded that no one in their right mind would open a public house in such an inhospitable place. The elements were too violent and the customers too few. He correctly grasped that such a business could never break even, and that its owner must therefore have had an ulterior motive in setting it up. Not knowing that Peter was searching for a Roman fortune hidden in the cliffs, the Supervisor naturally concluded that Peter was using the premises as a front for the smugglers. In 1831 he applied to his superior in Newcastle for extra officers, and his request was granted. Within days, a new unit of Customs Officers was stationed in South Shields to work alongside the original contingent. Their task was to covertly monitor the goings-on at the *Tam O' Shanter.*

The officers – often known as the *Preventives* or *Preventatives* – decided to make their presence felt immediately. As well as carrying out covert surveillance they also decided to intimidate Peter – two activities that were mutually contradictory, for had Peter really been involved in smuggling the intimidation would only have served to warn him that the Preventives were on his tail. Nevertheless, the intimidation began.

Peter had been warned of the new officers' arrival, and tipped-off by a local smuggler that it was the *Tam O' Shanter* itself that was to be the focus of their interest. Peter did not – could not – take this suggestion seriously. Despite his difficulties with the previous Supervisor over his selling of liquor, he found it hard to imagine that they would think of him as a smuggler. Until the Preventives arrived on his doorstep, that is.

To be truthful, they didn't *literally* arrive on his doorstep. They simply made a habit of riding along the cliff top, directly above the *Tam O' Shanter*, and staring down icily at the premises and the locals sitting outside. Peter was outraged, and bellowed up to them that they should keep their distance, and that dire consequences would follow if they should make a nuisance of themselves. The Preventives laughed and rode away. On the surface of things Peter's actions seemed foolhardy. Was it not asking for trouble to challenge the Queen's men? To a degree, yes; but we must bear in mind that by 1831 Peter had become quite friendly with the smugglers. True, he *wasn't* a smuggler, but the *Tam O' Shanter* was a perfect meeting place for the contrabanders. Here, in comfort and security, they could make their plans and discuss business. They could arrange to meet others of like mind at a pre-arranged time to pass on information. They could work out strategies for deceiving the Excise, and hide out there when things were hot. In fact, it is likely that several of the hidden rooms in the *Tam O' Shanter* were used to hide smugglers from the Preventives from time to time. All in all, then, both Peter Allan and the *Tam O' Shanter* were valuable to the smugglers, and they would not have allowed two priggish Excise men to ruin things.

Marsden was still a remote spot, remember. When Peter Allan was excavating inside the *Tam O' Shanter* a number of skeletons were uncovered. Most showed signs of having died a violent death. Others were found later. In June 1836, whilst some workmen were digging a hole near the *Tam O' Shanter* to receive a tent pole, a body was discovered three feet below the surface. The skeleton, that of a male, had been carefully buried, and several flat stones placed underneath and around his head. A flattened lead bullet was found in his rib cage, showing that, whoever he was, he had died violently.

On the grassy bank above the *Tam O' Shanter*, Peter's son – Peter III, we may call him – discovered no less than thirteen (some accounts say eighteen) skeletons. Others were found at the base of the cliff. Who were they? Some were undoubtedly the bodies of sailors washed up on the shore. Others may have been the remains of those who had drowned by ignoring the treachery of Marsden's tides. But many had bullet wounds and sword cuts. These were in all probability the bones of pirates or smugglers who had come off worst after a falling out with their colleagues. One or two may even have been Preventive Officers, caught red-handed by the smugglers and then quickly dispatched and buried. Interestingly, the partial remains of a skeleton – but including, bizarrely, two skulls – were found by Peter as he was excavating the ground outside of the premises in preparation for the building of the patio and sea wall, which now front *The Grotto*. Two silver buckles were found with the remains, and for a while they were displayed at a farmhouse on the cliff top where curious visitors could inspect them. The bones were found buried almost directly under the window which had been part of the original construction made by Blaster Jack, but whether the old quarryman knew of their presence is debatable.

Given the degree of violence, which Marsden Bay had witnessed, and mainly at the instigation of the wreckers and smugglers, there is no doubt in, my mind that they would have quite happily added another couple of Preventives to their tally had the opportunity arisen. Peter's threats, then, carried some weight.

An uneasy truce developed between Peter and the Preventives. They no longer intimidated him publicly, and resorted to more subtle methods of investigation. This involved sending in to the *Tam O' Shanter* undercover agents posing as drinkers and tourists. Of course this was a highly risky operation. Had the smugglers suspected that a stranger in their midst was a Preventive they may well have killed him on the spot. There was little point in visiting the *Tam O' Shanter* during the day. Only a handful of drinkers would be there, and they would know each other. A stranger would stick out like a sore thumb, immediately causing everyone else to maintain a discrete silence until he had left. But nights were a different matter. To Peter's pleasant surprise some of the local farmers and fishermen were now beginning to pop in to the *Tam O' Shanter* for a glass of ale or a drop of the hard stuff after their work was done. Sensing a means of making a little more money, Peter hastily erected a stage at the southern extremity of the Ballroom, and encouraged some 'local lasses' to sing for the clientele with the promise of free gin. He also added a bar at the northern extremity, thus saving drinkers from having to walk through to the original bar in $C_1$. Several nights a week the *Tam O' Shanter* would play host to a party of local merrymakers, and on each occasion someone new would come along to see what all the fuss was about. The seasoned Preventives at South Shields knew that this was the best time to 'hit' the *Tam O' Shanter*. With the drink flowing and the locals dancing, a stranger would be far less likely to stand out.

In July 1831, then, the Preventives moved in. Their plan seems to have been that several officers would enter the inn posing as drinkers, no doubt with some suitable yarn at the ready to fend off awkward questions. Whilst seemingly enjoying the revelry like everyone else, they would really be listening out for information regarding the smuggling activities at Marsden and Whitburn. Of course, the Supervisor would have been unlikely to allow his officers to enter the premises without back up, so we may safely assume that other Preventives were hiding outside in case of trouble.

What happened next is a matter of debate. There are literally dozens of written and oral variations of the legend, each one differing slightly from the rest. In some accounts one of the key players in the drama is not an Excise man at all, but a soldier. In another the villain is said – incomprehensibly – to be Blaster Jack. What follows is a composite of these variations, putting together the most plausible aspects into a realistic scenario. It is also composed of the elements of the legend, which virtually every variation agrees upon, and which are compatible with the known historical facts.

One of the regular drinkers at the *Tam O' Shanter* was a smuggler whose name is now lost to us. By all accounts he was a young man who possessed a devil-may-care attitude and who enjoyed the dancing and drinking which was now part of the *Tam O' Shanter* scene. One evening he was standing at the second bar, which Peter had erected in the Ballroom, enjoying a pint of ale. He was drinking from a plain but well-crafted pewter tankard. Having one's own tankard in the bar was a sign of some status. It identified the drinker as a regular who was known to and accepted by the management.

It is obvious that the tankard of ale before him was not the first he had downed that evening. His senses were now a little dulled, and perhaps for that reason did not set any alarm bells ringing when a polite and friendly stranger idled up to him and offered to buy him a drink. "Why not?", he thought.

A conversation ensued between the smuggler and the stranger, the stranger enquiring politely what his newfound companion did for a living. Was he a farmer, perhaps, or a fisherman? The young man laughed: not hysterically, but enough to draw the attention of Peter Allan who was himself behind the bar and serving the ale that evening:

"'Am I a farmer? A *fisherman*? Not exactly, my friend. I'm a smuggler!"
"Really?" said the stranger, his face now betraying a well-crafted expression of curiosity married to wide-eyed innocence. "So tell me; how exactly does one … 'smuggle', then?"'

To Peter's horror, the alcohol had loosened the young contrabander's tongue to such an extent that he then proceeded to divulge to the stranger the most guarded secrets of the smuggling operation. No amount of coughing, winking or nudging on Peter Allan's part had any effect, and the young man carried on with gusto. Peter had no way of knowing whether the man was a Preventive or not. He certainly didn't recognise him, but that counted for nothing. The boy was playing with fire.

At some point, even through his alcoholic fog, the smuggler seems to have realised that the stranger who was plying him with beer seemed unusually interested in what he had to say:

"Why are you asking me all these questions, my friend?" he enquired.

"Because I'm an Excise man, 'my friend', and you are now under arrest." The young man felt the barrel of the gun pressing firmly into his ribs.'

Suddenly sobered by the horror of what he had done, the smuggler reacted with a speed that contradicted his obvious inebriation. He instinctively lashed out at the Preventive and caught him on the head with a powerful blow. As the officer sprawled backwards towards the floor, the smuggler was already taking off through the door, which led from the Ballroom onto the wooden patio outside. With one leap he jumped over the sea wall and landed upon the sand. He had to escape, but which way to go? South was out of the question. The tide was in, and he could go no more that one hundred yards before hitting a large outcrop, which would bar his escape along the beach to Whitburn. He would have to head north towards South Shields.

Despite his drunken state, the youth worked up an impressive speed. The wet sand and shale was substantially firmer under foot with the tide being in. If he could make it to the myriad of caves, which encircled the Velvet Beds, he could hide in any one of them, and the Excise men could search for a year and a day and still not find him, bastards that they were.

By the time the young smuggler had made his mind up which way to run, the Preventative had already regained his feet and was in pursuit, leaving behind him a gaggle of bemused farmers, fishermen and smugglers. And of course, a concerned Peter Allan.

As his feet planted themselves on the wet sand, the Preventive immediately glanced to his right and his left. *There he is.* Dark though it was, the moonlight shone just brightly enough for the officer to catch sight of the inebriated smuggler racing northwards in the direction of South Shields. *I'll have you, you greasy, bloody whippersnapper.* Half a mile away lay Velvet Beds. *If he reaches there I'll never catch him.* Other officers had now emerged from various hiding places and joined the chase. They lagged behind, however, and the Preventative knew that his chances of catching the smuggler were slim. Breathing deeply he raced across the sands, but the man was pulling away. The officer had still not fully recovered from the blow to his head, and his legs began to feel heavy. It was at this point that he made an instinctive, snap decision, which would colour the legend of Marsden Bay forever: he raised his pistol and took aim. *Turn around, you bloody bugger*, thought the Preventive. *Let me see your face or at least the silhouette of it.*

The smuggler noticed that he could no longer hear the *skish-skish-skish* of the Preventive's boots as they hit the sand. There was silence now. *Don't look back.* He stopped and turned. The officer was there, but he was standing still. *Don't look back!* The Preventative's pistol was raised and pointing directly at him. He turned to run again, but it was too late. The ball of hot lead hit him directly between the shoulder blades, and he fell to the ground dead.

The smuggler fell next to a large, stone pillar, which has graced Marsden beach for millennia. It is a natural formation, roughly twenty feet in height. It has the appearance of an elongated saltcellar, and bears faint traces of having been worked or shaped in a bygone age. For as long as anyone could remember, the pillar had been called *Lot's Wife*.

By now the other Preventives had caught up, and a patrol, which had been passing along the cliff top, had dismounted and was making its way down Blaster Jack's stairs. Every single reveller from the *Tam O' Shanter* had raced out of the inn to watch the mêlée. There were too many officers to even consider making a fight of it, and to do so would have ultimately seen the end of the premises forever. Peter would lose his license to sell liquor, and the Excise would be crawling around morning, noon and night for years to come. Silently they filed back inside as the officers dragged the body towards the steps.

Once back inside, Peter asked Elizabeth to fetch him his toolbox, which she duly did. Opening it up, he removed his hammer and a large nail. Behind the bar was a pillar, which, to all appearances, looked as if it had been cut out of the rock. It was one of a number of such pillars that graced the Ballroom. Taking up the hammer, Peter drove the large nail into the limestone at the rear of the pillar as the clientèle of the *Tam O' Shanter* looked on curiously. Then Peter's eyes fell upon the pewter tankard, which stood upon the bar where the smuggler had left it. It was still half-filled with beer. He poured out the remainder onto the floor of the Ballroom and then hung the tankard upon the nail. Seething with anger he instructed everyone present, "Let no man drink from this tankard from this day forth, lest he be accursed." [3]

The above account is, as I have stated, a synthesis of several oral and written traditions that I have managed to uncover. There is absolutely no doubt in my mind that the tankard, which is central to this story, is the one that sat in *The Grotto* until it was stolen several years ago. It is this tankard, which Nick Garvey filled up reverently every evening and left upon the bar in the Ballroom. It was this same tankard which was often found empty the following morning. It was the tankard of which Peter Allan said, "Let no man drink from it from this day forth, lest he be accursed", a rule, which was subsequently ignored from time to time, with dire consequences.

\* \* \*

In 1832 Lizzie gave birth to their fifth child, also called Elizabeth after her mother. Peter, busy as ever, was still excavating further into the cliff face. Since the death of the young smuggler the Excise had continued to keep a watchful eye on the *Tam O' Shanter*, but they had not made any further attempts at covert infiltration of the inn itself. But they once again started to harass Peter, and we have a graphic illustration of this, which has survived to demonstrate to us just how dramatic life could be at Marsden Bay.

As the balmy summer nights began to fade away, and the first chill of the strong north-easterly winds started to bite, Lizzie and Peter would begin to spend more and more evenings at *The Highlander*. As detailed previously, they would eventually move into *The Highlander* permanently over the winter and not return to *The Grotto* residentially until "the swallows returned" the following spring. One evening in the autumn, when Peter and Lizzie were at *The Highlander*, the Preventives decided to pay the *Tam O' Shanter* a visit. They had, according to the author of *A Ramble to Marsden Rocks*[4], been tipped off that Peter and his wife would be spending the evening at Whitburn, and not returning to open up the *Tam O' Shanter* till the following morning. They had also been tipped off that a consignment of contraband brandy was due to be smuggled ashore and stored at the *Tam O' Shanter* itself. On arrival they rooted around, in all probability looking for the brandy kegs, according to Robinson[5], but found nothing.

Assuming that Peter and Lizzie were now residing permanently at *The Highlander* due to the imminent onset of winter, they decided to return the following evening. Unfortunately for the Preventives, the master of the *Tam O' Shanter* was waiting to bid them welcome.

Whether Peter had been tipped off about their visits, or whether he had decided to stay over at the inn for some other reason, we will never know;

but there he was, and he saw the officers coming. Keeping a discrete eye on the officers from one of the inn's windows, Peter watched in astonishment their audacious behaviour. The author *of A Ramble to Marsden Rocks*[6] takes up the story, '... He was very surprised to see them very coolly lighting their pipes on his quay, very close to his own door. Snatching down his gun, he rushed out among them, like Samson against the Philistines'.

Peter's hunting gun hung behind the bar in C1, and every written and oral account I have came across agrees that, at this point, he fired it over their heads and terrified the life out of the officers, shouting, "Ye villains! How dare you intrude upon my property? Be off with you!" Robinson[7] states that the Preventives were so scared they probably hid in the caves further up the beach till they believed the coast was clear.

At this juncture the tale takes a curious turn. All available sources state that almost immediately after this altercation with the Excise there was a sudden change in the relationship between Peter and the officers. What had previously been a bitter hatred mysteriously turned into a warm friendship and mutual respect. The author of *A Ramble to Marsden Rocks*[8] stated that, 'he was soon on the best possible terms with the Preventive men, and continued to be so till the day of his death.' What could have brought about such an extraordinary reversal? History remains silent, but we may hazard a guess or two. Most historians and researchers have concluded that, 'having seen that Peter Allan was really a hearty good fellow', the officers suddenly had a fit of conscience and realised that he was innocent of any grave misdemeanours. For the life of me I cannot see that this could be the case. The man had *shot* at them and *threatened their lives*.

So how do we explain the change? Safely ruling out the notion that the Preventives had suddenly gone all soft and cuddly on Peter Allan, we must conclude that a deal of some sorts was struck which was mutually beneficial to both sides – a deal which allowed Peter to go about his business without harassment, and the Preventives to at least control the small part Peter played in the smuggling activities, if not exactly stop it. More than one person from Marsden has suggested that Peter was receiving a backhander from the Excise to supply them with information. I doubt this very much. Peter was too principled to engage in that sort of game, and would almost certainly have been caught out by the smugglers at some point had he engaged in it. Personally I lean towards the argument that the financial enhancements did not pass from the Preventives to Peter, but from Peter to the Preventives. At some point Peter may have approached one of the officers who he felt was most amenable to taking a bribe and proposed 'an arrangement' of some kind. Presumably the proposal was accepted, and cordial relations then developed.

But would the smugglers not have become suspicious of Peter's newfound friendship with their deadliest enemies? Not necessarily, for Peter could have convinced them quite easily that the arrangement was to their benefit. Peter could have told the contrabanders that he was paying the Excise Officers a regular sum to ensure that they would not harass him, or continually make their presence felt at the *Tam O' Shanter*. This would have seemed reasonable enough, and it would certainly be an advantage to the smugglers, for, if the Excise were spending less time watching the *Tam O' Shanter*, they were also spending less time watching the smugglers themselves. And so the acrimonious game of cat-and-mouse between Peter and the Preventives ended. But this was not the end of the affair. Peter still wanted to know who had tipped off the Excise that he would be away from home that night.

## References

[1] Alan C. Robinson, *The Story of Marsden and Peter Allan* (published privately by the author, 1971).

[2] *Chambers Journal*, September 1875.

[3] Anon. *The History of Marsden Grotto*, (Vaux Breweries, date unknown) p 18.

[4] Anon. *A Ramble to Marsden Rocks*, (publisher unknown), p. 21.

[5] Alan C. Robinson, *The Story of Marsden and Peter Allan* (published privately by the author, 1971), p.8.

[6] Anon. *A Ramble to Marsden Rocks*, (publisher unknown), p. 21.

[7] Alan C. Robinson, *The Story of Marsden and Peter Allan* (published privately by the author, 1971), p.8.

[8] Anon. *A Ramble to Marsden Rocks*, (publisher unknown), p. 21.

# CHAPTER 21

# THE SETTING UP OF JIBBER JOHN

Peter knew that *someone* had tipped of the Excise men, but who? Marsden had a sparse population indeed, and so figuring out who the guilty party was should not have been that difficult. The farmers and fishermen who frequented the bay area were unlikely candidates. They drank in the *Tam O' Shanter*, but did not mix with either the smugglers or the wreckers on an intimate level. Neither did they like to be seen in the company of the Excise men, lest people should get the wrong idea. They were also unlikely to be acquainted with the comings and goings of Peter Allan outside of licensed hours. The other locals did too well out of the smugglers, receiving cut-price rum and tobacco, and would be unlikely to jeopardise their own creature comforts for a one-off back-hander. Also, being an informer was a very risky business. Make one mistake or utter an indiscreet word and you would have effectively signed your own death warrant. You may have also precipitated the ostracism of your entire family from the community forever. Too risky indeed.

So who was the informer? He or she would have to be someone who had no family in the vicinity to jeopardise. They would have to possess an intimate knowledge of the Bay, and, if they were in the pay of the Excise, an even more detailed knowledge of the contrabanding activities that went on there. This process of deduction pointed the finger of suspicion firmly at one of the smugglers themselves being the informer.

Peter lost no time in speaking to some of the dyed-in-the-wool smugglers who frequented *The Tam O'Shanter*. Naturally he would have had to choose carefully whom he talked to. There was a very real possibility that he may have ended up voicing his fears and suspicions to the informer himself. It has to be said at this juncture that there is no actual record of such a meeting having taken place between Peter and the smugglers, but we cannot imagine that *no* discussion took place. It was in everyone's interest to identify the informer as quickly as possible and then act appropriately.

With the presumption that such a meeting did occur, we can assume that it did not take long for one or two likely names to rise to the top of this motley broth of characters who supped their ale at the *Tam O' Shanter*. Indeed, one name did spring to the lips of more than one person present – that of Smuggler John.

We know precious little about Smuggler John. We do not know his surname. We do not know anything about his parentage, place of origin or trade, if indeed he had one. What we do know is that he was a smuggler of some repute, but not someone whom his comrades felt could be entirely trusted. The smugglers knew that someone had been informing on them to the Excise. The Preventives had been enjoying a suspiciously high number of successes of late, successes that hinted at an inside knowledge of just when and where their contraband would be off-loaded and stored.

Exactly why Smuggler John aroused the suspicions of his mates we do not know; but there must have been some rationale behind it. The problem was that no one could produce any real proof. Ruthless though the smugglers were, they were not about to lynch one of their own unless his guilt could be established beyond doubt. What was needed was a plan – a means of testing out Smuggler John and establishing whether or not he was trustworthy. Such a plan would have to be executed quickly, and for two reasons. Firstly, an informer in the ranks was a perilous threat to the others involved in contrabanding. For all they knew, the Excise could turn up *en masse* at the next shore drop and arrest everyone involved. Secondly, there was always the possibility that one loose tongue could inadvertently warn John of the plan, and the longer it took to affect the strategy the greater the likelihood was that he would find out what they were up to. Eventually the smugglers came up with a plan that was daring, ingeniously simple and would need little in the way of organisation. In fact, all they would need was the loan of thirty old brandy casks from Peter. Peter knew that the smugglers were setting up John, and had little sympathy for the traitor. But what he didn't know was that the contrabandists also had other plans. They would teach the Excise a lesson they'd not forget in many a year.

One of the idiosyncrasies of the *Tam O' Shanter* was the difficulty that its location posed in terms of deliveries. There is some evidence that barrels of rum, beer and brandy etc. sold at the *Tam O' Shanter* (at least, those which came from legitimate sources) were lowered down to the inn by a rope and pulley system. What the brewers were not interested in, apparently, was "collecting the empties". Before long a huge collection of empty barrels was being stockpiled on the sands next to the inn. Eventually, some of these barrels were stored in the *Tam O' Shanter* itself. In all probability they would have been stocked in the hidden rooms of the inn, which were not in use. Later, others would be stacked in the multitude of caverns, which dotted the cliff face and surrounding rocks. Alan Robinson told me how, as a child, he stumbled across just such a cave filled with barrels with his brother. The cave had been filled with barrels and then walled up with heavy boulders. After Alan and his brother removed the boulders the barrels were washed out to sea. It is not beyond the bounds of possibility that other barrels may be still hiding in the caves waiting to be found, although personally I think it unlikely. Finding a few barrels to help execute their plan, then, would be no problem. The next step was to set up Smuggler John.

Within a day or two John wandered into the *Tam O' Shanter* for a drink. Before long he was approached by one of the leading lights within the gang who asked for a quiet word in his ear. Probably their impromptu meeting took place in one of the discrete niches set into the wall of the Ballroom. Once they were seated, the other smuggler lost no time in putting forward a proposition to John. A cutter was coming in on Wednesday evening under cover of darkness, and it would be loaded with thirty barrels of contraband – a mixture of brandy and tobacco. The haul needed to be offloaded quickly, and every spare pair of hands would be required. The gang needed to know quickly whether John was up for the job. (At this point it seems that John must have made an excuse for not joining the operation, for records from the time indicate that he was not present. This, however, would only have served to make Peter and the smugglers even more suspicious.)

Having apologised in advance for his absence, John nevertheless wished the rest of the gang the best of luck. He enquired as to where the contraband was to be stored. Now *why is he asking me that, the wormy leechgreaser?* He was told that they would be offloaded at Jackie's Cove two miles to the south. The goods would then be brought overland and stored in Smugglers Cave, and then distributed to various safe houses till they could be fenced.

This arrangement probably struck John as a wee bit strange. Why not just take the goods straight to the safe houses? *Because we think the Excise are watching them, John. But when nothing turns up a' Wednesday night they'll be gone. Then we'll move the stuff in a' Thursday night. It'll just have to stand one night in Smugglers Cave, John; just one night, and as long as the Excise don't get wind of it we'll be fine.*

Meanwhile, several trusted smugglers were making the strangest delivery imaginable on their boss's orders. Thirty empty barrels were to be taken by cart to Seaburn, and then ferried out by boat to a cutter, which was waiting offshore. The captain – a good friend of the smugglers – grinned from ear to ear as he saw the boat heading towards his ship. *Aye*, he thought, *this will show you Excise bastards. This will show you, and right enough.*

# CHAPTER 22

# SMUGGLERS CAVE AND PETER'S PSYCHIC PETS

Smugglers Cave – also known as Smugglers Hole – was the largest cavern in the Marsden Bay area. It is recorded that on one occasion at least over 200 people sheltered there when a sudden storm broke out. (What on earth 200 people were doing on Marsden beach is not explained). The cave also had a very peculiar feature; a vertical shaft ran from the roof of the cavern to the cliff top up above. The shaft was, as far as I have been able to determine, between six and eight feet in diameter, and it has to be said that its origins are shrouded in mystery.

One of the orthodox views regarding the shaft's origins is that the hole was artificially created, and that its architect was none other than Blaster Jack. This assumption is admittedly quite logical. After all, Jack had used his blasting skills to create the flight of steps to the north of the *Tam O' Shanter*, and he had also enlarged C1 itself. Who better than Jack to blast a shaft from the roof of Smugglers Cave to the cliff top? Unfortunately, although the idea is logical up to this point, it is fraught with difficulties when explored further.

The first difficulty arises when we try to ascertain what Jack's motives may have been for creating such a shaft. Most commentators [1,2,3] suggest that the shaft was initially made so that farmers could transport barrels or baskets of *guano* (bird dung) and seaweed to the cliff top. From there it would be taken to the fields and used as fertiliser. There was certainly no shortage of guano at Marsden Bay. According to current scientific wisdom it had had literally millions of years to accumulate there. The question we must ask, however, is why such a shaft would be necessary. A simple joist and pulley system would have been just as effective and far easier to construct. There are, in fact, many places adjacent to *The Grotto Inn* where such a hoist could have been set up. And even if such a shaft had been thought of as advantageous, why would Blaster Jack wish to be the one to create it? Blasting a perfectly vertical shaft, over one hundred feet in depth, even through soft magnesian limestone, is a complex and arduous task, and when one considers that neither Jack nor Jessie had any use whatsoever for barrel-loads of guano and seaweed, any idea that the old quarryman could have been responsible for creating the shaft evaporates like the morning dew. And further, even if Jack did have some obscure use for all that guano, why would he want it taken to the cliff top when he resided at the bottom? We can safely say that Blaster Jack did *not* create the vertical shaft above Smugglers Cave.

So what of Peter Allan? Again we lack a motive, and interestingly, the *earliest* commentators on this matter were not comfortable with the idea that either Jack or Peter Allan had been responsible for excavating the shaft. One researcher tentatively suggests that the shaft was the work of Peter Allan, but in a September 1875 edition of *Chambers' Journal* one commentator noted, 'It is not known when or by whom the shaft was made; some accounts state that it was one of Peter Allan's enterprises but it is clear it was made before his time.' So then, if Blaster Jack or Peter Allan did not excavate the shaft, are there any other likely candidates? We can discount the idea that the farmers excavated the shaft as a means of hauling seaweed and guano up to the cliff top. As I have demonstrated, there were far easier methods of taking fertiliser to the top of the cliff than that.

And the smugglers and wreckers? Wouldn't a shaft have been a distinct advantage to them? Surely, hauling contraband up a hidden shaft is far more discrete than hoisting it up an open cliff face. The problem with this theory is that the visibility factor was not really a risk whilst the contraband was being hauled *up* the cliff. The danger of being spotted by the Preventives would present itself when the contraband was *on* the cliff top. The excise patrols were carried out on horseback, and the officers were given to leaving their station at South Shields and riding along the cliff tops as far as the next (smaller) station at Seaburn. The flat leas on the cliff top provided excellent visibility, and once goods had arrived at the cliff top itself, whether via the shaft or a hoist, it was then that the danger presented itself that a passing patrol may stumble upon the activities of the contrabanders.

But there is an even greater reason for discounting the notion that the smugglers were responsible for excavating the shaft. During my research I uncovered a little-known fact about the shaft. *During Peter Allan's day the mouth of the shaft was topped by a large wooden gantry and a hoist.* The gantry consisted of four small walkways, together forming a square. In the centre stood a large tripod made of stout timber. From the centre of the tripod a pulley-rope descended into the shaft. So then, there is no doubt that the shaft *was* used for lowering and raising goods to and from the cliff top. So why can we say that the smugglers did not use it, in addition to the reasons given above? Firstly, we know that the boats, which brought the contraband ashore, did not always use Marsden Bay as a landing point. Most local legends declare that Jackie's Cove and Souter Point to the south were the drop-off points for the sea smugglers. The unpredictable sea at Marsden Bay was just too dangerous to make it a viable proposition. Secondly, the shaft was *not* a secret shaft. Surmounted as it was by a huge gantry and tripod, its presence would hardly be missed by the Preventives. If they had thought for one moment that the shaft was being utilised by the smugglers they would have had it filled in or blasted away. The reason they allowed it to remain was simply because they knew that the shaft *was of no use* to the smugglers at all. It was simply too far from the drop-off points. It was not even of any use to Peter Allan as a means of lowering supplies down to the *Tam O' Shanter*. Between the inn and Smugglers Cave there is a large rocky escarpment, which would make it exceedingly difficult for anyone hauling barrels of ale to the *Tam O' Shanter*. Peter Allan, we know, had his supplies lowered down by a joist and pulley situated next to the stairway to the north of the inn.

But the gantry and tripod over the mouth of the shaft indicates that it had certainly been used by *someone* to haul up something from the beach below. It seems likely that it was indeed used by the farmers for hauling up guano and seaweed to the cliff top: used by them, yes; but as I have demonstrated, not *created* by them. The farmers merely utilised the shaft because it was already there. So at this juncture we are really no further forwards in trying to determine who originally excavated the shaft.

But there are three other possibilities yet to be considered, the first of which is that the Romans may have created the shaft during the time when they occupied *Arbeia* and operated the quay at Velvet Beds. This is an intriguing possibility, for the Romans certainly had the engineering skills necessary to create such a shaft. They were master builders, construction experts and technicians. But again we are faced with the difficulty of providing the Romans with a credible motive for engaging in such an operation. There is just no fathomable reason for them to excavate the cliff in such a manner.

Another theory is that the shaft had been created long before the Roman occupation of Britain, by unknown hands and for unknown purposes. Just who these ancient excavators may have been we do not know, but if the shaft was even more ancient than the Roman occupation we are then led to ask, could the shaft have been part of the tunnel complex that exists in the area? Before examining this possibility we need to discount one other notion; and that is that the shaft was simply a natural fissure in the ground – in other words, the product of natural geological processes as opposed to human ingenuity.

Mackenzie & Ross in their *History of Durham*[4] stated that the shaft had been 'made' as opposed to being formed naturally, which gives us our first clue. However, it is the writer of the aforementioned article in *Chambers' Journal*[5] who really provides a definitive answer. He examined the shaft personally, and described both it and the cave beneath it thus:

> The largest of these [caves] with an irregular domed roof, has a *perfectly cut circular hole* [emphasis mine] in its loftiest portion, through which, by standing directly underneath, we could detect daylight. We found that this hole opened on to the surface of the cliff, unrailed and unguarded, amidst and partially hidden by thick and stunted foliage.

This shaft, then, consisted of a 'perfectly *cut* circular hole'. It must also have been perfectly vertical, for the writer states that you could immediately see daylight by standing underneath it. Indeed, had the shaft not been perfectly vertical it would have made the raising and lowering of goods exceedingly difficult. There can be no doubt then that this was a man-made shaft and *not* a natural fissure.

But what of the theory that the shaft was connected to the larger complex of tunnels which we have proved beyond all doubt exists even to this day? If this was the case, then we need to determine at which point the shaft was linked to the network. Obviously it could not have been connected to any tunnels or caves at its upper extremity, for to our knowledge there were none, but what about the lower extremity of the shaft?

The lower extremity of the shaft ended in the roof of Smugglers Cave. It is possible that other tunnels may have led from the cave, thus indirectly connecting the vertical shaft with the larger complex. Unfortunately, some time before 1875 – we cannot be sure when – Smugglers Cave collapsed after a ferocious storm. But here we must digress for a moment, for we are faced with yet another historical puzzle. In the September 1875 edition of *Chamber's Journal* we read, 'It [Smugglers Cave] was a huge, natural cavern … but for some years *before its destruction* [emphasis mine] it was much reduced in size due to the raising of the floor level by silted sand.'

The difficulty we are faced with here is that most contemporary historians believe that Smugglers Cave collapsed as late as 1913. Robinson[6] quotes the late R. P. Fernandes as stating, in the pages of the *Shields Gazette*, that:

> The cave is now a matter of history, for its disappearance is complete, the cliffe [*sic*] having fallen right away from the summit. The landslip occurred about five o'clock on Thursday (April 3rd 1913) and fortunately no one was about at the time; it was accompanied by a great noise which brought practically the whole of the inhabitants of Marsden to the spot.

So then, according to *Chambers' Journal* the cave was destroyed before 1875; and yet according to Fernandes it collapsed on April 3 1913. To solve this discrepancy we need to initially set out all the possible solutions:

> 1. That some local historians unwittingly gained their information from an incorrect source which identified the collapse as having taken place in 1913, when in reality the source should have read *1813*.

> 2. That the cave only *partially* collapsed before 1875, and that there was a second and complete collapse in 1913. This theory would allow that both dates are correct and mutually compatible.

> 3. That the writer of *Chambers' Journal* is talking about a different cave.

Firstly, it seems that we can clearly identify the cave mentioned *in Chambers' Journal*. The writer describes a shaft, which led from the roof of the cave to the top of the cliff, thus apparently removing any ambiguity. He was, to all intents and purposes, talking about no other recess in the cliff wall than Smugglers Cave, just to the south of the inn. Enigmatically, however, we also know that the year 1913 *was* correct, and not an inaccurate transcription of *1813*, for a photograph exists of the cave taken in *1913* just before its collapse. This cave, too, seems to be Smugglers Cave, for many witnesses also mention the shaft, which led from the roof to the cliff top.

Could the writer who detailed the collapse of the cave pre-1875 have been wrong? Hardly, for in his account he mentions how he had examined the remains of the cave himself. Could Robinson and others have been wrong? No, for the photographic evidence and written testimonies exist to support their argument. On the surface of things, then, there appears to be no way of reconciling the conundrum. Two impeccable sources detail the collapse of Smugglers Cave. One source gives a date of pre-1875, the other a date of 1913, and they can both be proven correct.

So what about the idea of a partial collapse prior to 1875, followed by a complete collapse in 1913? Initially this idea seemed to carry some weight. Fernandes, writing in the *Shields Gazette,* states that the cave's 'disappearance is now complete'. One could put forward a *prima facie* case that if the 1913 collapse *completed* the destruction of the cave, then the pre-1875 collapse must therefore have been *in*complete. Unfortunately, what the writer of *Chambers' Journal* has to say scotches this notion thoroughly, for he talks about the complete 'collapse' of the cave. He also states that the upper entrance to the shaft was still visible from the cliff top (although obscured totally by foliage), and implies that the lower entrance was no longer visible from the beach. Today, the western aspect of the shaft is just visible at its upper portion, but the lower portion, which would have been just above the roof of the cave, is totally missing. We can deduce from this that when the cave collapsed, at some point before 1875, the *entire roof* of the cavern collapsed and destroyed the lower part of the shaft with it. There was no *partial* fall of the cave before 1875, then, but rather a *complete and utter collapse* of the entire cavern from its entrance back to the cliff face.

Bewildering though it may seem, we can only reach one conclusion, and that is that the 'Smugglers Cave' mentioned in *Chambers' Journal* and the 'Smugglers Cave' detailed by Robinson and others are two different caverns altogether. But how can this be? Don't both sources insist that the 'Smugglers Cave' they mention in their writings contained the shaft which led from the roof of the cave to the cliff top? Indeed they do, but there is a startling answer to the mystery.

When Alan Robinson published his comprehensive history of Marsden Bay, he quoted from both *Chambers' Journal* and the recollections of R. P. Fernandes in the *Shields Gazette.* Robinson himself gives the cave's location as being 'two hundred yards south of The Grotto'[7].

In the booklet *A Ramble to Marsden Rocks*[8] the author recounts the narrow escape had by three youths who nearly drowned when the tide suddenly cut them off at Marsden Bay. (We will deal with the incident later in this book.) The youths were only saved by being drawn up on a rope through the shaft that led from a nearby cave to the cliff top. Elizabeth Allan, wife of Peter, told the story of the dramatic rescue to a Mr. Robert Ward whose account was published in a booklet entitled *Summer Excursions.* Robinson states, 'This story, told by Mrs. Allan to Mr. R. Ward, shows clearly that it was the Smugglers Cave on the south side of *The Grotto.*'[9]

And so it seems, until we dig further.

The youths who nearly fell victim to the perilous seas at Marsden were, according to the account, 'playing hide and seek…heedlessly roaming round the abutting rocks.' True, the account also says that this took place at the 'southern extremities of the bay', but we have several reasons for doubting that this was correct.

Firstly, the account in *Summer Excursions* states that a peculiar hermit known as 'Hairy Man' at one time inhabited the cave in question. Robinson himself then displays the instinctive hesitancy of the good researcher when he fully admits that some versions of the legend place the Hairy Man's cave not at the extreme south of Marsden bay, near Smugglers Cave, but at the extreme *north* of the bay at Velvet Beds [10]. William Yellowly certainly believed that Smuggler's Cave and the Hairy Man's Cave were different.

Secondly, the caves at the southern end of the bay simply run in series with each other, like pearls strung on a necklace, as recesses in the cliff face. It takes a large stretch of the imagination to think of how a successful game of 'hide and seek' could be accomplished here. But the *northern* end of the Bay is a different proposition altogether. Here, a myriad of caves and 'abutting rocks' intermingle and dovetail with each other in quite bizarre fashion. Standing in amongst the rocks adjacent to Velvet Beds is like standing on the surface of the moon. Huge caverns and small niches stand next to each other; tunnels, holes, fissures and caves of infinite size and variety make for an *excellent* game of hide and seek. The landscape at Velvet Beds fits perfectly with the description given in *Summer Excursions*.

A third and final reason for doubting that the cave 'to the south of *The Grotto*' is the one discussed by Fernandes is the picture that was taken of it in 1913. It is abundantly clear that the cave in the photograph is composed of rock which bears no resemblance to the striated, laminated limestone found to the north of the Bay, but it bears a *perfect* resemblance to the rocks at Velvet Beds. In fact, the site of the cave can still be seen at Velvet Beds to this day.

So why did the writer of *Summer Excursions* state that the cave was at the 'southern extremity' of the Bay? This is not difficult to fathom. The writer had seen the remains of Smugglers Cave – this we know for a fact. He also knew that there was a shaft leading from the roof of the cave to the cliff top. So, when Elizabeth Allan told the story of how the three youngsters had been hauled to safety through the shaft, her interviewer automatically assumed that the shaft *above Smugglers Cave* was the one she was talking about. But he was mistaken.

Despite the difficulties, some researchers still plump for Smugglers Cave as being not only the location of the dramatic rescue, but also the abode of the mysterious Hairy Man. Why? Because in each instance the cave in question is said to have a shaft leading from its roof to the cliff top. Naturally, then, Ward, Robinson and others seem to have been irresistibly drawn to the conclusion that the different accounts and stories all refer to the same cave. But as we have seen, they *could not possibly* have been the same cave. So, what is the answer?

There were, in fact, two caves. One – Smugglers Cave – was situated at the southern end of the Bay. The other – known as the Hairy Man's cave – was situated at the northern end of the Bay. Incredibly, *both* caves had shafts leading from the roof to the cliff top above, hence the confusion between the two in the literature that exists concerning Marsden Bay.

So what are we to make of this? Quite simply, the existence of a second shaft of this nature strongly supports the idea that they belonged to a network of tunnels within the Marsden area. Indeed, it is possible that more may yet be found.

After this considerable digression, we may now return to the point of our narrative, and ask once again whether there were any connecting apertures between the shaft above Smugglers Cave and the rest of the tunnel network. What used to be the back of the cave is still visible, now forming part of the cliff face surrounding the cove. There are no horizontal apertures or entrances to be seen leading into the cliff face, so if an entrance did exist into the tunnel complex within Smugglers Cave, where may it have been situated? The answer almost certainly is that the entrance was to be found in the floor of the cave itself. But how do we know this?

Let me draw the reader's attention once again to the aforementioned quote from Chambers Journal, 'It [Smugglers Cave] was a huge, natural cavern … but for some years *before its destruction* [emphasis mine] it was much reduced in size due to the raising of the floor level by silted sand.' The 'raising of the sand', of course, would provide a perfect cover for a vertical entrance down into the tunnel network under the beach.

It is also possible that there may have been one or more horizontal shafts leading off the vertical one, and if such horizontal shafts existed these too may have connected to the larger network at some point. And here, almost unconsciously, we may have stumbled upon the reason behind Peter Allan's decision to move steadily southwards as he systematically blasted his way into the cliff face. If Peter Allan suspected that the vertical shaft which sat above Smugglers Cave one hundred yards to the south was connected to a larger complex of tunnels, then logic would dictate that he head in that direction in an effort to connect his own rapidly expanding network of caves to the larger one. Of course, all this is, at least up till this point, based purely on assumption and guesswork. Is there any historical evidence to suggest that Peter's motive may have been entirely consistent with the one I have just suggested? Indeed there is.

To understand why the shaft above Smugglers Cave may have been significant to Peter in his excavations we must first consider an aspect of his character and personality which, admittedly, would seem to have no bearing on the matter whatsoever: his fondness for animals and wildlife. Bizarre though it may seem, his love of animals may very well help us solve this aspect of the puzzle.

Peter Allan Snr. had a passionate love of wildlife, as we have seen. This passion was no less intensely felt by Peter Allan Jnr. In fact, there is little doubt that young Peter had an affinity with animals, which was little short of shamanic.

Like his father before him, Peter kept a hive of bees in the *Tam O' Shanter*, only removing them with great reluctance at the insistence of his regular customers, who, even though they had not been stung, were disconcerted by the small creatures buzzing around their heads. Peter had an affinity with the bees and would let them crawl all over him. He would stroke and tickle them, and never once got stung. It was as if the bees sensed that he was a friend, and demonstrated a genuine affection for their human protector.

But if Peter's relationship with his bees was unusual, his relationship with other species was nothing short of staggering. One day, whilst browsing around the docks at South Shields, Peter met the captain of a foreign vessel berthed there. What conversation took place we do not know, but Peter ended up purchasing two pigs of a peculiar Russian breed from the man. He took these home to Marsden Bay, and promptly set up a 'smallholding' just north of the *Tam O' Shanter*, which became known as Peter's Farm. Here he kept the two pigs, which he affectionately named Jack and Jessie after Jack the Blaster and his wife.

Pigs are not – it goes without saying – the most domesticated of animals. And yet within a short space of time Peter had Jack and Jessie behaving like well-trained gun dogs. They would obey his every command, and seemed to sense exactly what Peter required of them. Jack and Jessie (particularly Jessie) went everywhere with Peter, following faithfully at his heels. When they produced a litter of piglets nothing changed. Peter could still be seen waltzing around the streets of South Shields, Newcastle and Sunderland with Jessie, Jack and their 'children' following closely behind.

According to contemporary accounts, people became so used to seeing Peter and his pigs they would automatically assume the worst if he passed them without the porkers being in tow. They would, according to one writer, say, "What has become of Jessie to-day, Peter?" or something similar.

But Peter had other pets, too. There is an almost mystical association between Marsden Bay and the birds that frequent it. Currently the vast bulk of the birds at Marsden are common sea gulls, kittiwakes, fulmar petrels, cormorants, herring gulls, lesser black-backed gulls, shags, and razorbills. Other species, such as guillemots, buntings, and sandpipers can also be seen from time to time. But in Peter Allan's day it was different. The raven was in the ascendancy then, and was revered by the locals as an almost sacred animal. Bad luck would befall anyone who was foolish enough to kill or even taunt a raven on Marsden sands, for according to local legend the ravens protected both the dead and the living at Marsden Bay.

Peter was a good friend to the ravens. Stories abound at Marsden about Peter's psychic relationship with the ravens. He could, for instance, call a raven as it passed and it would immediately come and land on his shoulder. In 1833, Peter became firm friends with one particular raven whom he named Ralphy. Ralphy was a constant companion to Peter, always perched on his shoulder as if guarding his master. Ralphy later died in tragic circumstances – we will deal with these in a later chapter – but he was, previous to his demise, also injured in a shooting accident like Peter's brother John. Like John, he also lost a limb.

Tommy Stokes was a well-known sporting celebrity from Seaham Harbour. He was also by some accounts a bit of a braggart who was not averse to boasting of his athletic prowess. Tommy had taken to frequenting the Marsden Bay area with a gun, shooting birds that would later end up in a pie. One day, Stokes saw what he believed to be a crow flying near the *Tam O' Shanter*. He shot it, and the creature fell to earth in an instant. Perhaps sensing that something was wrong, Peter left the inn and found Ralphy on the sands, seriously wounded. The shot had not killed him, but it had taken off one of his legs.

As Peter Allan looked down incredulously at his wounded avian friend lying on the beach he became aware of Stokes walking towards him. The sportsman had shot the bird and aimed to claim it. What happened next was brief but bloody.

Peter stared at Stokes and asked, "Did you shoot him?"

"Aye, I did that," answered the grinning celebrity.

Peter fell upon the man with such ferocity that the sportsman had little chance of defending himself. As he collapsed under a torrent of hammer-like blows he could only have wondered what on earth he had done to deserve such treatment. Several of Peter's pals raced from the *Tam O' Shanter* and pulled him off the man, who by this time was unconscious and virtually unrecognisable due to the pummelling Peter had dished out to him. One contemporary writer said that they "had to tyek him hyem in a cart."

Ralphy survived the attack by Stokes, which the author of *Summer Excursions* says was made 'in sheer wanton ignorance.' After this event, the psychic bond between the raven and the innkeeper seemed only to become deeper. Peter taught Ralphy how to play tricks and pranks on people, both man and bird seemingly revelling in the consternation they wrought upon the unsuspecting tourist. The writer also mentioned Ralphy's 'supernatural instincts'.

But the psychic bond did not exist solely between Peter and his pets. Extraordinarily, the pets seemed to develop a psychic cohesion between themselves that manifested itself in the most bizarre ways. One of Peter's two pigs, for instance (Jack in most accounts), used to like nothing better than to scamper up and down the sands in the warm sun. Nothing strange in this – except that he would invariably have four ravens clinging on to his back! The birds seemed to take it in turns to ride upon Jack the pig, this strange mobile menagerie squealing and squawking as they danced play-fully upon the beach.

In some strange way the animals of Marsden Bay seemed to recognise Peter Allan as their master and protector. Even Peter must have sensed, by this time that the incredible affinity he had with the animals was beyond anything, which could be simply put down to natural and mutual empathy. Those who knew the innkeeper say that his relationship with the birds of the air and the beasts of the field was truly uncanny. Peter, by this time, was also beginning to realise that nothing really dies or ends at Marsden bay. Everything reincarnates in a subtle but unmistakable way. Places, events, relationships, incidents, ideas and even names are continually recycled in a surreal drama being played out upon a strange stage.

We also know that, of all the animals with which Peter bonded, his relation-ship with the ravens was the most wondrous. Just as Peter protected them, they protected him. There is very real evidence that the ravens at Marsden Bay, in some unfathomable way, understood both their role as Protectors and Peter's special place in the history of the area. William Yellowly gives a breathtaking account of how the ravens fulfilled this responsibility, although he almost certainly did not understand the importance of this except on the most superficial level:

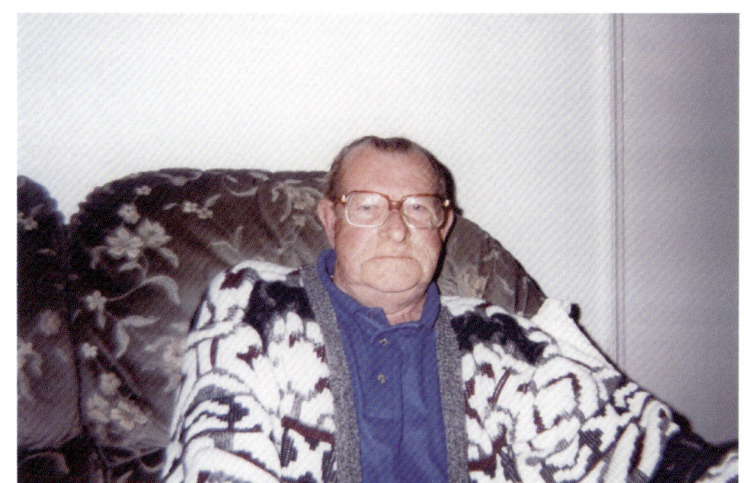

1 Ronnie Ward, the "Hoist Man" at The Marsden Grotto.

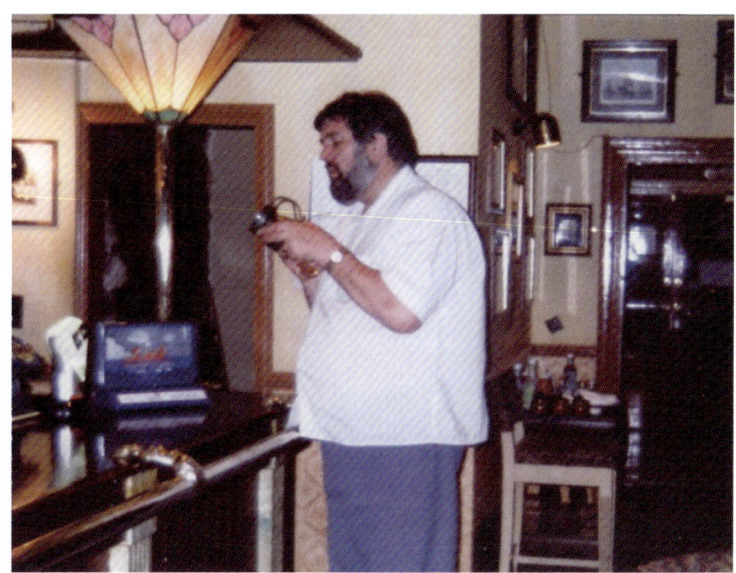

2 Nick Garvey, former landlord at The Marsden Grotto, examining the infamous Smuggler's Tankard.

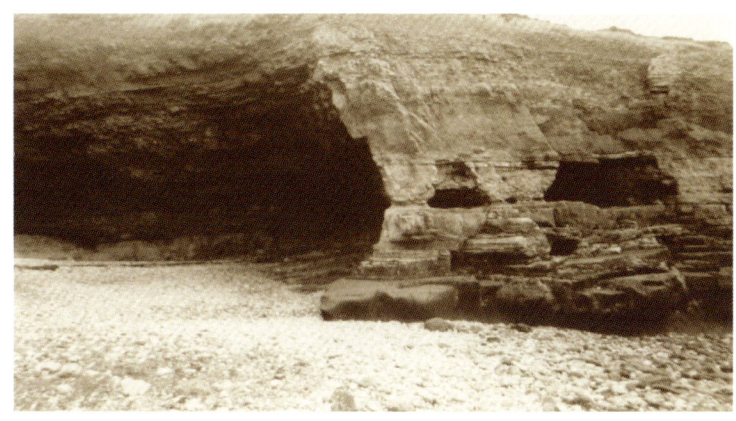

3 Caves at Marsden Bay. The naturalist William Yellowly spoke of the complex and interconnecting caves and tunnels at Marsden.

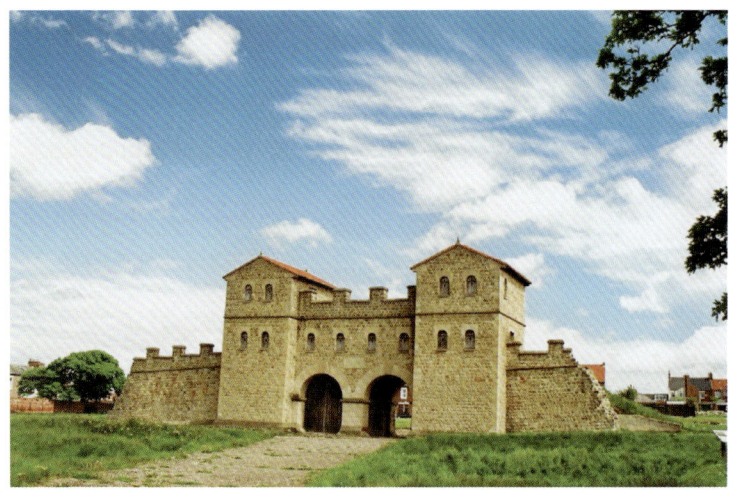

4 The reconstructed West Gate of the Arbeia Roman Fort, South Shields (Courtesy of Darren W. Ritson).

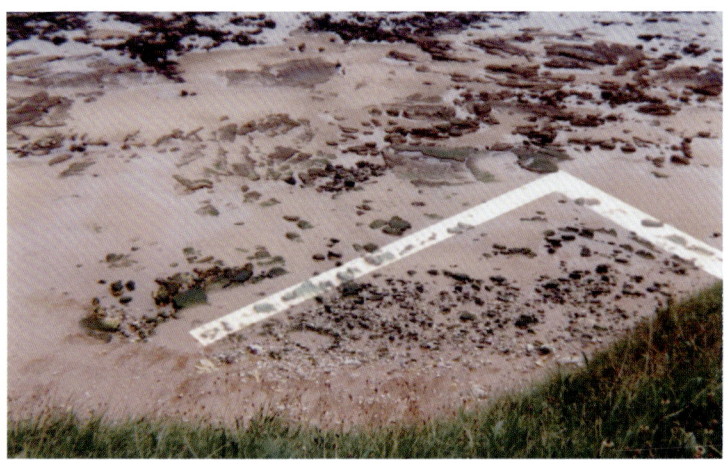

5 The first of two possible sites for the Roman quay at Marsden. This one lies to the south, and what could conceivably be the outline of a quay wall is just visible.

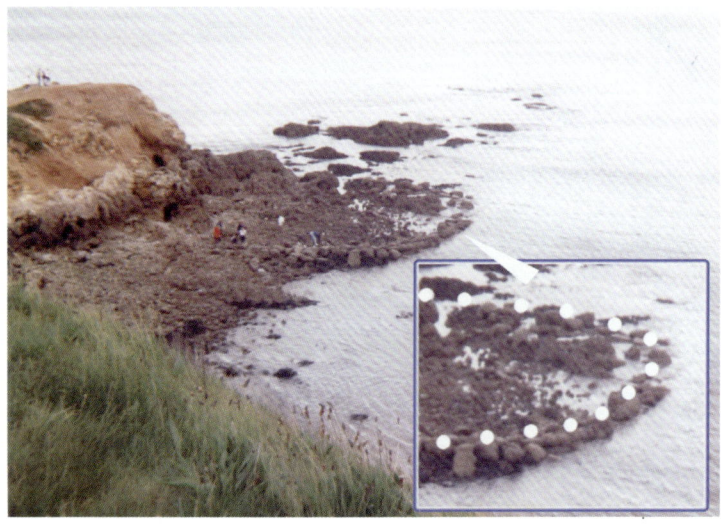

6 The second and more likely site of the Roman quay at Velvet Beds to the north. The shape of part of the quay, semi-circular, can clearly be seen (inset), although it is impossible to identify the site with absolute certainty.

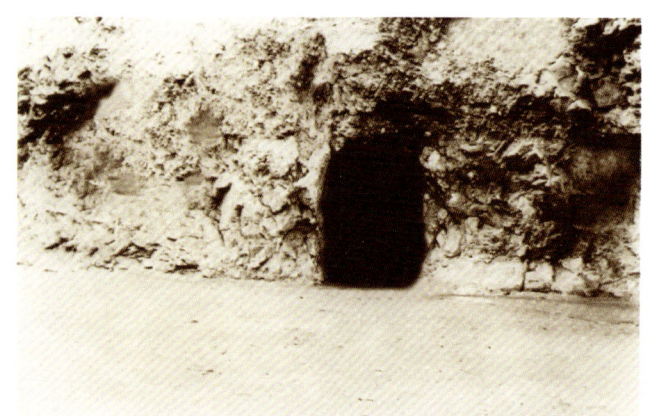

7 Blaster Jack's Cave as it would have looked before his excavation.

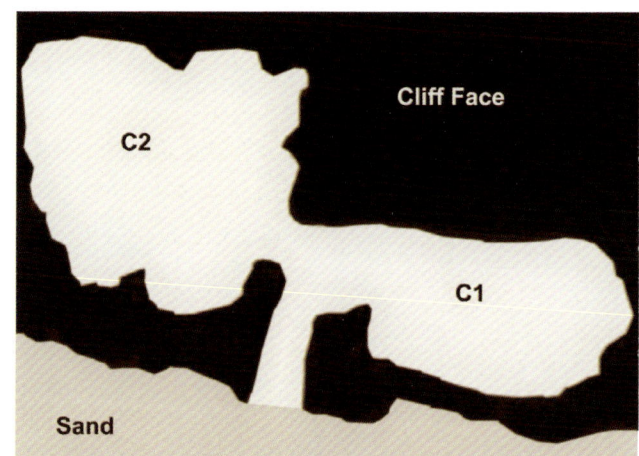

8 (Fig. 1) The layout of Blaster Jack's Cave showing the original two rooms.

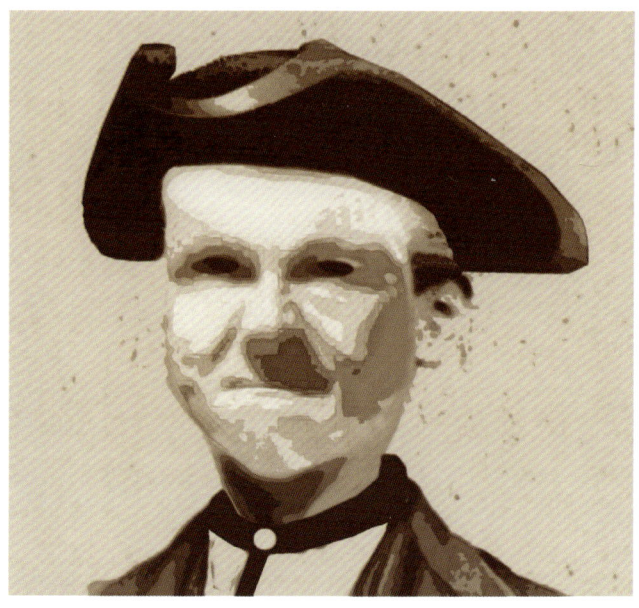

9 An artist's impression of Blaster Jack.

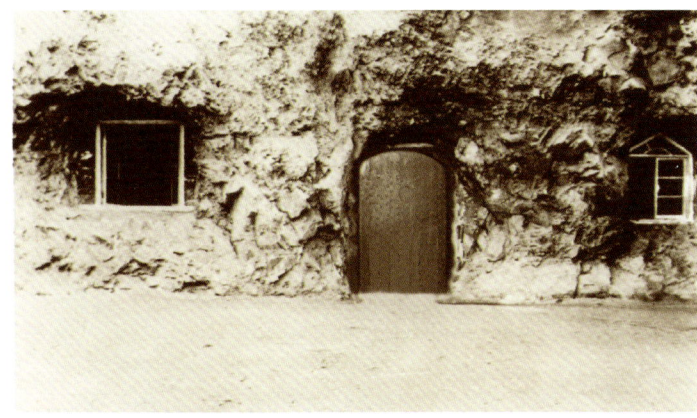

10 (Fig. 2) Blaster Jack's cave as it looked from the outside after the door and windows were added.

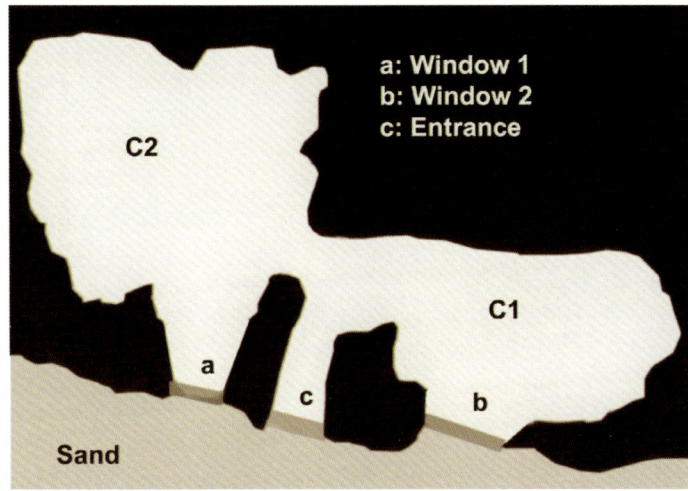

a: Window 1
b: Window 2
c: Entrance

C2

C1

a

c

b

Sand

*Left:* 11 (Fig. 3) A floor plan of Blaster Jack's cave after further apertures were added.

*Below:* 12 (Fig. 4) A floor plan of the cave complex after Peter Allan's initial excavations.

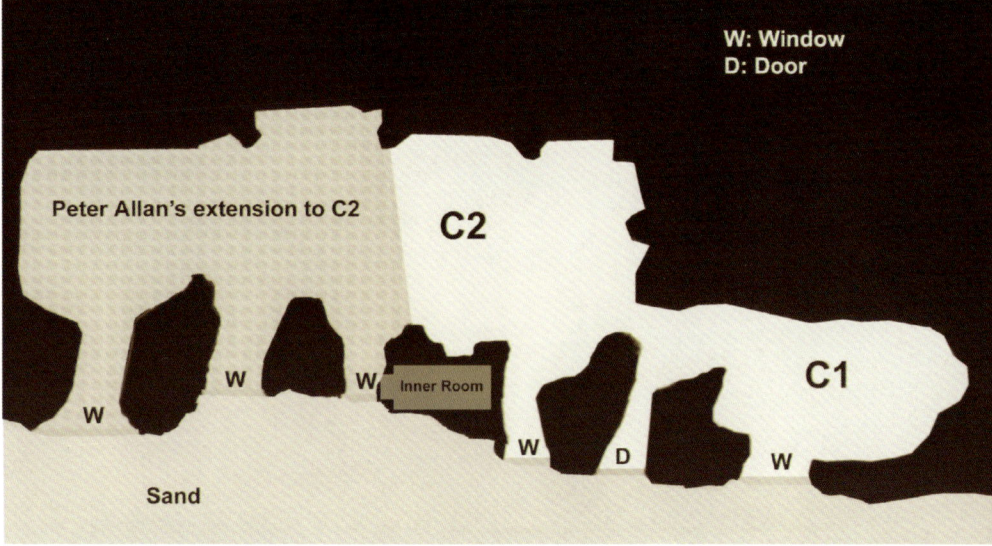

W: Window
D: Door

Peter Allan's extension to C2

C2

C1

W

W

W

Inner Room

W

D

W

Sand

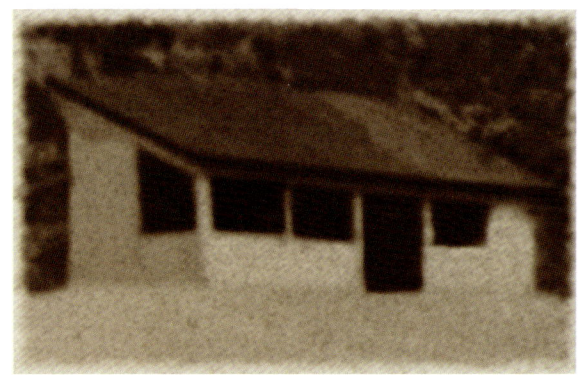

13 The temporary porch added to cover the entrance to the complex shortly after Peter Allan moved in (Courtesy of Evelyn Waugh-Almond).

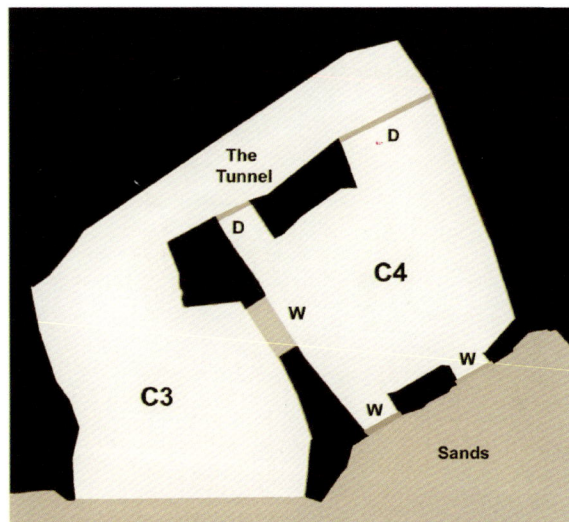

*Right:* 14 (Fig. 5) Floor plan of the Gaol and the Devil's Room.

*Below:* 15 (Fig. 6) The floor plan of the excavations on the upper level.

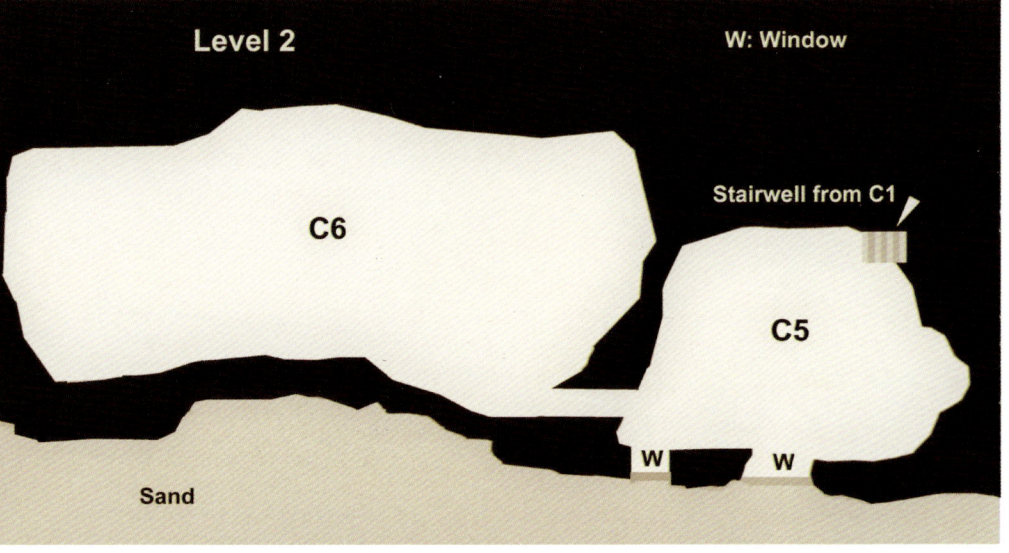

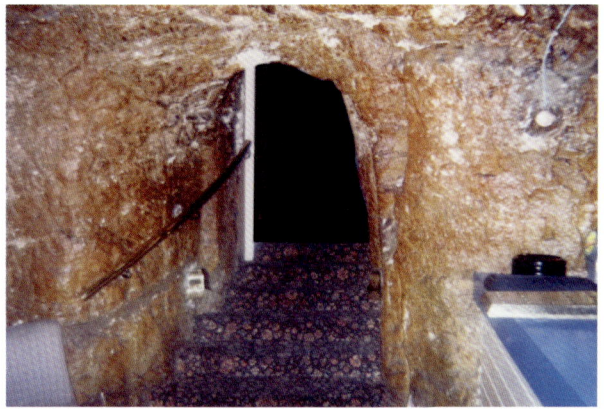

16 The upper part of the stairway between Levels 1 and 2.

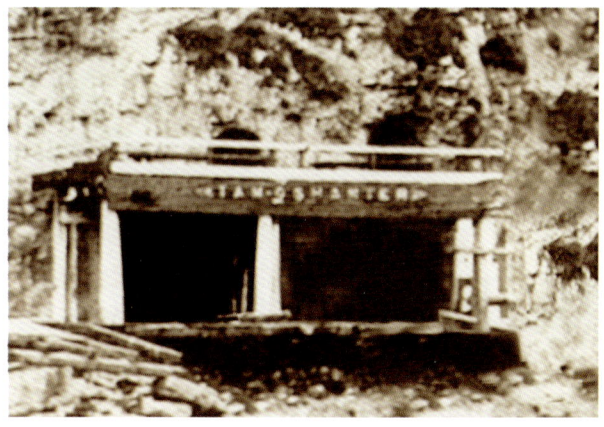

17 The Second Porch added to the front of the cave complex after the excavation of the second level (Courtesy of Alan Robinson).

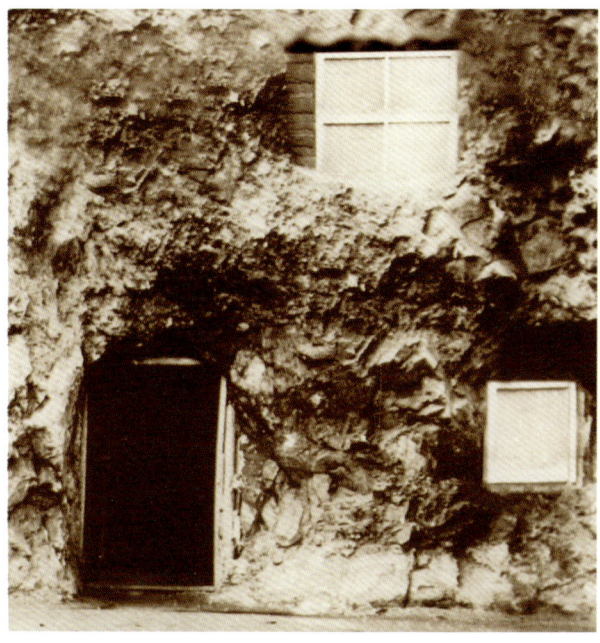

18 A glazed window on the upper floor is now visible after Peter began to excavate above the ground-level complex.

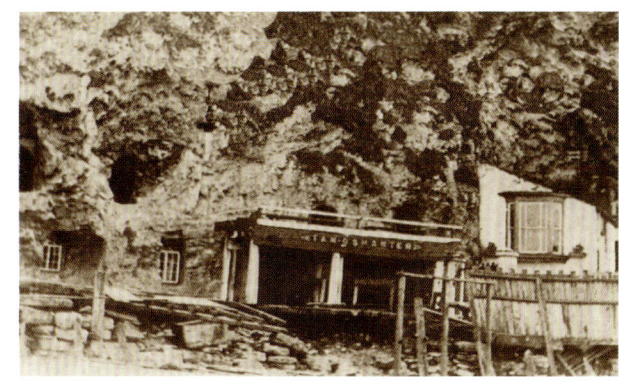

19 The cottage, the Allan family's living quarters, can be seen to the right of the pub frontage on this photograph (Courtesy of Alan Robinson).

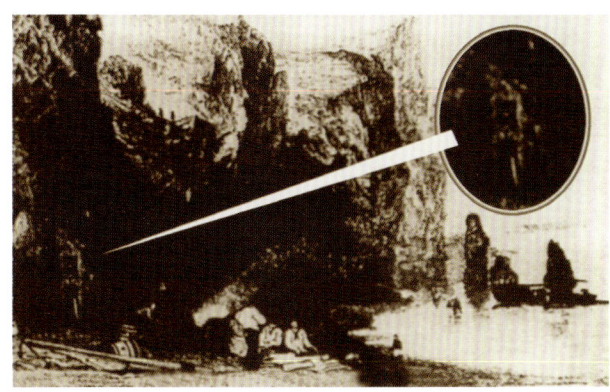

20 An early view of Marsden Bay, allegedly composed in 1820, although the author suspects it was actually composed after 1829, as Peter Allan's "cottage" can clearly be seen nestling against the cliff face.

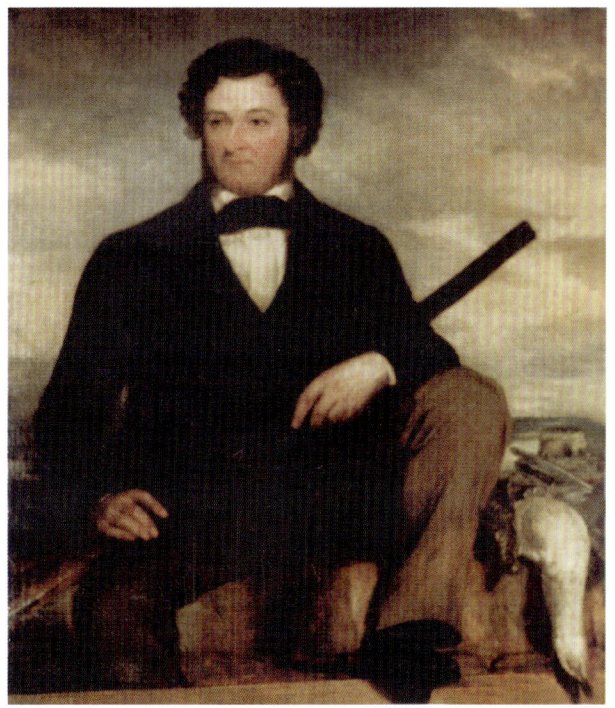

21 Peter Allan – the legendary character behind The Marsden Grotto (Courtesy of Pat Moore).

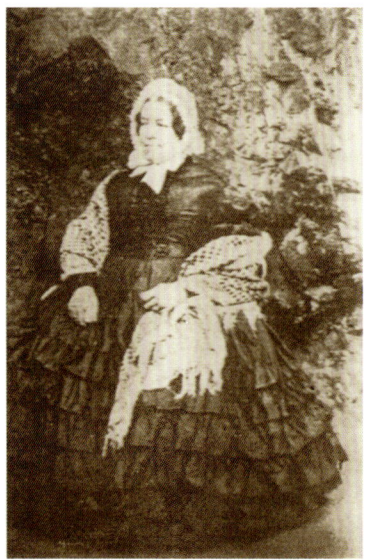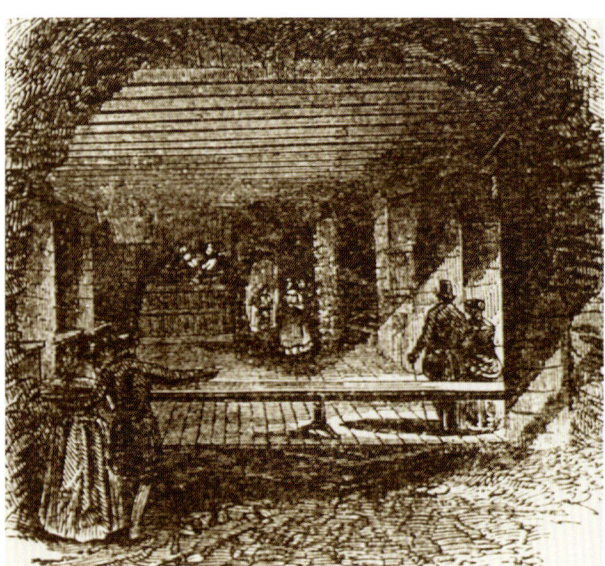

*Above left:* 22 Peter Allan's wife, Lizzie.

*Above right:* 23 The Ballroom before 1849, above which the substitute wooden ceiling can be seen.

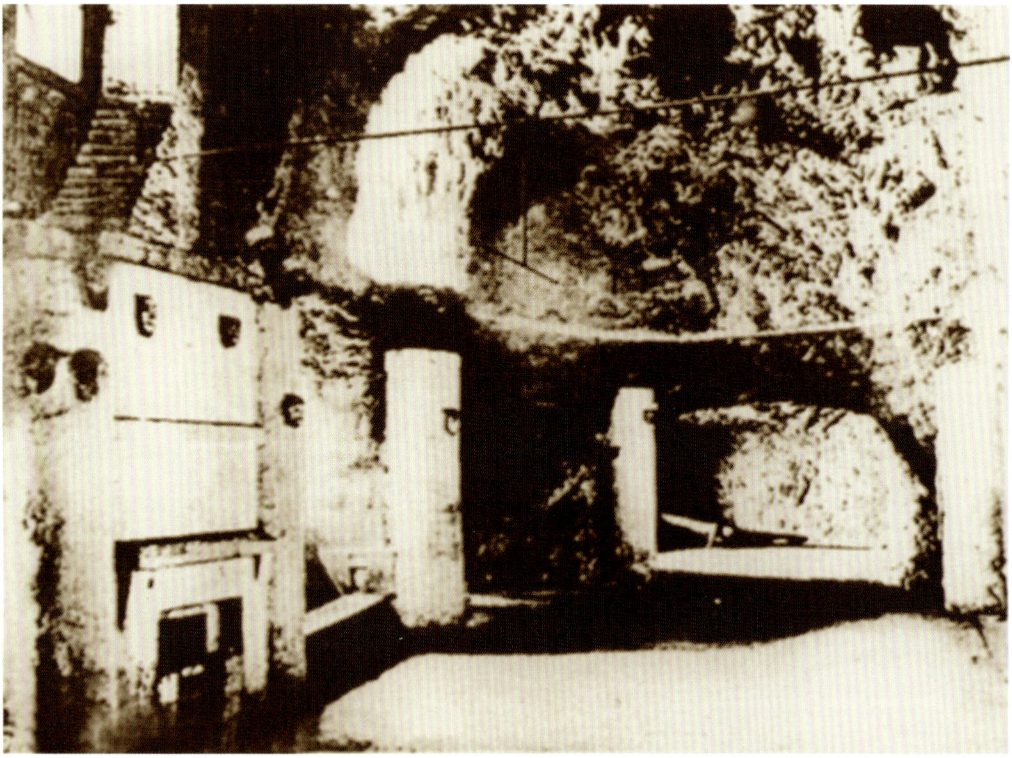

24 The Ballroom after 1885, when the substitute wooden ceiling had already been removed.

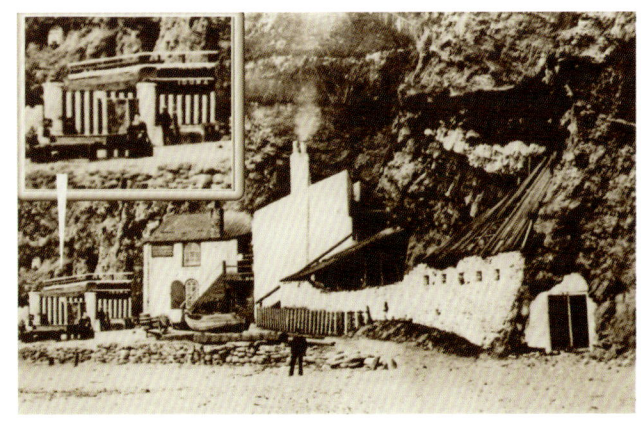

25 An old photograph of The Marsden Grotto, in which several stone pillars can clearly be seen, which may well have came from the demolished Lambton Castle.

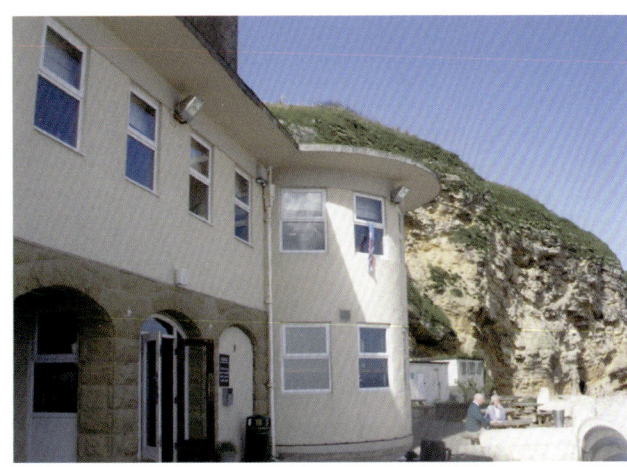

26 The Marsden Grotto now, showing the frontage which was added in 1938.

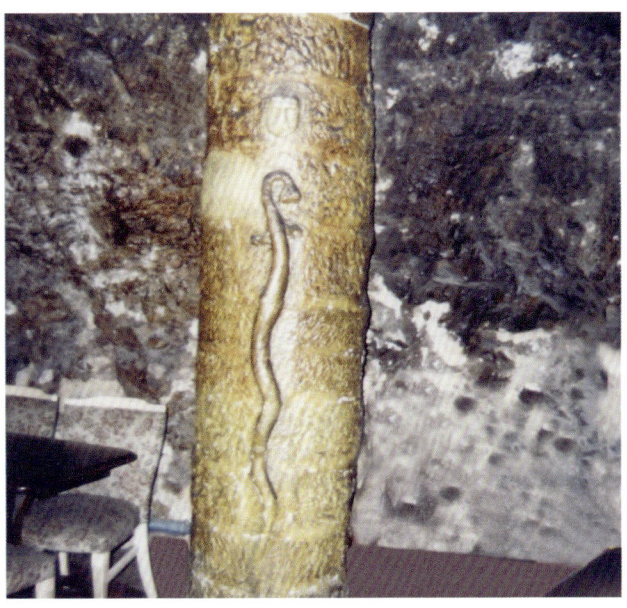

27 The Lambton Worm and the head of Sir John Lambton on one of the pillars which grace the Back Bar of The Marsden Grotto.

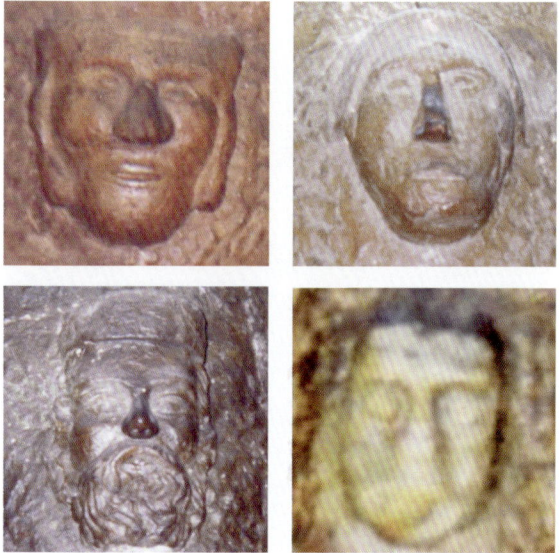

28 Four of the faces of the "ten Lords of Lambton" which can be found on the pillars inside The Marsden Grotto.

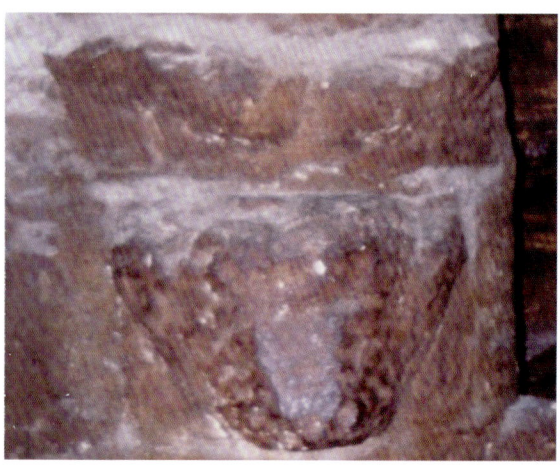

29 Face of the Dragon: A stylized head found on one of the pillars at the northerly end of the Back Bar, used to warn off overly-curious patrons.

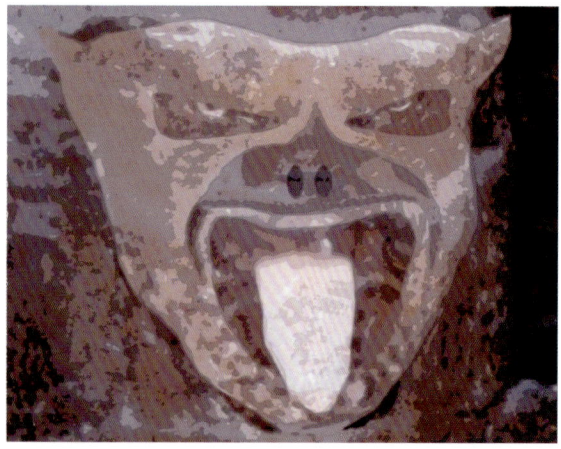

30 A digital reconstruction of the dragon's head to illustrate what it may have looked like before the elements took their toll.

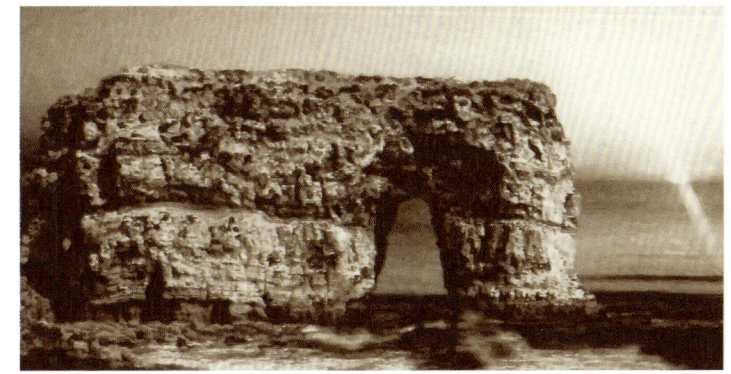

31 An oil painting of Marsden Rock.

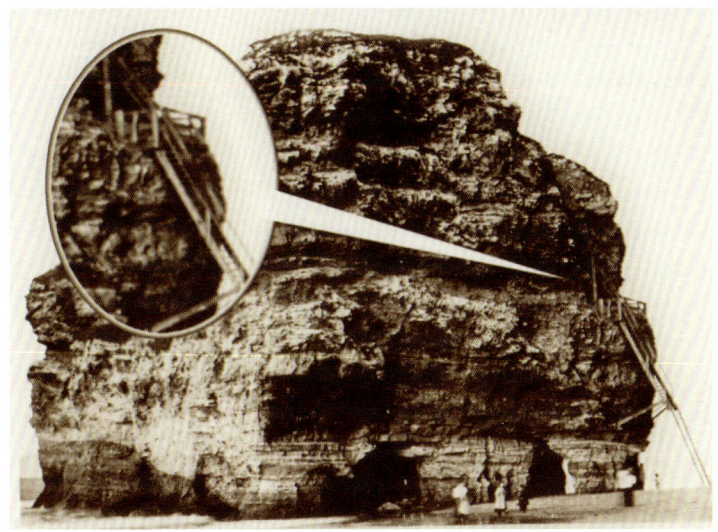

32 The Stairway ascending Marsden Rock. The inset shows a small gantry half way up, upon which climbers could catch their breath before making the final ascent (Courtesy of Alan Robinson).

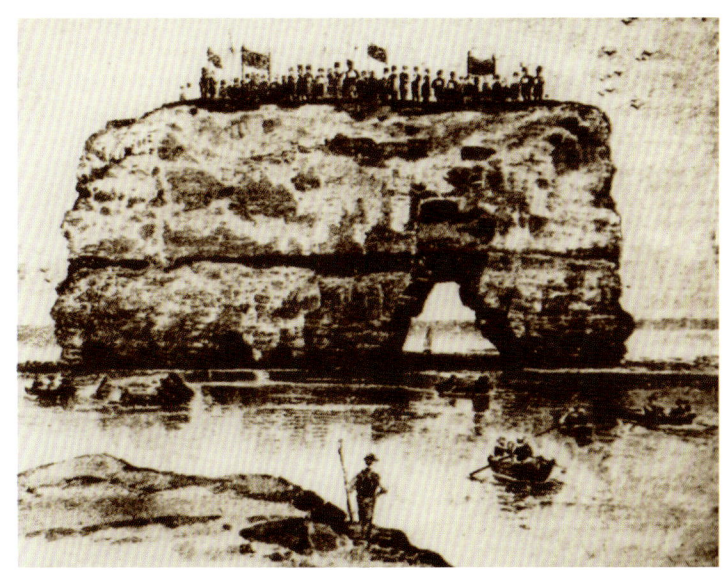

33 One of the many religious gatherings which took place upon Marsden Rock in the 19th century.

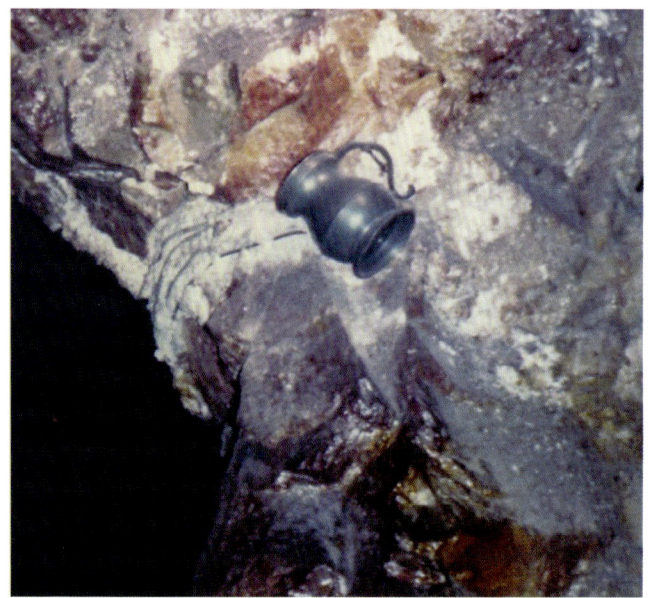

34 The Smuggler's Tankard which hung upon the cave wall until it was stolen in June 2000.

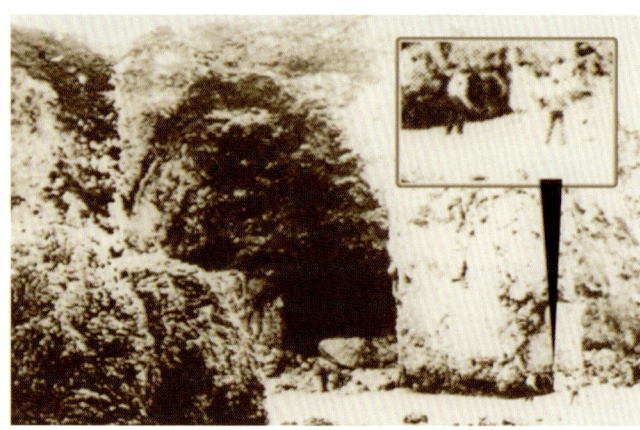

35 The Hairy Man's Cave before its collapse in 1913. Note how the enormity of the entrance dwarves visitors (inset) (Courtesy of Alan Robinson).

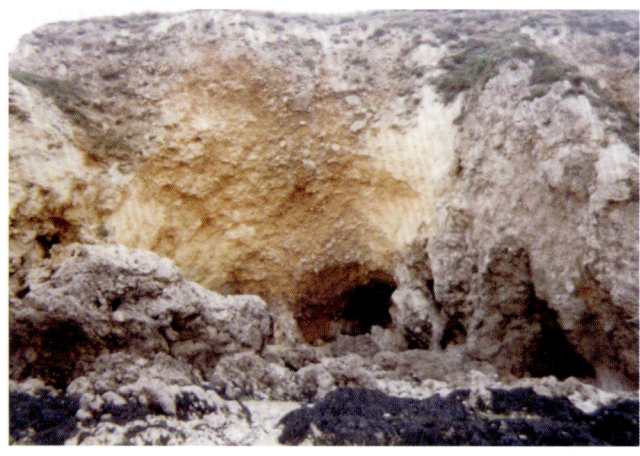

36 The remains of The Hairy Man's Cave today.

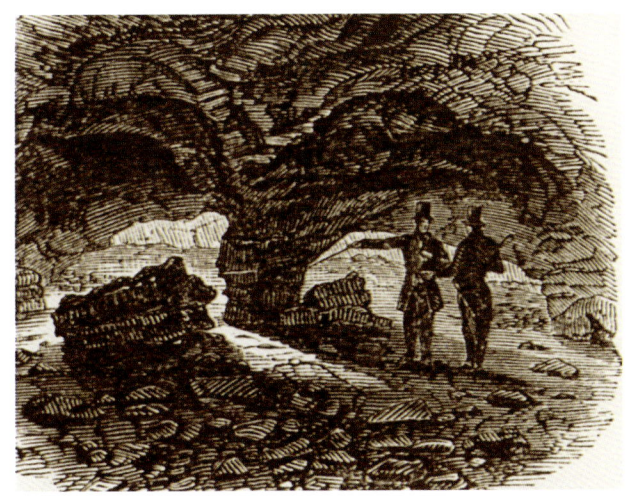

37 A line drawing of the interior of The Hairy Man's Cave made in the mid 19th century.

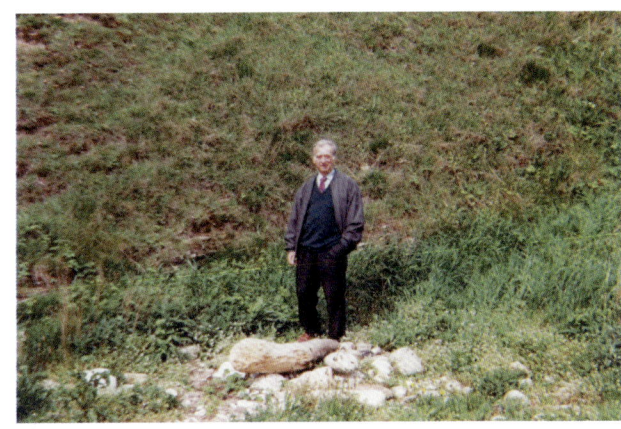

38 Grotto researcher and author Alan Robinson, photographed several yards from one of the smuggler's hidey-holes at Whitburn, the location of which is known to only a handful of people today.

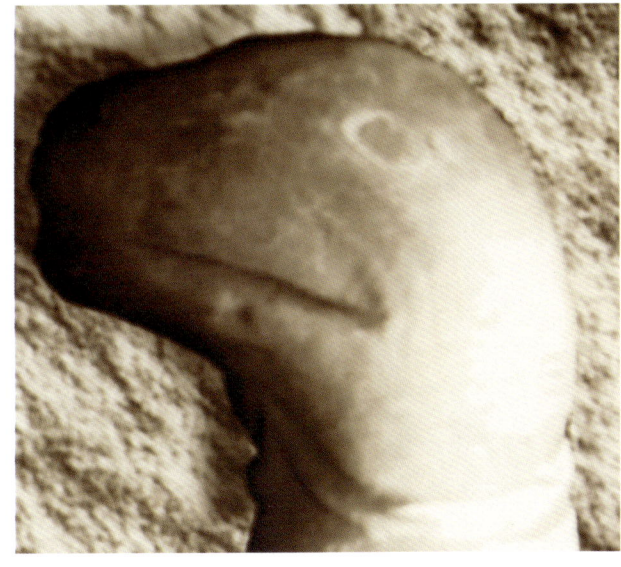

39 The Shony; South Tyneside's legendary sea monster which was intimately tied up with the dragon legends that had become embedded in the region's folklore. This dragon's head original stood outside of St. Peter's Church, Monkwearmouth, and now resides in Sunderland Museum (Courtesy of Evelyn Waugh-Almond).

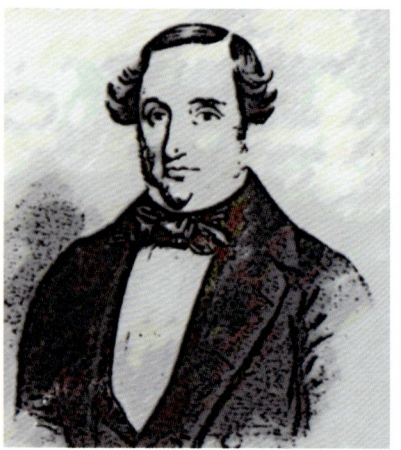
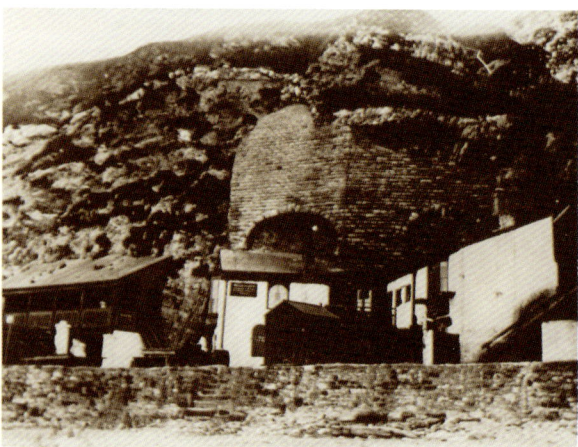

*Above left:* 40   J. Twizel Wawn, one of the influential personages involved with the efforts to remove the Allan family from The Marsden Grotto.

*Above right:* 41 The cliff face behind The Marsden Grotto after the buttress had been added to prevent further rock falls (Courtesy of Ivor Muncey).

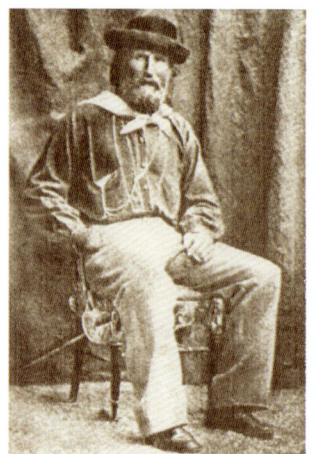
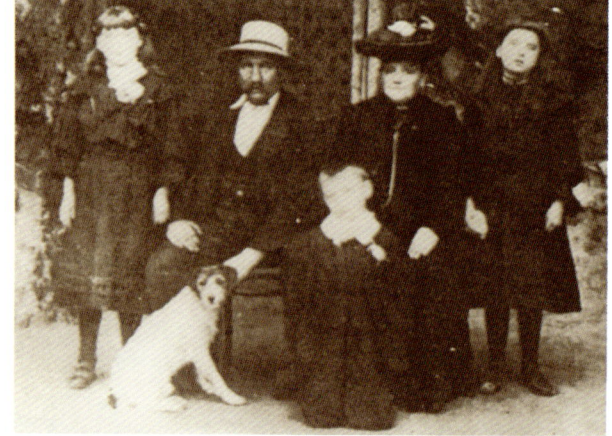

*Above left:* 42 Patriot and activist Giuseppe Mazzini, wearing the sword he was given by his supporters on Tyneside (Courtesy of David Bell).

*Above right:* 43 William "Segar" Robinson and his family, posing for a family portrait outside of The Marsden Grotto (Courtesy of Alan Robinson).

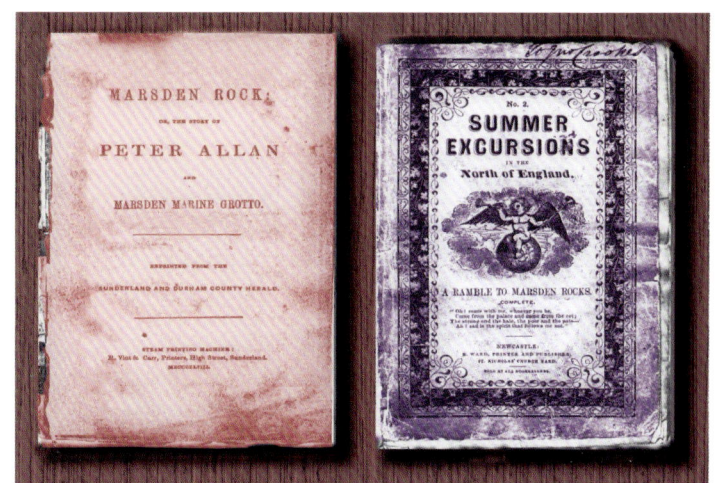

44 Two rare publications dealing with the history of the mysterious Grotto Inn.

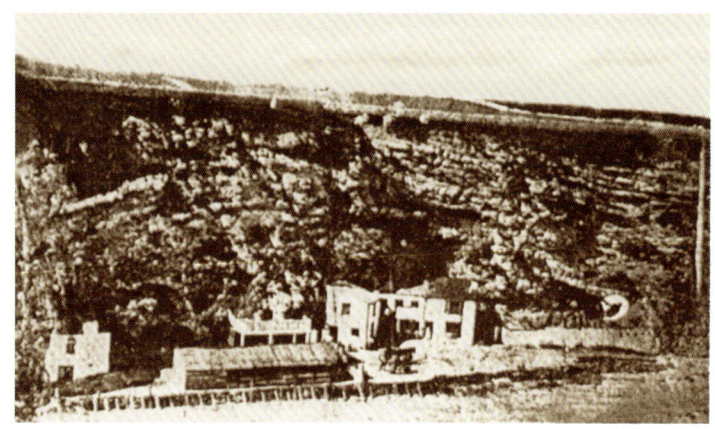

45 A view of The Marsden Grotto taken from the top of Marsden Rock in the year 1889 (Courtesy of Ivor Muncey).

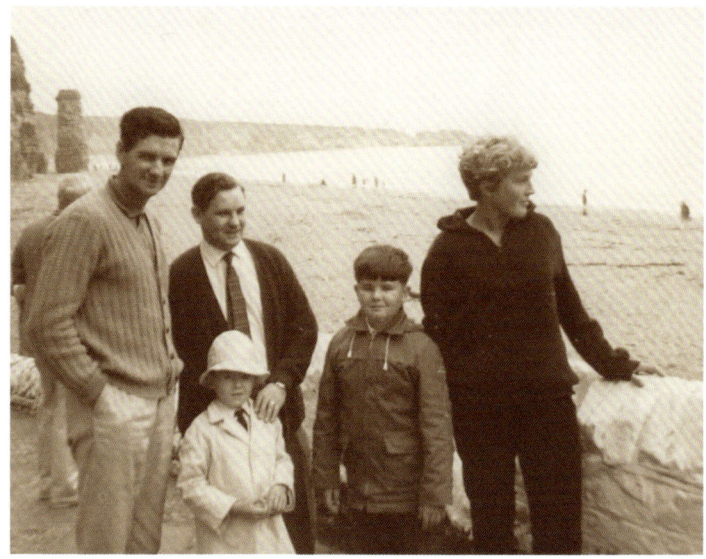

46 The author [second from right] visiting the Grotto with family and friends in 1967.

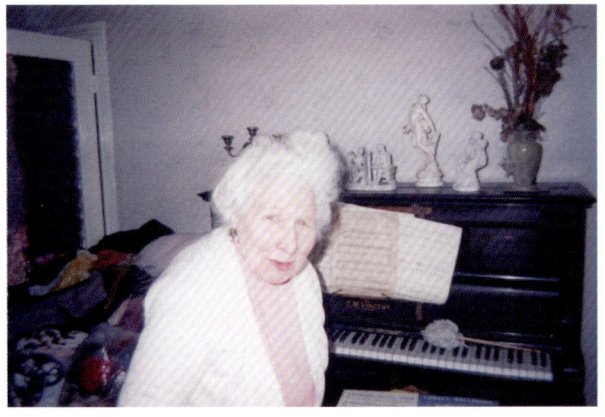

47 The late Evelyn Waugh-Almond, archaeologist, who supplied the author with much information about the hidden history of The Marsden Grotto.

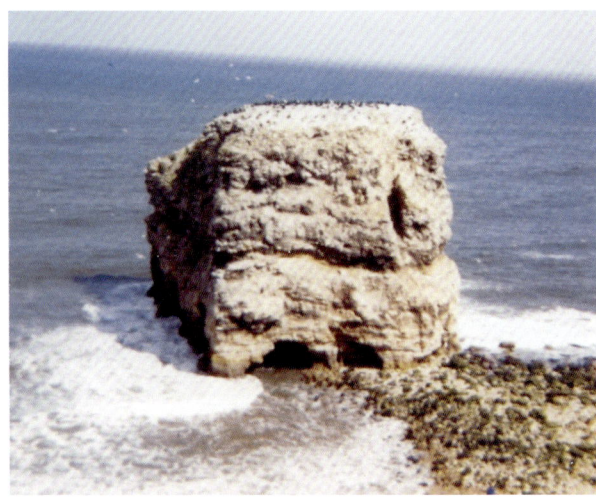

48 Marsden Rock as it is today.

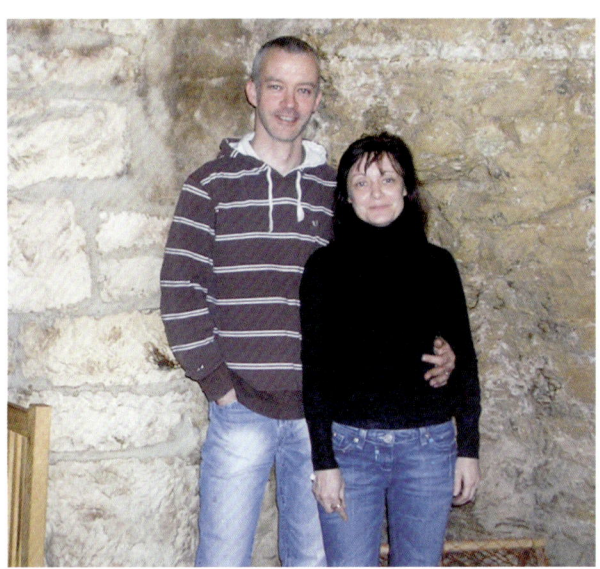

49 Bev & Paul Wright-Simpson, current tenants of The Marsden Grotto.

' ... When going between Marsden and Whitburn, where he kept an inn, Jessie would be seen trotting alongside, while a pair of tame ravens would accompany him all the way, flying before for a hundred yards or so, alighting on the stone walls till Peter came up, and then flying forward again, so as always to keep a little in front.' [11]

This account begins to open our minds to the fact that something very mystical and wonderful was being worked out on this beautiful stretch of English coastline.

So where did these ravens come from? Yellowly himself gives an explanation, but it is so at odds with everything we know about Peter Allan's character that we must immediately discount it. In fact, probably the only reason Yellowly gives this explanation is that he was unaware of the profundity of what was really taking place at Marsden. To Yellowly, the tame ravens were merely extraordinary pets.

According to Yellowly, Peter took the ravens from a nest 'a little to the south of *The Grotto*' [12]. That Peter would desecrate a ravens' nest in such a manner is unthinkable in the light of what we know. So how did William Yellowly – a friend of Peter's, remember – come to embrace such an extraordinary notion about the master of the *Tam O' Shanter*? The reason is that Peter was quite happy for William to harbour this misconception, *and almost certainly helped to establish it in his mind.*

To understand what is going on here we need to examine in some detail an incident that occurred, as far as I have been able to establish, in or around 1832. This incident was recorded for posterity, again by the taxidermist William Yellowly [13], but is little known even amongst those who have studied the history of Marsden extensively. When I showed the documentary evidence of what I am about to relate to one researcher he gently shook his head and said, "This is fascinating. I've never read anything about this before."

In Peter's day the raven population at Marsden was colossal, and had he wanted to steal young ravens from their nest he could have found far more accessible ones than those which nestled in the cavities half way down the steep cliff face. This aside, Yellowly goes on to tell us how the theft of the raven chicks was apparently accomplished:

John Allan, a brother of Peter's, who had only one hand, the other having been lost through a gun accident, was sometimes lowered over the rocks to take the young ravens from the nest. On one of these occasions, some fishermen from Whitburn hurried up to the farm to procure a pair of cart ropes; for, in lowering John over the cliffs, the rope had got fast in a crevice, and the fishermen were afraid that the jutting edges would cut the rope, in which case the poor fellow would have been dashed to pieces, the cliffs being upwards of a hundred feet in height. However, he was got up without sustaining any serious injury.

We are being asked to believe, then, that the man who loved ravens so much, and had such an empathy with them that they escorted him like a troop of soldiers escorting a royal entourage, would actually stoop to pinching the chicks of his raven friends from their nests. One of the most startling aspects of the colourful character known as Peter Allan was his psychical relationship with the *fauna* of Marsden Bay. We have also seen how anyone who dared flout the kindness to animals, which prevailed in the innkeeper's protectorate, would be dealt with most severely. Although he was not averse to hunting game for food, Peter *hated* cruelty to animals. Peter was friend and protector to the ravens. He would not steal their young.

A careful reading of Yellowly's account (his use of the word 'sometimes', for instance, and the phrase 'on one of these occasions') makes it clear that this was not a one-off incident. Peter was supposed to be lowering his brother over this dangerous cliff *regularly* to pinch young raven chicks. This is unthinkable. But nevertheless, there is no doubt that Peter did frequently lower John over the cliff for some reason. If not to pinch raven chicks, then for what?

If one stands on the shore in front of *The Grotto* today and looks at the cliff above the building, and lets one's eyes drift to the left, a number of small holes can be seen in the rock face. These appear to be entrances to small caves or hollows in the cliff itself. Today they are totally inaccessible, and any attempt to reach them would be highly dangerous. What are these holes? My belief is that they are apertures, possibly created over a long period of time through the erosion of the cliff face, exposing the easterly side of one or more horizontal shafts, which probably connected to the vertical shaft above Smugglers Cave further south. I say *possibly* created by erosion, but not certainly, for there is another explanation for how these holes appeared.

Peter tunnelled south in the direction of the vertical shaft above Smugglers Cave, suspecting that he would break into the larger complex at some point. For reasons unknown to us this plan became unworkable, and Peter found himself unable to continue in a southerly direction. He therefore had to find some other means of entering the larger complex. The obvious solution would be to lower someone down the cliff face, further south and to the correct height, and get them to chip away at the soft limestone at various points until they found and broke into one of the horizontal shafts. This is exactly what Peter's brother John was doing when his safety rope got jammed in between two rocks, necessitating his rescue by some passing fishermen. John was not pinching raven chicks at all, that was just a cover story. What John Allan was really doing was looking for an entrance into a very ancient tunnel complex.

It is possible, of course, that Peter hadn't worked out the location of the tunnels in this way. It may indeed be that natural erosion simply exposed some of the horizontal shafts and Peter spotted them as he meandered up and down the Bay. But however he discovered them, he certainly knew that they were there.

Currently, there are only faint traces of the westerly aspect of the shaft, which sat at the rear of Smugglers Cave. True, there are no visible signs of horizontal shafts leading from it into the cliff wall, but these may have either collapsed or been filled in over the years.

We must finally ask if the apertures, which can be seen on the cliff face, really are entrances to the tunnel complex or simply holes made by John Allan as he excavated. As they are currently inaccessible we do not know. Only a detailed examination of the caves carried out under controlled conditions will give us the answer. Several contemporaries of Peter Allan and his family held the belief that they were "dovecots", but this too was simply a red herring created by Peter to divert their attention from the truth.

## References

[1] Mackenzie, E. and Ross, M. *An Historical, Topographical and Descriptive View of the County Palatine of Durham*, (Mackenzie & Dent, 1834).

[2] Anon. *The Marine Grotto Today* (Vaux Breweries, date unknown) p 4.

[3] Anon. *A Ramble to Marsden Rocks*, (publisher unknown), p. 9.

[4] Mackenzie, E. and Ross, M. *An Historical, Topographical and Descriptive View of the County Palatine of Durham*, (Mackenzie & Dent, 1834).

[5] *Chambers Journal*, September 1875.

[6] Alan C. Robinson, *The Story of Marsden and Peter Allan* (published privately by the author, 1971), p.31.

[7] *Ibid*.

[8] Anon. *A Ramble to Marsden Rocks*, (publisher unknown), p. 19.

[9] Anon. *A Ramble to Marsden Rocks*, (publisher unknown), p. 25.

[10] Alan C. Robinson, *The Story of Marsden and Peter Allan* (published privately by the author, 1971), p.25.
[11] *The Monthly Chronicle*, May 1887, p. 128.
[12] *Ibid.*
[13] *Ibid.*

# CHAPTER 23

# BARRELS O' BILGE WATER

The larger numbers of smugglers were gathered at Jackie's Cove, and two smaller detachments had been stationed elsewhere: one at Smugglers Cave, and the other at Souter Point. At Jackie's Cove, several of the smugglers sipped rum, but none dared suck on their pipe. The distinct odour of tobacco could carry a long way on the wind, and no one wanted to alert any Excise men who may have been snooping around. Besides, the glow of a burning pipe-bowl
was no help either!

They could not see the lugger, but they knew it was there.

The plan was simple. The lugger would attempt to come into Jackie's Cove when signalled, and the land smugglers would then off-load the contraband. If this phase of the operation were completed successfully, the goods would not, as Smuggler John had been led to believe, be stored at Smugglers Cave. Instead, they would be stored in a secret chamber that had been excavated on the beach itself. The smugglers would then return at a later time and spirit the contraband away when the Excise men were elsewhere.

But if Smuggler John really was an informer, then it was likely that the Preventives were already secreted around the cliffs waiting to pounce as soon as the lugger dropped anchor. Probably they would make their move as soon as the contraband was ashore. To counter this threat the smugglers had placed their own lookouts on the cliff top and in the surrounding fields. Should the Excise Officers make their presence known, the nearest lookout would immediately discharge his firearm and thus alert the captain of the lugger. The captain had already been given instructions that, should he hear a gun shot, he was to instantly change course and head to Souter Point. There, the second team of smugglers would quickly off-load the spirit and tobacco and hide it in a nearby field. The smugglers at Souter Point were extremely confident that their role in the plan was risk-free. If John had tipped off the Excise, the Preventives would be split between Jackie's Cove where the goods were to be off-loaded, and Smugglers Cave where they mistakenly believed they were to be stored. None of them would suspect that anything would be happening at Souter Point.

After dark, two of the smugglers from the detachment at Jackie's Cove carefully crept towards the outcrop at the southern end of the bay. One of them carried a large bundle of kindling, the other a bottle of lamp oil. They entered a small cave at the distal end of the outcrop and began to prepare a fire. As soon as it was ignited, the flames could be seen for two miles or more out to sea. Importantly, however, the walls of the cave prevented the fire being seen by any Preventives who may have been on the cliffs. Normally the gang would have just used lamps, but under the prevailing circumstances that was far too risky. As soon as the fire was blazing, the two men made their way back to their comrades, being careful not to make a noise by accidentally stumbling or dislodging loose rocks.

Twenty minutes later, the lugger became visible to the smugglers at Jackie's Cove. Its eerie silhouette bobbed and weaved upon the choppy waves. Within another few minutes the lugger would anchor; the crew would then lower a boat and begin to bring the contraband ashore. If the Preventives were around, it wouldn't be long before the smugglers knew about it. Meanwhile, on board the lugger, the captain stood on the deck and strained his ears.

Upwards of twenty smugglers were scattered around the cliff top above the cove. One of them was secreted near a hut, which stood on the grassy top. (The site is now occupied by an Army rifle range). With him were two ferocious dogs, fanatically loyal to their master.

At some point the smuggler became aware of the presence of the Preventives. Perhaps it was the sound of boots padding on wet grass, maybe the sound of whispered instructions. Whatever, the smuggler heard it and immediately sprang into action. Leaping up from behind the hut he discharged his gun, and the thunderous report carried right across the cove and out to sea.

"Bark, boys, bark!" the smuggler urged the hounds. And they did. If the captain of the lugger had needed a second hint, this was it. He immediately bellowed out instructions to his crew, and a frantic flurry of activity took place upon the deck. Quickly the lugger sheared off and away from Jackie's Cove, and began to head north towards Souter point.

The smugglers on the shore below immediately ran for cover. Breaking into gangs of three, each 'set' made for one of the many 'hidey-holes' which had been constructed by contrabanders over the decades. These hidey-holes could hold up to three men, and were accessible through a trap door that was covered with sand and rocks. Frantically, leathery hands tossed boulders to one side, thereby uncovering stout oak doors with an iron ring for a handle. *Get the door up! Hurry, for God's sake!* With cat-like speed and stealth the men dropped down into the hole below.

One smuggler from each set – chosen beforehand – remained above to cover over the trap door so that the Preventives could not see it as they searched. When their job was done, these fleet-foots made off for the caves to the north. There they would stay until the coast was, quite literally, clear.

Within minutes a remarkable change had taken place at Jackie's Cove. All human life had disappeared, all activity ceased. The lugger, still pulling away sharply, was once again only a silhouette.

In the hidey-holes the smugglers began to relax. Each hole contained a small lamp, a shelf on which to stand it and old wooden crates which doubled as stools. The trapdoors had been carefully constructed so that no light could escape and give the game away. A smuggler's hidey-hole wasn't exactly the Ritz, but it was safe.

But if all was quiet on the beach, all was certainly not quiet on the cliff top above. Startled by the report from the smuggler's gun, the Preventives charged towards the old cabin with pistols drawn. The lookout, knowing that he had absolutely no chance of escaping, had already dropped his weapon and raised his hands. He would have to talk his way out of this one.

One of the Preventives – the Supervisor – bounded across the turf and placed his pistol at the head of the contrabander. Calmly and quietly, he spoke, "Who are you, Sir, and what are you doing here?"

The smuggler gave his explanation. He was an itinerant farmhand, accustomed to drifting from one job to another. He'd been walking his dogs along the cliff top, "takin' in the night air, Sir" – when suddenly he heard voices:

And I looks over, Sir, and sees these men tryin' to break-lock the cabin. Well, I set off the dogs, Sir, and then let off me gun to send them runnin'. Off they went, like shiverin' rabbits, if you like, Sir. Damn the ragamuffins, I say. And I'm sure you'd say so too, Sir. Am I right? Run like buggery, they did.

The Supervisor, of course, didn't believe a word of it. He ordered several of his men to look over the cliff and see if there was any sign of life down below on the sands, "Nothing. Not a bloody thing, Sir. Looks all quiet to us."

And so it was.

As the senior Preventive was considering his options, two other officers came running towards him. They'd seen the lugger when she was close in, and got a good look at her in the moonlight.

The smuggler continued to protest his innocence, and the Supervisor eventually decided to let him go. There was no way they could prove any connection between him and the ship:

"What about the ship, Sir?"
"Would you know it if you saw it again, officers?"
"Yes, Sir".
"Definitely, Sir".
"Well, the chances are that it has some proper cargo on board apart from the thirty barrels of stuff your informer told us about. My estimation is that the captain might just try to off-load his contraband at Marsden Bay, and then take his legal load to the dock at South Shields on the morrow."
"What now, then, Sir?"
"We head for Marsden, and quickly."

By the time the Preventives got half way to Marsden, the Supervisor was stunned to see the officers who had been keeping watch above Smugglers Cave walking up the track to meet him:

"What are you men doing? Why aren't you at your watch?"
"We saw the lugger pull out and away through a glass. We could see no sense in waiting, and thought to join you, Sir."
The Supervisor blasphemed.
"It may interest you to know, officer, that the lugger you saw pulling away is in all probability discharging its cargo of rum and 'baccy-oh as we speak. I would suggest we all make haste to Marsden before I decide to put you on a bloody charge!"

When the Preventives arrived at Marsden they gingerly approached the cliff top. What astonished the officers was the scene on the beach below. There, large as life, sat a party of ten or so smugglers. They were laughing, smoking and drinking rum by the bottle. "Bastards. They've taken the stuff off already and have broken open a bottle to toast their fortune! Well, we'll have 'em this time and no mistake".

Silently, the Preventives ran along the cliff top and filed down the steps, which old Blaster had long ago cut into the rock. "Thank the Lord for old

Blaster. Thank the Lord for the old lag's steps, I say".

As the officers raced along the sands towards Smugglers Cave, Peter Allan and Lizzie peered out of their bedroom window.

"What are they doing, Peter?"

"Making an ass of themselves, Lizzie, and no mistake. Truly they're making an ass of themselves, girl."

Clambering over the outcrop of rock that separates Marsden Bay proper from Smugglers Cove, the Preventives expected to see the motley band of smugglers run for their lives. But they didn't. In fact, during the time that it had taken the Preventives to reach them they had even kindled a fire.

"Bastards! Are they mad?":

"Good evening to you, Mr. Supervisor, Sir. Can we offer you a drink?"

"Shut it, you slimy toad. Officers! Search the cave and remove anything you find to the beach!"

"You seem troubled, Sir, as if something's amiss. What ails you?"

"I'm warning you. One more quip and I'll cleave your scalp with a ball of best lead. *Now shut it!*"

"The cave's empty, Sir."

"What did you say, officer?"

"The cave, Sir. There's naught in it."

Suddenly, the Supervisor realised exactly what had happened. The smugglers had hoodwinked him good and proper. They'd never intended to drop their contraband off at Smugglers Cove at all. Either Smuggler John was playing fast and loose with him, or his mates had realised he was an informer and had fed him duff information. Well, John was on his own now whatever the truth. Embarrassments like this could cost the Excise dear, even make them a laughing stock. If anyone's blood were to be spilt – literally or metaphorically – it would be John's and not that of the Preventives.

But the Supervisor was not finished yet, not by a long chalk. If they had been foiled from discharging their illegal cargo at Jackie's Cove, and had never had any intention of unloading it at Smugglers Cove, where else could they off-load it? Souter point? No; too exposed, too risky – or so they thought. The smugglers would know – or at least assume – that there was a risk of being seen by the Supervisor's officers. What the Supervisor did *not* know was that the contrabanders had already been made privy to far more than he realised. The smugglers knew that the Preventives were all gathered at either Jackie's Cove or Marsden Bay, and that their booty could be safely off-loaded at Souter Point after all, "No, they wouldn't dare try for Souter Point. The sons-of bloody-urchins must be planning to unload their hooch and 'baccy-oh at South Shields itself."

As the Supervisor pondered, a smartly painted lugger was already dropping anchor at Souter Point, and the detachment of smugglers hiding there was preparing to receive the contraband stored on board.

\* \* \*

Before dawn, an exhausted group of Preventives arrived at South Shields docks. They had been made to look stupid, and all they wanted was revenge. "Good, she hasn't docked yet."

Shortly after the officers' arrival, the lugger heaved-to, and the Preventives lost no time on storming aboard. They knew exactly what they were looking for – thirty barrels full of rum and tobacco. And they found them. Or to be more precise, they did find thirty barrels. Unfortunately for the excited Preventatives they were filled with nothing more than stinking, foetid bilge water.

The roars of laughter could still be heard from below decks as the Supervisor and his men stormed out of the dock.

\* \* \*

The contraband which had been unloaded at Souter Point was stored in a beetroot field at a nearby farm. For days the Preventives passed the spot, never realising that the goods they were determined to seize were under their noses all the time. [1]

Early one morning, about a week later, the regular Excise patrol passed the field. They noticed that a large patch of earth appeared to be freshly dug over. It had not been dug over at midnight. Then they knew, and realised it was too late. They had been "done, and done good."

The young officer started off, his companion following close behind. "Ne'er mind." He said. "There'll be other days. We'll see them smugglers away yet."

And they did, but not until the young officer was a very old man.

## References

[1] *The Monthly Chronicle*, May 1887, p. 130.

# CHAPTER 24

# AYE, AYE, JOHN

Revenge upon Smuggler John was meted out with stunning swiftness, and in the following manner.

The very day that the Excise Officers were humiliated at South Shields, the smugglers moved against John. They had to act swiftly, for there was a real possibility that the Preventives may have tried to warn him about the events of the previous evening. Also, word was spreading throughout the town like wildfire about how the Excise had been upstaged by the contra-banders, "Thirty barrels of stinking bilge water." John was still in bed when they came:

> "What do you want? I'm still a'bed!"
> "Aye-Aye, John. It's us! Move swift with your pants and boots!"
> "What the hell's up with ye?"
> "No time! We need to move the haul from the cave! We have an hour at most before the Excise will be there!"

Cursing, John dressed and headed off for Smugglers Cove with his compatriots. When John entered the cave, two things entered his head. The first was the realisation that something was wrong. Where was all the contraband that needed shifting? The second thing to enter his head was the grip of a heavy flintlock pistol, which cleaved his scalp open and possibly fractured his skull. Quickly, the smugglers dragged John's prostrate form to the back of the cave, a steady drip-drip-drip of blood leaving its mark upon the golden sand. John groaned. When he came-to, John was puzzled: he was in semi-darkness, and could hear voices. They were distant voices, but he recognised them. They were the voices of his smuggling companions. John began to panic. They had shut him in some sort of box. A round box, and he could barely move. Wait.

It wasn't a box at all. It was a *barrel*. His head throbbed, but he managed to crane his neck slowly so that he was staring upwards. At once he knew exactly where he was. The shaft. Above him he could see daylight streaming in through the upper entrance. He could also see the wooden tripod. And the rope; the rope that connected to the barrel in which he had been stuffed. "Help."

"You'll get no help, you stinking jibber. That's what we'll call you from now on, you greasy, stinking bastard jibber. Jibber John. John the bloody Jibber. How are you, Jibber John? Like your new home? You'll rot there, you bastard jibber."

"Please? Help."

[Only the sound of laughter.]

After a while the smugglers departed. Within a few minutes John realised that they must have gone up to the top of the cliff, for one of the smugglers was now staring down at him, "Light getting in your eyes, John?"

"Please. Help. I done nothing."

"Never mind, bucko. This'll stop the light hurting them pretty eyes."

A grinding sound echoed down the shaft as a huge stone was placed over the upper entrance. Only a tiny gap remained where the rope fed through. John was in darkness.

Word soon spread round that John had been strung up in the shaft. No one dared help him, and many probably didn't want to. He was a jibber. His pitiful cries could be heard day after day. Every evening, after dark, they would lower the barrel down from its height of thirty feet and give John a sip of water and a crust of bread. Sometimes they would leave the barrel on the ground and let John watch them as they roasted a rabbit on a spit inside the cave. As they drunk rum, and joked. And then they'd hoist him up again.

The conditions that John would have found himself in are unimaginable. According to legend he was not allowed to leave the barrel either to urinate or defecate. The stench would have been unbearable. Especially after sixty days, which is how long some say Jibber John lasted. And then, mercifully, he died. His body was never found, but is believed to be buried in the vicinity of the cave itself.

Peter had nothing to do with the slow and terrible death of John the Jibber. Undoubtedly he would have wanted the man punished, but not in such a cruel manner. Those who knew Peter Allan are unanimous in stating that he was a man with a furious temper, yes, but also a tender-hearted man who possessed great compassion. But it was too late for sentiment now. The Jibber was dead.

# CHAPTER 25

# THE FORGE

One of the main difficulties I have faced whilst writing this book is the fact that we just do not know exactly what the nature of the treasure was that the Romans secreted away in the cliffs at Marsden. I spoke to an archaeologist who specialises in the Roman period and told him of my theories. Initially he was sceptical. It wasn't that the theory of the Romans hiding their valuables in the cliff face was impossible *per se*, but just that it is difficult to see what they could have hidden which would have been of any great value *now*.

There are several possibilities. One is that they secreted away large sums of money. Another is that they hid precious valuables and artefacts. They may also have hidden away a combination of the two, of course.

But there are two other possibilities. To be rational in our analysis we are forced to accept that they may have hidden something which had no direct monetary value, but which was extremely valuable in terms of what it could raise from the highest bidder. I am thinking specifically of works of art, manuscripts or whatever. But yet another possibility – and an admittedly outlandish one – is that the caves contained treasures of a more spiritual nature – artefacts that, although of no financial worth, were of huge religious significance. The pages of history are full of people who have searched for Solomon's treasure, the Ark of the Covenant, the Holy Spear, the true cross, etc. etc.

So which of these possibilities is likely to be correct? The blunt answer is that we can't be sure, but we can make some educated guesses.

There is no doubt that there is a strong spiritual aspect to the whole Marsden Bay enigma. Jon, Richard and I discovered how a dragon-based cult once exercised considerable influence at Marsden Bay, and it is not beyond the bounds of possibility that the physical treasure hidden within the cliffs may have had some religious or spiritual significance to them in the same way that it had financial significance to Peter Allan.

But this means that if there is a religious or spiritual treasure hidden at Marsden, then there is also a pecuniary one; and here we are on a much safer footing. Such 'earthly treasure' would almost certainly have been coins and/or valuables, which belonged to those stationed at the Arbeia fort. Unfortunately, this is where archaeologists rightly point out an all too apparent problem.

Let us suppose for one moment that coins were a substantial part of the treasure. The bulk would be made from relatively low-value metals such as copper. A smaller proportion would be made from silver or even gold. However, the combined weight of such coins would have a relatively small value when smelted down. Another obvious problem is the fact that the coins would have had no buying power as such, as they were no longer legal tender.

These problems compel us towards two possible solutions. Firstly, that the number of coins was so vast that the value of the hoard really did have an enormous value. A second solution is that the hoard was comprised of coins almost exclusively made from precious metals.

One archaeologist told me was that there was a suspicion on the part of some experts that Arbeia had been used as a stopping-off point by the legionnaires tasked with delivering the soldiers' wages across the entire length of Hadrian's Wall. In other words, not long before pay-day, a colossal sum of money, in all different denominations, would be delivered to Arbeia before going on the final leg of its journey further north. This money would have been held in a strong room at the fort, and during my research I made enquiries as to whether the remains of such a building had been excavated yet. "Yes," the archaeologist told me. "In fact, *two* strongrooms have been excavated there."

The existence of two strong rooms, although not that unusual, does hint that a fair amount of coinage was kept at the fort on a regular basis.

But what about other valuables, apart from coinage? Here the archaeologist was sceptical; "Probably the only metal artefacts of any great value would be things like the cutlery and dishes in the Commander's silver dinner service. I just can't see that there would have been anything that would have been *that* valuable, even when melted down."

Nevertheless, a large hoard of precious-metal coins, combined with other valuable artefacts, could well have been sufficient to create a treasure trove of at least moderate proportions. This idea is enhanced even further when we realise that legionnaires were only paid once every four months at one of the three 'pay parades' held every year. The system worked as follows. Every four months the quartermasters would submit their ledgers to the battalion adjutant or Cornicularius, and Imaginifer or Standard-bearer. Before the salaries were doled out, accountants withheld enough money to cover all the standard deductions, which legionnaires were subject to, plus any other bills that they may have ran up in the previous trimester. Before such deductions were made, however, it is clear that a large amount of money would have been in situ once every four months.

There is also a possibility that valuables from other places may have been stored in the caves at Marsden. But if Peter did find such a hoard, what on earth would he have done with it? He could hardly have waltzed into the local blacksmith's shop and said, "Excuse me; could you possibly be a decent cove and melt down this Roman treasure for me?" No, if Peter was going to reduce the metal to ingots he would need to do it somewhere secure. He would need to do it in an environment where those around him could be trusted. Interestingly, there is evidence that Peter did exactly that.

In the booklet *A Ramble To Marsden Rocks*, the author discusses his saunter through the villages of Cleadon (which, although now the most desirable part of South Tyneside to live in, was then apparently a bit of a dump) and Whitburn. 'But see, we have arrived at the sweet little village of Whitburn, which presents a striking contrast with the description we have just given of Cleadon. Ha! Here is the smith's forge, formerly the property of Peter Allan; and there stands the cottage of Peter's parents ...'[1].

Peter Allan – gamekeeper, valet, cobbler, quarryman, publican and foreman – also apparently fancied himself as a blacksmith. But if Peter operated a forge, why do we not see any mention of it in contemporary documents relating to his life? Only *A Ramble to Marsden Rocks* mentions the fact to my knowledge, and then only in passing. Indeed, the booklet wasn't written until after Peter had died. So if Peter operated a forge, he operated it very discreetly indeed. My belief is that this forge probably had only one purpose: to smelt down coins and other metal artefacts, which Peter had found at Marsden Bay.

Research has enabled me to determine that Peter purchased or built the forge at Whitburn in 1836. This was just after the departure of the Hairy Man from Marsden, and at this juncture we would do well to explain, albeit briefly, just who this enigmatic Hairy Man was.

In July 1835, a ship docked at South Shields. On board was the ship's mate, a man somewhat over twenty years of age, and pretty much the only thing we know about him is that he was depressed. Local legends say that a long-standing relationship with his childhood sweetheart had just come to a bitter end, which may or may not be true. In any event, the man seems to have decided there and then that he was not going to go back to sea. He wandered from South Shields southwards towards Marsden and somehow found himself sitting in the bar of Peter's inn. Feeling sorry for the young man, Peter and Lizzie allowed him to stay at the inn as an unpaid helper. He could do a little work, and be recompensed with free board and lodgings.

Some time after the man's arrival at Marsden, a dramatic incident occurred in which fourteen young people got trapped in a cave near Velvet Beds. The incoming tide would have drowned them all, but the sailor and three others rescued them. There was a long, vertical shaft leading from the cliff top down to the roof of the cave, similar to the one northward in Smugglers Cave. The rescuers lowered a rope down and, one by one, hauled the youngsters to safety.

This incident seems to have had a dramatic affect upon the sailor. He started to dress in the most peculiar manner – wearing sandals, clothes and a hat – the latter two being fashioned from rabbit skins. He also grew his hair long and eventually took up residence in the cave, which had almost become the coffin of the aforementioned youngsters.

His unkempt appearance eventually earned him the nickname of the Hairy Man, and we believe that, during his stay at Marsden Bay, he became associated with the dragon cult. At some point he began to excavate the cave, just as Peter was doing in the complex further north. According to contemporary records he cut no less than three expansions into the cave, and it seems obvious that he was looking for something.

One day, a furious storm blew up and the Allan's pleaded with the Hairy Man to leave the cave and travel to Whitburn with them. He refused – a decision that almost cost him his life. The cave flooded and extinguished a fire that the Hairy Man had built to warm his small complex of caverns. A toxic mixture of steam and smoke flooded the cave and almost choked him to death. He was pulled out after the tide had ebbed by Peter Allan, barely alive. After the Hairy Man recovered, his brother arrived and took him away for a longer period of rest and recuperation with his family.

Several years later, whilst down in London on 'business', Peter apparently had the luck to 'bump into' the Hairy Man 'by chance'. By all accounts he had recovered from his ordeal and was once again back at sea.

There is little doubt that the Hairy Man was living in the cave for a reason, and one of those reasons was that he was searching for something hidden within the cliff. To my mind, it can only have been the Roman treasure reputed to have been stashed there by the legionnaires around the time they departed from Arbeia. Whatever his motivation, he felt that whatever he was searching for was of such importance, even if only in his own mind, that the threat of death itself could not dissuade him to abandon his mission.

I believe there is a distinct possibility that Peter thoroughly excavated the cave at Velvet Beds immediately after the Hairy Man left. We can say this with some confidence, for, when dealing with the near-death of the Hairy Man, some documents state that the waves penetrated not one, or even two, caverns, but *three*. In *Marsden Rock – Or the True Story of Peter Allan and Marsden Marine Grotto* [2], the author states:

> The most perfect cavern [the Hairy Man's cave] is one which is entered between the drooping wall of another exterior to it, formed by the face of the rock. In this a door, neatly cut in the far side, admits to a third, which should be inspected with a light. This was excavated under very singular circumstances, by a youth who, some years ago, took up his quarters at *The Grotto*.

However, we know that there were not three caves in the Hairy Man's abode when he lived there, but only *two*. The author of the aforementioned booklet works to the assumption that the three caves present when he wrote his booklet (1848) were all excavated by the Hairy Man himself. Peter Allan, being the prime 'mover and shaker' behind the work, was also quite happy to let the author labour under this delusion, for it deflected the attention drawn by the excavating activities away from himself. However, there is no doubt from contemporary accounts that there were only two caves there – the original, large cavern and the excavated cell at the rear of it – on the evening that the Hairy Man survived his close encounter with the Grim Reaper. He was taken from *The Grotto* by his brother just days later, and had neither the time to excavate a third cave or, quite frankly, the inclination. Up to the point of his leaving Marsden Bay forever he was, apparently, severely traumatised. The third chamber in the Hairy Man's cave can, then, only have been excavated by one other person – Peter Allan himself.

If Peter Allan's excavations in the Hairy Man's cave were successful, and he found a stash of Roman coinage, then we should not be surprised. Remember, the cave was only yards away from the remains of the Roman quay, which had been constructed to facilitate the taking of cut limestone from Marsden quarry to the fort at South Shields. At the very least we must admit that this is an astonishing coincidence, and I personally cannot accept that it is coincidental at all.

An even more astonishing coincidence – apparently – is the fact that Peter Allan purchased or constructed a forge almost immediately after the Hairy Man's departure. This too, I think, leads us to the conclusion that Peter Allan found more that sand and pebbles in the cavern at Velvet Beds.

But what of the other possibility, that Peter may have found not just coins but precious artefacts? The aforementioned archaeologist was sceptical that anything found at Arbeia could have been translated into a huge amount of money by sale, and initially I had to agree with him. But then I checked with the British Museum. An expert in the *Department of Prehistoric and Romano-British Antiquities* at the museum, was immensely helpful, and agreed to help me in my research.

We know that, after the Hairy Man departed from Marsden with his brother he went back to the south of England and once again joined the navy. Apparently by coincidence – and I find this very hard to believe - Peter Allan 'bumped into' his friend three years later whilst in London. Two oddities arise here. Firstly, even in Peter Allan's day, the capital was a large place and the chance of bumping into someone in such a manner was unlikely indeed. Secondly, this was one of several mysterious trips that Peter Allan made to London, and no one seems to know what their purpose was. I think there is a *prima facie* case to answer here that something very strange indeed was going on. The question is, what?

I came to believe that Peter made journeys to London – no mean feat, in those days – in an effort to sell coins and artefacts, which he had found in the caves at Marsden Bay. What I wanted to know was whether Peter Allan had made any attempt to sell antiquities to The British Museum between the years 1835 and 1839, the time period in question. I received an answer, which should have deflated me, but actually convinced me more than ever that I was on the right track.

I was informed that there was around a 1% chance that I would be able to find what I was looking for. Record keeping was poor during that time period, and there was simply no proof whatsoever that Peter Allan had sold any Roman antiquities to the British Museum. However, what I discovered next added a totally new dimension of credibility to my theory.

In the eighteenth century the study of Roman history was almost an obsession in England. In the 1730s archaeologists had began excavating the buried city of Herculaneum in earnest. Pompeii, to the southwest, was also buried under tons of solidified lava. In 1594, some workmen who were digging a channel almost stumbled upon the hidden city. They discovered a plaque bearing the words, *decurio Pompeiis,* and assumed that it referred to the Roman statesman Pompey the Great. It did not, but the error determined that Pompeii would stay buried until 1748. From then onwards excavations were carried out sporadically for a while, and then abandoned completely. Not until 1828 did work resume, and then the incredible glory of a buried Roman city eventually came to light. Before long, the civilised world went Roman crazy. In Britain, municipal and public buildings were all created in Greco-Roman style, and Latin became the essential language of mottoes, signs and document headings.

During the 1830s this obsession with all things Roman was showing no signs of abating. It was no surprise, then, that Peter Allan had not sold his finds to the British Museum for there were at that time hordes of wealthy collectors in the capital who would pay huge amounts for Roman treasures. Peter Allan would have had no problem at all in selling any Roman items he may have found. I now believe that Peter Allan *did* visit the British Museum, but *did not* sell his wares. Instead, I am sure, he offloaded them onto one of the many rich antiquity collectors in London who would have basically written him an open cheque.

During my research into this period in Peter's life, I also came across an elderly resident of Marsden who told me that his grandfather had known one of Peter's sons, and that he had been told explicitly that Peter had constructed a *second* forge situated near the village pond at nearby Cleadon. Why Peter would have needed a second forge is baffling, but it demonstrates beyond doubt that something extraordinary was going on in his life at that time which cannot be explained in conventional terms. If he wasn't smelting down Roman coinage, *just what was he doing?* Further, Alan Tedder [3] details in his book that a tunnel was said to have ran from Whitburn to Cleadon village. If this is the case, and Peter Allan had access to these tunnels, as surely he must, then he would be able to travel between the two forges in absolute secrecy. The question is, what evidence exists to prove that Peter Allan did possess – or at least have access to – a second forge at Cleadon?

The information I had to go on was scant. This second forge was apparently 'near the duck pond', and it must, presumably, have been close to the entrance to the tunnel, which led, either from Whitburn or Marsden Bay to Cleadon Village. Working on descriptions of Cleadon Village recorded during that era, I narrowed the possible location down to three specific areas; a) an old manor house called Cleadon Tower, b) an old pub called The *Brittannia Inn* (now the *Toby Carvery*) and c) another, smaller private residence nearby.

Cleadon Tower was an unlikely candidate. How could Peter's activities be kept secret from the household staff, even if he had permission from the owners? Besides, there is no historical record of a forge being constructed at Cleadon Tower. The Britannia Inn? Impossible. Firstly, the inn did not exist in Peter's day, although another one apparently did. Secondly, building a forge in the grounds of a public house would have been absurd. That left only one option; the nearby cottage.

I spoke to the current owners, and asked them if they knew anything about a forge ever having existed on their land, "Sure", said the husband immediately. "It used to stand in the back garden."

The couple told me told me how they had uncovered the forge – which dated from the late eighteenth century – when they purchased the property. They didn't want to destroy it, so they donated the forge to Beamish Museum in County Durham where it has apparently been restored and rebuilt.

The astonishing thing is that a tunnel apparently connects this cottage to both Cleadon Tower and Whitburn. This being the case, then the existence of the forge at that very spot cannot be coincidental. Actually, a thriving blacksmith shop existed at the rear of the cottage – hence the existence of the forge – but what degree of ownership Peter had over it we cannot say. What we can say is that this was almost certainly one of the two forges used by Peter in his smelting operations.

Peter almost certainly *did* find Roman treasure, either to smelt down, sell or both. However, I suspect that he did not find all of it. Had he found the main cache this would, I think, have became demonstrably obvious. Instead, he seems to have found enough to make him moderately wealthy. So why didn't Peter and his family retire and move to what most people would think to be more hospitable surroundings? The answer to this question lies in the change that was wrought in Peter during the time he lived at Marsden Bay. Initially, Peter had seen the recovery of whatever valuables lay hidden in the cliffs as a means to an end. It was his family's passport to a happier life. Once he had found what he was looking for, he planned to move on. However, as we have seen, Marsden Bay exerts a powerful effect upon the psyche of all who are connected with it. Eventually, Peter's *raison d'etre* became not the finding of riches at Marsden Bay, but the consummate 'meaning' behind the Bay itself. Peter *no longer wanted* to leave Marsden, no matter how much treasure he found. He would keep looking for the treasure, yes: but only to make his family as comfortable as possible. The supreme irony is that Peter moved to Marsden Bay in the hope that he would find a fortune that would enable him to move somewhere else. Then he realised that the somewhere else he wanted to move to was actually Marsden Bay itself.

By smelting down coins and selling Roman antiquities I believe that Peter made a reasonable profit. This provided enough income for him to turn *The Grotto* into a first-rate inn and place of entertainment. It enabled him to send all of his children to Newcastle to be privately educated (and remember there were eight of them) and for both Lizzie and himself to live comfortably for the rest of their lives. The spiritual essence of Marsden Bay had soaked into Peter's bones, and it was not about to let him go.

## References

[1] Anon. *A Ramble to Marsden Rocks,* (publisher unknown), p. 25.

[2] Anon. *Marsden Rock – Or the True Story of Peter Allan and Marsden Marine Grotto* (publisher unknown, 1848), p.9.

[3] Alan Tedder, *Ghosts, Mysteries and Legends of Sunderland* (Black Cat Publications, 1992), p. 91.

# CHAPTER 26

# 1836–1839

From 1836 onwards, until the latter part of Peter's life, we know relatively little about what transpired at Marsden Bay. Those documents that survive simply give us a series of vignettes, which are largely detached both chronologically and circumstantially.

We know that Peter became friendly with the Newcastle poet William Mitford, who began to frequent the inn and entertain the clients there with his rhymes, poems and ballads. Peter described him as "one of my favourites".

The excavation of the cliff seems to have slowed to a crawl during this time, although we know that Peter never gave it up altogether. Marsden seems to have become Peter's universe, a world that he rarely left except to make his trips to London and the odd visit to Newcastle or Whitburn.

What follows are the accumulated narratives, which survive from the period 1836–1839, placed in their chronological order as best as I can determine. They portray a wonderful side to Peter Allan's character. His humour, honesty, morality and largeness of heart are self-evident.

## MORE BONES

In 1836 Peter and Lizzie decided to hold a party, to which any and all were welcome. The large marquee tent that Peter had erected on the cliff-top in 1827 to help finance his excavating of the cave was still doing a brisk trade, largely manned by his brother John – or "One-hand John" as he had become known locally, since his shooting accident. Peter arranged for the tent to be brought down to the beach and erected next to *The Grotto* so that guests could shelter from the sun/rain/wind or whatever element prevailed on the day.

Once the tent had been lowered down the cliff, Peter arranged for some labouring friends to dig a series of holes in which the tent poles could be placed. One labourer, whilst clearing away the sand, struck a curious flat rock with his spade and excavated it. With some difficulty he managed to turn it over and was shocked to discover a skeleton underneath.

The skeleton's former inhabitant had obviously been buried with great care. Two square stones lay underneath the skull, forming a strange pillow. A lead bullet was also found in his ribcage, indicative of the man's violent mode of death

Peter ordered that the remains be covered over. Who they belonged to we do not know. Shortly after this incident Lizzie gave birth to her seventh child, Archibald.

## LOOK INTO MY EYES

In January 1837, an incident occurred which demonstrated Peter's intense dislike of dishonesty. One lunchtime he had been sitting in the Upper Room with some friends, enjoying a quiet drink and a bite to eat, when he saw a stranger in the group acting rather furtively. Peter hadn't seen the man before, but was well familiar with the friend who had introduced him. With well-disguised anger the innkeeper watched as the man toyed with a silver teaspoon, cradled it in his hand and then, when he thought no one was looking, slipped it into the pocket of his jacket. Peter carried on as if nothing had happened.

At some point Peter left the table and went down stairs, discreetly telling one of the serving girls they had hired what had transpired. He then told her of his plan to get back at the thief in his own inimitable style.

Peter re-entered the Upper Room smiling sweetly as if he didn't have a care in the world and quickly joined in the conversation. After a few minutes the serving girl came in and began to place the used crockery and cutlery on a tray. "Oh dear", she said. "There seems to be a spoon missing".

"Really?" replied Peter, making a show of looking on the floor and under the tables. "I wonder where it can be?"

"Well Sir; if it's not here then it must have been pinched."

At this suggestion, of course, several of Peter's friends protested strongly. How dare a young serving girl insult her master's guests in such an outrageous manner? "But supposing the spoon *has* been stolen." Peter retorted. "What then?" He then told them that there was a sure-fire way to find out if the spoon had been taken. "Did I ever tell you that I am a worker of magic? Oh, aye! I can see into the hearts and souls o' men just by staring into their eyes. With just one glance I can tell ye who our thief is!"

The guests all thought Peter had flipped his lid, of course, but as he was the host they decided to humour him. With some amusement they watched as Peter went round the guests one by one. "It's not thee Sir, I can tell by your looks … and neither is it thee … nor thee …".

And then he came to the guilty party. Looking gravely into the man's face he bellowed, "Thou art the man! I even know which very pocket the spoon is in!"

Of course, the man adamantly denied that he was the thief, but Peter then grabbed him in a bear hug and promptly removed the spoon from his pocket. As you may well imagine, the onlookers were amazed.

Peter then dumped the man unceremoniously on the seat of his pants and would have left it at that, but the thief had been publicly humiliated and was determined to exact his revenge. This was a decision that would prove to cost him dearly.

Rising to his feet, the man charged at Peter and began to pummel him with his fists. Without breaking sweat, Peter grabbed hold of the man 'by shoulder and thigh' and promptly carried him out of the upper room and down the stairs. Followed by a crowd of bewildered onlookers, Peter waltzed through the bar, across the patio, down the steps and across the sand. The thief, frantically struggling to break Peter's vice-like grip, even resorted to biting, kicking and gouging, but to no avail. As soon as he reached the sea Peter dumped the man in it and held him under the water. Then he lifted him out, only to push him under again seconds later. And then he did it again. And again, and again, and again.

Eventually, Peter's friends had to pull him away, saying, "Peter! You'll kill him if you don't stop!"

"I don't want to *kill* the humbug." Peter replied, "I just want to teach him to be honest. He's yelpin' because I sent him into the sea. He could have been goin' *over* the sea!" [Peter was here referring to the practice of sending thieves to penal colonies abroad.]

## THE DRUNKEN JOURNALIST

1837 also saw Lizzie give birth to their seventh child, Mary-Ann (sometimes referred to as Mary-Anne and Marianne). Shortly after the birth, Lizzie was involved in a dramatic incident, which could, potentially, have resulted in the loss of three lives.

One day Lizzie Allan was sitting on the patio outside *The Grotto*, with her newborn daughter in her arms, when she was passed by a customer from the inn. The chap was a journalist from Newcastle [1] who had downed several ales and decided, stupidly, to go for a swim. Swimming at Marsden bay when you're sober gives pause for thought enough, but to swim there when you're drunk is to beg for trouble. Nevertheless, he staggered past Lizzie and into the brine.

After a while Lizzie noticed that the man appeared to be waving. Concerned, she walked down towards the shore to get a better look. Suddenly she saw two arms go up, and then slowly sink beneath the waves. The man was *drowning*. Without a moment's pause Lizzie placed her new baby on the sand and hurled herself into the water.

Beating against the waves, Lizzie Allan ploughed through the water towards the desperate wordsmith, rising and sinking, rising and sinking, and each time getting weaker. Lizzie knew that it was only a matter of a minute or so before he disappeared altogether. Suddenly she was there beside him, and her arms spun him over so that his mouth was free of the water. Then she began the dangerous and difficult task of getting him back to the shore.

Eventually they made it. Lizzie hauled the drunken writer up on to the sand – no doubt cursing his idiocy – and then went to check on her baby. To her horror, Lizzie found the child on the verge of suffocation. At some point the child had turned over and buried her frail head in the sand. Her mouth and nose were now full of the stuff, and she was choking. Desperately she cleared her daughter's airway with her fingers, scooping out the sand as fast as she could. To Lizzie's relief, the child recovered and suffered no lasting harm.

## The Lime Kilns

After the summer of 1837 was over, Peter gave up his work at Monkwearmouth docks. Some famous characters were now coming to the inn 'to busk', such as the aforementioned Willie Thornton the music hall star, and the ever-thriving business demanded more of Peter's attention. The takings at the inn were steadily rising, and a less demanding supplementary job was now needed. Within a few weeks Peter took up the post of foreman yet again – this time with a certain Mr. Mordey of Wallsend, who employed him at the limekilns at Marsden. This cut down Peter's travelling time considerably, but we know little or nothing of his experiences there.

Evenings began to take on popularity at *The Grotto*, which pleased both Peter and Lizzie. Peter himself acted as a 'people magnet' due to his charm and charisma. A friend of Peter Allan's – known only to us by his second name of Smith – once commented, "His heart seemed all in a glow, and therein lies the secret of his success and popularity."

## TIDAL WAVE

From 1838 onwards hardly a night passed by without a succession of fiddlers, buskers singers and dancers taking to the stage at the southern end of the Ballroom. Ale and spirits flowed, and "the wild gypsy music" could be heard the length and breadth of the Bay. But it was all good, clean fun as they say. Peter never allowed any sexual debauchery to go on at the premises.

The normal routine was for the Allans to rise early and prepare the food that would be sold on the premises that day. Mid morning, if the opportunity arose, Lizzie would take a rest in the Ballroom sitting on her rocking chair, which stood by the bar.

One day, in 1839, Lizzie happened to be sitting not in her customary position but at a table with her daughter Mary-Ann on her lap. Without warning, one of the huge, freakish waves, which can attack Marsden beach from time to time, burst the door open as if it were made of balsa wood and came careering through the room. Within seconds Lizzie found herself waist-deep in water and her child wrenched from her grasp. Just as suddenly as the water had entered it then began to recede, and, to her horror, Lizzie saw her toddler carried out of the door towards the sea.

Alerted by her screams, her oldest son, William, raced down the wooden stairwell and dove into the waters outside. By some miracle he managed to catch his younger sister by the hand and drag the child to safety.

This was not the only encounter the Allans had of this nature. On another occasion, Peter was sitting in the bar drinking with a friend – a local farmer, by most accounts – and nearer the door sat several labourers of Irish extraction who had been working at Monkwearmouth docks.

Suddenly, one of the labourers bellowed out a warning as a huge tidal wave raced up the beach at breakneck speed. The Irishman, to his credit, made a brave attempt to drop the latch on the door to prevent the water from entering. He didn't know what hit him. He was just a split-second too late in getting to the latch, and the wave tore the door from its hinges and sent both it and the labourer hurtling across the bar.

Peter and the farmer, both being residents of the area, had seen this before, of course. As soon as they realised what was happening they both leaped up onto the table, at which point they grabbed hold of the beams above them, which supported the floor of the Upper Room. They lifted their feet just in time to see the table disappear to the other end of the bar.

After the waters had receded they lowered themselves down and found the bemused and befuddled labourer sitting in the corner soaked to the skin. After finding his mates – also half-drowned – they raced up the steps to the cliff top, shouting that if Peter and his family had any sense they would follow. Peter and his friend simply collapsed with laughter.

## References

[1] It is just possible that this may have been Sidney Milnes-Hawkes, who will figure in our story later, but we cannot be sure. At this time Milnes-Hawkes was a reporter with *the Newcastle Chronicle* but frequented the Marsden area and actually lived there for some time.

# CHAPTER 27

# THE FARM AT FARDING LAKE

There was, in 1885, a farm situated at nearby Farding Lake. The holding was called Fardenlake Farm and was owned by a man named Ness. I have been unable to determine his first name with any degree of accuracy.

The writer of *A Ramble To Marsden Rocks* gives us the first hint that there was something odd about Fardenlake Farm when he states that he had been 'much struck with the peculiarities of the place' [1]. The farm itself had been there from time immemorial, but by the late 1830s it had apparently fallen into disrepair. The buildings were dilapidated and the fields overgrown with weeds. However, in 1885 the mysterious Mr. Ness purchased the land and set about restoring the entire place. The farmhouse was rebuilt and a beautiful front garden added.

Contemporary descriptions of the farmhouse indicate that it was nothing short of a delight to the eyes. The walls were painted brilliant white and sheltered by a beautifully shingled roof. At either side of the front door stood, like sentries, two carefully painted figureheads rescued from the wreckage of stricken vessels.

A trelliswork porch covered in golden honeysuckle surrounded the front door, and the garden itself was apparently filled with exotic flowers and shrubs, along with fruit trees. An ornate bamboo fence encircled this beautiful piece of land.

Near to the farmhouse was a small hill, which extended into a narrow cliff. The writer of *A Ramble to Marsden Rocks,* not sure how to interpret the obvious signs that the cliff had been worked, suggested that 'it seems to have been a lime kiln'. This could well be the site of the original Roman quarry at Marsden.

Ness, apparently a retired sea captain, collected the 'bold headpieces' of many vessels and painted them. He then stood them around the hilltop and the cliff 'resembling stiff, old pensioners' and interspersed them with large cannons 'ready to pepper the enemy should he dare to land a hostile force in Marsden Bay.'

At the foot of the hill was a small trout pond. In its centre sat an island, and at the centre of the island was a small bush. It is also recorded that 'a neat skiff slumbered on its untroubled waters.'[2]

It is rumoured that there was a tunnel running from *The Grotto* to Fardenlake Farm. Vague stories that smugglers used the tunnel, still surface from time to time, but there is no documentary or physical evidence that the alleged tunnel actually existed at all. Nevertheless, there are certain peculiarities about the farm that deserve scrutiny.

Firstly, there is something distinctly fishy about the trout pond, if you will excuse the pun. The pond was 'small' according to all accounts, so why was it necessary for Mr. Ness to keep a skiff there? Not for fishing, as a line could easily be cast from the bank. The only purpose a boat would serve would be to act as transport from the shore of the lake to the little island in its centre. But why would anybody want to go to the island in the first place? All it contained was a solitary bush, apparently. I say apparently, for I believe that there may very well have been a secret entrance to the tunnel complex from the island, and that the shrubbery may have covered the entrance. Exactly what purpose this tunnel would have served is another matter, although one obvious explanation is that it provided yet another entrance to the cave/tunnel complex underground.

Another oddity is why Ness wanted to own the area in the first place. In *Marsden Rock; Or, the True Story Of Peter Allan And Marsden Marine Grotto,*[3] we read:

> The garden is a neat, well-disposed little place, and owes its existence solely to its owner, for, previously to his possession, it was nothing but the naked rock. This Mr. Ness was at great pains to cut and fashion into convenient form for the reception of soil, the choicest beauties of the flower garden, and a profusion of fruit trees, willows, sycamores, with the alderberry, snowberry, and other shrubs, make a little Eden of what, only a few years ago, was a wilderness. The effigies planted all around – a fanciful whim – are old ship figure-heads, and those in front of the house once passed current, with vessels of their name, as portraits of Lord George Bentinck and Sir Jacob Astley.

There is something here, which is both very strange and very familiar at the same time. Like Peter Allan, 'Mr. Ness' leaves a life of comfort to go and live

in an inhospitable place. In Peter's case it was a cave in a cliff. In the case of
Ness it was a broken-down farmhouse on a windswept hill. Like Peter, Ness
extensively remodels his new abode. Peter cut into the rock in the cliff; Ness
excavated the rock beneath his feet allegedly to create a pit in which soil
could be placed to receive plants. But there are other, striking similarities.
*The Grotto* was festooned with ships' figureheads. So was Fardenlake farm.
*The Grotto* was protected by iron grilles and hidden entrances. Fardenlake
farm was actually protected by cannon! Whereas the hidden entrances in
*The Grotto* were covered with limestone slabs, etc. the hidden entrance at
Fardenlake Farm, or at least the one that we know about, was probably hid-
den by the shrub on the island at the centre of the trout pond.

When we consider that there were rumours regarding a tunnel, which supposedly ran from *The Grotto* to Fardenlake farm, the connection becomes
complete. It is almost as if the farmhouse was an extension of *The Grotto*,
mirroring its appearance and character in great detail. If we could shed some
light on the owner of the farm, Mr. Ness, then we might be able to make an
educated guess as to what was actually going on here.

Ness, we know, purchased the farm in 1885, which was long after Peter
Allan had passed away. Bearing in mind that the population of Marsden
was quite small then, it is not impossible however that Peter could have
known "Mr. Ness" in his younger days. The problem is that we cannot get
to know him, for to my knowledge few biographical details of the man have
been passed down to us. Nevertheless, there are one or two peculiarities,
which need to be scrutinised.

Firstly, I think that the surname Ness is significant. It is very close to
Naestre, Anglo Saxon daughter of Thalphere the Thane, who was inextrica-
bly tied up with the history of the Farding Lake area. In local legend, Naestre
fell in love with a Viking berserker called Rolf Hadarsson, and the couple
enjoyed regular trysts in secret. Ironically, the venue for these secret assigna-
tions was none other than the cliff, which Blaster Jack had turned into a
seaside dwelling centuries later. The story ends with Naestre and her father
being killed, and the morose spirit of Rolf having to wander the coastline at
Marsden Bay for a thousand years.

Secondly, the word *ness* itself has two meanings. It may refer to a lake or
other body of water, and it may also describe a piece of rock or land that
protrudes into a body of water. One cannot help but wonder whether there
is an oblique connection here between the name of the farm's owner and the
lake adjacent to his dwelling. There may also be a link with the topography
of Marsden Bay, particularly Marsden Rock.

Thirdly, we know that for hundreds of years Loch *Ness* in Scotland has been the legendary home of a serpent-like creature which bears great similarities to both the 'Shony' – the North Sea's very own aquatic, dragon-like monster of legend – and the 'Worm' which lived in the tunnel complex. These 'coincidences' are not really coincidences. They are further evidence of an attempt to cover up the real secret of Marsden Bay and the part which the central characters within these pages played in its outworking. Although Ness's family later emigrated to Canada, I am not absolutely sure that our "Mr. Ness" was really called Ness at all. His surname may possibly have been assumed simply as a symbolic device to indicate his involvement with the Marsden Secret, whatever we may conceive that mystery to be. This is only a hypothesis, however, for which I have no categorical proof.

## References

[1] Anon. *A Ramble to Marsden Rocks*, (publisher unknown), p. 43.

[2] *Ibid.*

[3] Smith, Mr; *Marsden Rock; or the Story of Peter Allan, and Marsden Marine Grotto* (*The Sunderland & Durham County Herald*, 1848) p. 7.

# CHAPTER 28

# 1842–1847

No one reading this book could have failed to get this far without agreeing that Marsden Bay is, to put it mildly, a place with what paranormal investigators call a very 'High Strangeness Quotient.' Even if one discounts the notion of any paranormal activity having taken place at Marsden, the area must still count as one of the most peculiar stretches of coastline in the world, if only due to the odd assortment of characters who have, for one reason or another, inhabited its caves.

One of the strangest incidents of all has become known locally, as the Cotton-Ball Duel.

## The Cotton Ball Duel

The confrontation – held in the time-honoured fashion of 'pistols at dawn' – was the last recorded duel between two individuals held in South Shields. In 1842 – we cannot be sure of the month – two individuals from Sunderland had a falling out.[1] One chap was a magistrate by the name of Richard Spurr, the other a 'professional man' called Joseph Wright. One 'demanded satisfaction' from the other, which was a nice way of insisting upon the opportunity to put a bullet in his skull.

The duel took place on the sands directly outside of *The Grotto*, the name *Tam O'Shanter* having finally been retired. Lizzie Allan herself seems to have been Referee, Adviser and Chief Inspector of Weapons.

At dawn the two men stood back-to-back, walked the customary number of paces and then turned to face each other. The magistrate discharged his gun first – and missed. His opponent, most civilly, then fired his pistol in the air and an end was made to the matter. In fact, there is a tradition that the two duellists later became firm friends.

A week or two after the duel, the magistrate visited *The Grotto* for a drink and passed a group of youths who were sitting with their tankards and pipes at a table in the bar. One of the men shouted across to Lizzie, "Where's the cotton ball, Mrs. Allan?" The others then broke out into peals of laughter.

What puzzled the magistrate was Lizzie's reaction. Putting an index finger to her lips she chastened the boys to keep quiet and then asked them to go to the Upper Room out of the way: "What's that they say?"

"Why, its only the cotton ball you fired at Mr. Wright – or possibly the one he fired at you – and which Peter picked up on the sand."

"The *cotton* ball?"

"To be sure, and there it is." Said Lizzie, at which point she promptly handed him a corked bottle with a sooty ball of cotton in it. On the front was a label that read, 'A Penny Each To See This!'

In fact, Lizzie – not wanting any bloodshed on the premises – had loaded both pistols with cotton balls instead of lead balls, thereby ensuring that the worst thing the two buffoons could give each other during the duel was one hell of a fright when their guns discharged.

The magistrate could see the funny side of this of course, and laughed. There wasn't much else he could do under the circumstances. He did, however, in jest, insist that Lizzie Allan put the price up of viewing the cotton ball to sixpence. She duly obliged.

A publication known as *Latimer's Local Records* states that a man named Peter Flint wrote a ballad about the incident entitled 'Famous Battle of Marsden Rock – Between Sir Richard de Spurr and Sir Joe de Wright.' I have been unable to find a copy.

## WILLIAM TELL REBORN

One of Peter Allan's descendants once related to me a wonderful oral legend regarding Peter, which has been passed down in the family. I have since heard the same tale from another source, and have included it in this work because it demonstrates marvellously the innkeeper's coolness and dry wit.

One day, a local sportsman came into *The Grotto* and began bragging about how good a shot he was with a gun. Now Peter Allan excelled at many things, but, like his father before him, his accuracy with both pistol and shotgun was so good it was almost uncanny. *No one* was a better shot than Peter. Eventually the braggartly statements of the visitor began to get on Peter's nerves, and he decided to do something. Calmly he fetched his pistol. He then walked over to the sportsman, who was sitting with his ale, pausing momentarily to pick an apple from the bowl of fruit which always stood on the bar.

Peter then shouted to one of his sisters – it may have been Jane, for she was known to frequent the inn regularly – and threw her the apple. She caught it, found a suitable spot in the bar, and then placed the apple on her head. Without hesitating Peter calmly raised the pistol and let a shot off. The apple exploded into a thousand pieces, and Peter's sister walked away unscathed:

> "D'ye reckon *ye* could dae that?" asked Peter.
> The sportsman, appearing distinctly nervous, hesitated momentarily before saying, "Er ... yes."
> "Then go ahead."
> "Um...may I borrow your pistol, Sir? I haven't mine with me."
> "Of course".
> "And ... may I borrow an apple, Sir?"
> "Surely".
> "Now about your sister ..."
> "You can get your OWN sister, my friend!" said Peter, as everyone in the bar roared with laughter.

Guns seem to have been a quite natural part of life at *The Grotto*. Yet another story relates the incredible ability of Peter to handle firearms.

One afternoon Peter needed 'three or four brace of snipe' for Lady Williamson in Whitburn, as she was entertaining guests for dinner. Now when snipe are flushed from their hiding place they will fly extremely quickly and in a zigzag fashion. This makes them notoriously difficult to hit. Peter shot snipe all that afternoon, and never missed so much as a single shot.

## THE SHOOTING ACCIDENT

On July 5 1846 a tragedy occurred at Marsden Bay. A party of pleasure trippers had arrived from Westoe, and with them they brought a double-barrelled shotgun to shoot seabirds with. As we have seen, birds have a very mystical role to play at Marsden, and bad things tend to happen to those who show disrespect for their office. Shooting birds for food seems to have been permissible, but shooting them purely for sport was, apparently against the rules.

The majority of the group had came ashore, but two young men, known only as Mr. Marshall and Mr. Galloway, decided to stay at sea for a while longer. The exact details are not known, but it seems that there was an accident of some kind and the shotgun was inadvertently discharged. Marshall took the full blast in his stomach, and was in a critical condition. Galloway rowed furiously for the shore and carried his stricken friend to *The Grotto*. Peter and Lizzie did what they could, but to no avail. The youth died within minutes of arriving.

## ISOLATION AT MARSDEN BAY

The winter of 1846 was one of the worst on record, and its effect on Marsden Bay is a testament to just how barren and remote the place was during the middle of the nineteenth century.

That year, so much snow fell that all road and rail traffic ground to an undignified halt. Even the river was unusable, as the water under the Tyne Bridge had frozen solid, thus cutting off communication with the folks further downstream.

Contemporary records state that huge drifts of snow cut off every single road and path to Marsden Bay. The place looked like the Antarctic.

At *The Grotto*, Peter Allan had foreseen such a situation and prepared for it. He had purchased a large stock of cured, dried, desiccated, powdered and salted foods and stored it in the kitchen. It was just as well he did, for it would be six, long weeks before the Allans would have any contact with civilisation again.

Peter was desperately worried about the animals outside, which included his prized Russian pigs, goats and chickens. These were kept in a small-holding adjacent to the cave complex known as Peter's Farm. As the snow began to deepen, Peter apparently brought them inside the inn, and almost certainly kept them in one of the vacant rooms or caves he had excavated. Peter is also known to have slaughtered two piglets during their isolation so that his family had fresh meat to eat.

## THE DEATH OF POOR RALPHY

Among Peter's many pets were two greyhounds, which he kept in separate kennels. (One of the enduring traditions of *The Grotto* is that the landlord or tenant often keeps dogs, and normally two.) I have already detailed the psychic affinity that the animals had, not just with Peter, but also between themselves. One curious bond was that which existed between Ralphy, Peter's disabled raven, and one of the greyhound dogs. In fact, not only would Ralphy ride on the animal's back, but he also slept in its kennel at night. One evening, Ralphy and the dog must have had a disagreement. The next morning Peter found his feathered friend dead. It had been crushed between the jaws of the greyhound.

What Peter's feelings were towards the dog are not recorded, but he quite rightly decided that Ralphy was too good just to be buried in the sands of Marsden Bay. Peter contacted his friend William Yellowly the taxidermist. He wanted the remains of Ralphy preserved.

Yellowly used every trick of his craft to immortalise Ralphy in splendour, and by all accounts did an excellent job. Firstly he had constructed a cabinet of oak. We do not know the exact shape, but it was likely to be of the display-case type that was so popular with the Victorians. Inside Yellowly created a natural scene with branches, leaves and other bits and pieces. In the centre was perched Ralphy.

In front of the beautifully decorated scene was a small wooden stand, upon which rested a piece of blue paper. In ornate gold letters, Yellowly had copied a poem. The author is not known, although the author of *A Ramble to Marsden Rocks* states that it was 'a young man belonging to South Shields':

> *Poor Ralphy, though thy life is sped,*
> *Thou shalt not mingle with the dead:*
> *No after-life – no future state –*
> *Death through eternity's thy fate!*
> *Shall thy lov'd form in earth be laid,*
> *Forgotten, like the flowers that fade?*
> *In case of glass, thy plumage bright*
> *Shall ever glow in noonday light:*
> *From memory redeem the past,*
> *And seem to us as once thou wast.*

It takes no stretch of the imagination to think that the presence of Ralphy in the Upper Room, at least in bodily form, would have been a great comfort to Peter. He loved Ralphy, conversed with him and shared his dreams and ambitions with this the most intelligent and perceptive of friends. I have no doubt that he also 'chatted' to Ralphy after he was dead.

## ANOTHER NEAR-TRAGEDY AVERTED

In 1847, three youths came to play hide and seek at Marsden Bay. These also found themselves cut off in the Hairy Man's cave and had to be rescued, this time by Peter Allan himself, plus some locals and his eldest son, William. The oldest of these youths, Arthur, was aged twelve; the youngest, his brother Edward, just nine.

The account touched the heart of The Reverend R.C. Cox, Vicar of Newcastle and well-known local poet. Shortly after hearing about the incident he penned the following:

> *A romping party seek the sand,*
> *Where Marsden's tunnel'd rock,*
> *Wave-worn and rent and isolate,*
> *Still braves the ocean's shock.*

> *And off they go; their plotting heads*
> *Much thought and care combine!*
> *The senior sage twelve years has told,*
> *The youngest only nine.*

> *Their friends are gone – all's safe without*
> *But, ah! What's this within?*
> *They're found by one they heeded not!*
> *The sea comes hungering in!*

The poem goes on to describe how Arthur desperately tried to warn the youngsters of their dangerous predicament, and then continues:

> *But none would heed the tiny note;*
> *"Away!" bold Edward cried.*
> *"With baby-fears – they'll hear you speak –*
> *Who cares about the tide?"*

As the sea crept ever closer whilst the youngsters awaited rescue, Coxe captures the scene imaginatively with typical Victorian excess:

> *Cramped were those little hands, and cold,*
> *And all suppressed their breath;*
> *When o'er the rock a visage stole –*
> *What is it – life or death?*
> *The phantom speaks! – 'tis he – poor Ned!*
> *But oh, alas! How changed!*
> *He lives, but his big heart has burst,*
> *His wits are all deranged!*
>
> *And "Mother, dear!" he cries, as though*
> *The cold rock were his bed,*
> *And that lov'd form were near, to pour*
> *Her blessings on his head.*
> *"Dear, dearest mother, kiss your boy!*
> *Why look so wan and weep?*
> *I'm cold and weary, mother dear,*
> *I'm cold and fain would sleep."*

Imaginatively, Coxe then has young Ned repenting of his folly and encouraging the others to do the same:

> *"Down, down upon your knees, dear boys!*
> *Down on your knees!" he cried;*
> *"Thank God – the God of infinite love –*
> *Who has saved you from the tide."*

## References

[1] Anon. *A Ramble to Marsden Rocks*, (publisher unknown), p. 53.

# CHAPTER 29

# PETER'S GREAT BATTLE

During the final years of Peter Alan's life, *The Grotto* became a Mecca for eccentrics, thinkers, poets, singers, artists, journalists, writers and story-tellers, It was, in a sense, a precursor to the beat cafés which were popular in New York in the late '50s and early '60s. *The Grotto* was, in mid-twentieth century parlance, a *happening* place.

There is some evidence that there may have been a slight decline in Peter's level of health and fitness during this time, but not in his vigour. The author of *A Ramble to Marsden Rocks*[1] recalls one visitor's recollections:

> And he bids fair to outlive the accomplishment of all his little plans; for although his locks have now assumed the whitening hue of years, and his corpus is such as would reflect no discredit on the dinner circle of any London alderman. Yet is his step as elastic, his limbs as lithe, and his arm as strong as old; and you see, by the light beaming in his quick, dark, eye, and the compression of his firmly-set lips, that his mind is as originative, and his will as determined, and prompt to carry out its suggestions, as ever.

But things were about to change. For some time a local politician, banker and ship owner named John Clay, who lived in East Boldon, had been keeping a discreet eye on Peter Allan and his inn. Clay, who had fingers in many pies, had been instrumental in getting the town of South Shields registered as a municipal Borough. After receiving a muted response from local officials initially, several prominent individuals, including Clay, had formed the South Shields Incorporation Committee. Working both openly and covertly with colleagues from North Shields, across the Tyne, the group planned to get both Boroughs incorporated as soon as possible.

There was a sound financial motive for this move. The city of Newcastle, further up the Tyne, was beginning to dominate the river trade considerably. The city's success was strangling the life out of the smaller towns like North and South Shields. Clay and others believed that the only way to fight this domination of the market was to have the town enjoy Borough status, giving it a credibility, which would help retain the trade it was losing. This would also enable the town to demand a percentage of the revenue earned through river trade.

But the idea of incorporation did not go unchallenged. Several local politicians pointed out that if the town was granted Borough status it would be liable to pay for certain things, and the sum total of the things they'd have to pay for was not unadjacent to £2,500. To the 'canny folks of Shields' this was like a King's Ransom. Another dignitary pointed out that if the town became incorporated as a Borough it might be required to provide financial support towards the County Police. "Yes", replied another, " but if we're incorporated we won't *need* the constables from the County. We'll be able to have our *own* Police."

"Indeed? And who'll pay for *them*?" was the retort.

And so it went on. Eventually, a meeting was held on January 30ᵗʰ 1850. In the chair was local magistrate J. Twizel Wawn. Wawn may actually have been one of the four men who, in 1835 helped save over a dozen youths from drowning at the Bay when they were trapped in a cave by the tide. This connection is strange, for Wawn was a good friend of John Clay, thus providing at least an indirect link between Clay and *The Marsden Grotto Inn*.

Eventually a motion to have the current system of local government declared inadequate was passed. This motion had been proposed by John Clay and seconded by one J.W. Lamb. The town of South Shields was on its way to becoming a Borough, and a committee was immediately elected to steer the process.

The committee included both Clay and J. Twizel Wawn. There were also two other men named Wawn on the committee, both related to J. Twizel. These were all related to yet another Wawn, named Charles, who owned a rope manufacturing business in Fowler Street and sported a fashionable and well-furnished home at 5 Albion Terrace. Yet another Wawn, Thomas, lived at 3 Albert Terrace and was a successful shipbuilder. Elected with them was one William Brockie, author of several excellent books on the history and legends of South Shields and Durham. Brockie also took an unusual interest in what Peter Allan was doing at Marsden Bay, and we cannot but help note in passing that the writer was elected as the first vice-president of *The*

*Geological Club* when it was inaugurated on October 9ᵗʰ 1862. Brockie, it should be noted, had a keen and long-standing interest in both geology and palaeontology.

But I'm getting ahead of myself here. Let us regress to 1848. Whilst John Clay and his colleagues were pressing to have South Shields incorporated as a Borough, he also suddenly decided to purchase a short lease on a farm. This was unusual, for as previously stated his business was primarily in brewing, banking and shipping. The farm was called Marsden Rock Farm, and sat on the cliff top directly above *The Grotto*. It had formerly been the residence of two uncles of Peter Allan's good friend, the naturalist and taxidermist William Yellowly. In fact, Yellowly had owned the farm. No sooner was the ink dry on the bill of sale than Clay had made his first move against Peter Allan.

Clay claimed that as the leaseholder of the farm on the cliff top, he was also the holder of the slice of cliff and stretch of shore that lay before it. This, in effect, also made him the holder of *The Grotto* itself. Clay's ally in this matter was Andrew Stoddart, agent to the Chapter and Dean of Durham, whose office was in King Street, South Shields. Clay wanted Peter out for reasons which will become clear later, but to unceremoniously dump a husband, wife and eight children on the beach and leave them without a home would not only be immoral but also a public relations disaster. Instead he decided to charge Peter rent. The amount he would ask would be so high that it would, he hoped, press Peter and his family to move elsewhere. There is some confusion about the exact amount demanded of Peter, but we know that it must have been exorbitant. Peter refused to pay up, and told Stoddart and Clay to their faces that he would "never pay as long as I can wag a leg". This, of course, was exactly what Clay wanted. He immediately instructed Stoddart to serve Peter Allan with notice to quit.

At this point we need to look at some political changes which were going on during this period, for they help us to understand the motivation behind some of the actions of people like Clay and Stoddart. The leasehold of Dean and Chapter land was, by tradition, virtually as secure as freehold. Renewals were given as a matter of course – a situation that the residents of South Shields enjoyed, for it gave them a feeling of security and permanency, even if it was only the lease that was being purchased. There were other benefits too. Tenants could improve the property considerably, and yet there would be no re-evaluation of the lease price because of those improvements until the second renewal. You could even build extra property on the land, and again escape re-evaluation until the *third* renewal. But then came the University Act, and everything changed.

Because of the Act, the possessions of the Bishop of Durham were trans-
ferred to the Ecclesiastical Commissioners in 1836. Shortly afterwards
efforts were made to transfer the capitular estates to the Commissioners
also. The following year the Chancellor of the Exchequer, Spring Rice,
introduced a Bill that was aimed, supposedly, at improving the running of
the estates which now belonged to the Ecclesiastical Commissioners. The
problem was that the Bill paid no heed whatsoever to the custom and practice of automatically renewing leases. Families, which had held the same
farm for generations, now felt extremely vulnerable. What would their
future be if they suddenly found themselves denied the right to renew the
lease on the land?

At this point another interesting character joins the drama; Mr. Thomas
Salmon, a lawyer who owned a large mansion on the seafront at nearby
Manhaven called Salmon Hall. (Salmon Hall, legend has it, sat on top of a
tunnel, which ran all the way to a farm at Whitburn.) Salmon got together
a committee to lobby the government to amend the Bill. This committee
also contained John Clay, Andrew Stoddart, William Brockie and J. Twizel
Wawn. Through their lobbying and the lobbying of others, the matter was
passed to a Parliamentary Select Committee, which in 1838 agreed that the
matter of lease renewal should be decided locally. As everyone who mattered
in the town of South Shields seemed to be on their side, the leaseholders
were quite happy with this compromise and confidence was restored. Clay,
Stoddart, Salmon and Wawn later had streets named after them in South
Shields. They are still there to this day.

But the matter reared its head again in 1849. In that year, Lord Carlisle
introduced a Bill, which would have once again made the leaseholders' position vulnerable. For a second time, Thomas Salmon sprung into action. The
old committee was resurrected and pressure was immediately brought to
bear on the government. A Select Committee of the House of Lords was
formed in 1850 to hear the matter, and, once again, a decision was made
that the rights of the leaseholders should be respected.

But that was not the end of the matter. Extraordinarily, another Bill
was put before Parliament the following year, which would *yet again* have
removed the rights of leaseholders. The leaseholders of South Shields fought
this motion just as vigorously, and the Bill was amended 'with due regard to
the just and reasonable claims of leaseholders arising from the long-contin-
ued practice of renewal.'

John Clay now held the lease on Marsden Rock Farm. Through the support of his friends and colleagues, he also had the right to renew it for as

long as he wished. All he had to do now was get the Allan family out. The pair immediately instigated legal proceedings, and the case was heard at the Durham Assizes in early August 1849.

Clay and Stoddart were influential people, but Peter Allan did have some big guns on his side, not least of which were the members of the Williamson family at Whitburn, wealthy landowners themselves.

At court, both sides put forward lengthy arguments. Eventually a compromise was reached. Peter was granted a twenty-one year lease on *The Grotto*, but he would have to supplement that with an annual rent of £10. He was also instructed to pay court costs to the sum of £50. This may have sounded like a victory for Peter, as he could continue to live in *The Grotto*. In reality it was a defeat. When Peter had first moved to the Bay permanently and sold *The Highlander* at Whitburn, his motives were temporal and secular. He knew that there was at least one cache of gold and valuables hidden in the cliff, and he wanted it so that he could better the circumstances of his family. He had planned to vacate the Bay and move somewhere altogether more pleasant as soon as he had found what he was looking for. But then things had changed. In fact, *Peter* had changed. *The Grotto* was his home now, and he wanted it to be passed down to his family as an inheritance, whether or not his sons and daughters ever found the hoard of Roman treasure he knew was hidden in the cliff face somewhere. But now the Allan family was on borrowed time. They knew that twenty-one years hence Clay would use all of his considerable influence to attempt to wrest the lease from them. The law currently seemed to offer them protection, but as they had seen, the advantage had swung back and forth between the leaseholders and the landowners like a pendulum. Who could say that they would have a right to renew in twenty-one years' time?

But the result was also a defeat for Clay. His own efforts to make Parliament recognise the right of leaseholders to renew their use of the land had backfired on him terribly. The Allans now had a lease on *The Grotto,* and that did not serve Clay's purpose at all. For reasons that will become clear presently, Clay needed the Allans out of *The Grotto* very quickly indeed.

Despite the fact that John Clay hadn't gotten his own way entirely, Peter was devastated. What he had wanted, at the very least, was a lease with a *permanent guarantee* of renewability. After all, wasn't that what Clay and his cronies had been fighting for? Hadn't they argued vociferously with MP and Lord alike that the rights of leaseholders were being trampled upon because they had no right of renewal?

Both Clay and the Allans knew that Clay's own lease on Marsden Rock Farm was a short one. By the time the Allans' lease had expired, his own lease would have expired too, and if the law changed once again *he* may have found himself with no guarantee of renewability. Clay wanted access to *The Grotto,* and he couldn't wait two decades to get it. He *had* to find some other way to get them out before then. And John Clay certainly tried.

When Peter got home from Durham he went straight to bed. The next day he got up late, and left the running of *The Grotto* to the others. He sat moodily on the patio, sinking deeper and deeper into a state of melancholy. Lizzie made him food, but he refused to eat it.

After another week or so Peter was refusing to get out of bed. His weight was diminishing rapidly, and he had virtually stopped speaking. His father and mother came to *The Grotto* frequently and pleaded with him. His children begged him to rekindle his interest in living. Lizzie cried tears by the bucketful as she watched this big, brave Scot with the heart of a lion wasting away before her eyes.

By the 30<sup>th</sup> August Peter had lapsed into unconsciousness. The following day, with his family gathered around his bed, he slipped peacefully away. Lizzie – his dear Lizzie – was holding his hand at the time. Peter Allan had died of a broken heart.

Days later, the Allan family and a huge number of friends from all over the region gathered as Peter was laid to rest in the graveyard attached to Whitburn Parish church.

His tombstone, which can be seen to this day, bears the following inscription:

## Sacred
TO THE MEMORY OF
# PETER ALLAN
OF MARSDEN MARINE GROTTO
Who Died, August 31<sup>st</sup>
1849, Aged 51 years.
*Universally Respected.*
God is my Rock.
And my salvation.

## References

[1] Anon. *A Ramble to Marsden Rocks,* (publisher unknown), p. 36.

# CHAPTER 30

# TO THE MEMORY OF PETER ALLAN

*Where the deep-moaning billow is laving the strand;*
*Where the sea-mew is whirling aloft in the air;*
*Where the rock-covered grotto now margins the sand –*
*Where last we saw Marsden, poor Allan was there.*

*His dark eye was glowing with vigorous fire;*
*His step was elastic, his limbs strong and free;*
*His laugh rang as merry as joy could desire; –*
*Now Peter lies cold as the surf on the sea!*

*He told us his projects, explained all his schemes;*
*In fancy he saw every toil at an end;*
*But the bark that to-day sails on smooth-flowing streams*
*May to-morrow be wrecked, and to ruin descend!*

*Yet how fertile his brain, and how dauntless his breast!*
*Determined to conquer, disdaining to flee;*
*Still his heart every feeling of kindness possessed: –*
*Now Peter lies cold as the surf on the sea!*

*And whence came the serpent that wounded his heart?*
*Was it home – desolation – the loss of all dear?*
*Did his children, rebellious, occasion the smart?*
*Or did friendship forsake him when trouble was near?*

*Oh, no! As the noblest of stoics he died,*
*With his wife near his bed, and his bairns by his knee;*
*He had drunk of the hemlock that law can provide; –*
*And now he lies cold as the surf on the sea!*

*When the summer days come, we will wander again,*
*And visit his grotto, the work of his hands;*
*We will scale Marsden Rock 'mid the waves of the main,*
*And shed a sad tear as we move o'er the sands.*

*Then, when music and dancing have ceased in each cave, –*
*When the twilight is deep'ning o'er mountain and lea;*
*With his dear wife and children we'll mourn o'er his grave,*
*Where Peter lies cold as the surf on the sea!*

Robert Ward, author of *A Ramble to Marsden Rocks*, penned the above poem.

# CHAPTER 31

# LIFE AFTER PETER

Lizzie knew that the lease on *The Grotto* would eventually pass from her family. She also knew that John Clay would not wait twenty-one years to get his hands on it. Sooner or later he would make a move. It was just a question of how and when.

Peter's children all turned out well. William, in his early twenties, more or less stepped into Peter's shoes and became the proprietor of *The Grotto*, if not legally then practically. Thomas took over the forge his father had purchased in Whitburn and became a blacksmith. Peter became an able seaman. John became an apprentice joiner and cartwright. Jane married a clock and watchmaker from Bishopwearmouth named Charles Hutchinson. Hutchinson then took on Peter's son Archibald as an apprentice. Elizabeth Marsden Allan decided to help William and her mother run *The Grotto*, whilst Mary-Ann still attended private school in Newcastle.

William, of course, knew all about his father's plans to excavate the cliffs. Indeed, he had helped him carry them out. Although William himself had been infected with the spiritual atmosphere that surrounded the inn, although he had not been caught up with it to the same degree as Peter. Whereas the possibility of finding Roman treasure in the cliffs diminished in importance somewhat to Peter Allan, to William Allan, young and adventurous, it still held an irresistible allure. Before long, William carried on where his father had left off. He began excavating the cliff with gusto.

Life in *The Grotto* carried on much as before in some ways. It would never be the same again without Peter's presence, but Lizzie and her family made sure that the character of the inn was maintained fully. Peter may not have been there in the flesh, but he was certainly there in spirit.

For the next few years' life seems to have been relatively uneventful at Marsden. In 1850 John Clay was elected Mayor of South Shields. He was then re-elected the following year. Meanwhile, the smugglers carried on with their nefarious trade as best they could. Even the wreckers still made an occasional attempt to bring a ship ashore so they could plunder it.

## THE *ROB ROY*

In 1851 a former Excise cutter turned schooner named the *Rob Roy*, wholly owned by smugglers, was captured off the coast of Marsden [1]. On board the customs officials found 8,000 lbs. of tobacco and cigars. As tobacco retailed at the equivalent of around 3p per ounce, the total haul had a street value of around £4,000. Having impounded the ship, the officers found even more of the boat's illicit cargo, already off-loaded, stored in Smugglers Cave. This second cache weighed 600lbs.

## IN PRAISE OF A SMALL DOG

On May 16 1858, tragedy struck the Allan family, or at least someone close to it. Four young men from North Shields had decided to take a large boat named the Delhi out to Marsden Bay. They set out after lunch on the day in question, and on board were Mr. Alexander McDonald, an assistant with the North Shields booksellers Philipson & Hare, and John Cookson, an assistant at Williamson's the chemist, also of North Shields. Also on board was McDonald's small dog, named Grip.

McDonald, although young, was a well-known character in North Shields. He had a tremendous physique and was rated to be one of the finest swimmers in the area. He had been awarded numerous medals for swimming, including a silver medal from Tynemouth Swimming Club, which he had been presented with in the summer of 1857

McDonald had also been awarded two medals by the Royal Humane Society. One was for rescuing a man whilst he was working for a company called Simpkin & Marshall, in Blackwall, London, and the other for having saved a woman from drowning at Chorley, with the help of one R.M. Tate.

Also on board was a sailor named R. Coatsworth and a young man named Wheatley, who was apprenticed to a South Shields cabinetmaker called Smith.

The men crossed the mouth of the Tyne and headed south down the coast for Marsden. Suddenly, heavy waves started to buffet the boat, one of which hit the *Delhi* on the quarter and capsized her, promptly throwing the four men and the dog into the sea. On one side of the boat were Coatsworth and Wheatley, to the other side of the boat clung McDonald. Cookson, meanwhile, was clinging to an oar and floating nearby.

Suddenly another wave hit the boat and actually righted her. Unfortunately it also separated the three men from the Delhi, leaving them floundering in the water as was Cookson. McDonald was stunned, and in an effort to save him Cookson held out the oar hoping that his friend would grasp it. The waves were too strong, however, and McDonald was carried away. Now desperate for his own safety, Cookson headed for the boat, which was rapidly filling with water. As he struck out he was astonished to see McDonald's dog, Grip, heading towards him. In his mouth the terrier carried a piece of wood, which he offered to the man as a means of help. It was, of course, too small, but the selflessness of the little dog is touching in the extreme.

Coatsworth, by now, was also nowhere to be seen. Cookson and Wheatley did manage to make it back to the boat and cling on, but their respite was only temporary. Suddenly, a huge wave made for the Delhi at frightening speed. Cookson was fortunate in that he saw it coming. This gave him a split second in which to act, and he dove under the water to avoid being struck. Wheatley was not so lucky. When Cookson came up for air he saw no sign of his companions. Their bodies were found later, further down the shore.

Cookson was now desperate. Grip, McDonald's dog, was swimming faithfully by his side, but he knew that if he didn't make for shore now the sea would claim him as it had the others. He estimated that he was seventy yards from safety, and struck out. After what seemed an eternity, John Cookson found himself standing exhausted on the sands. In front of him was *The Grotto*, and by his side McDonald's brave little terrier.

He was vaguely aware of footsteps on the sand running towards him. Then, as if from nowhere, a pair of female hands was supporting him and helping him towards the inn. His helper was Mary-Ann Allan, daughter of Peter and Lizzie:

"How many were on the boat?"

"Four, including me. And the dog, here".

"It's a pity that Alexander McDonald wasn't here. He's the best swimmer in the area. He'd have saved your friends."

"But he *was* with us. Alexander was my friend, and the sea's taken him too."

Mary-Ann Allan ran screaming into *The Grotto*. She had recently become engaged to be married, and her fiancé had been one Alexander McDonald, a booksellers' assistant from North Shields. The above conversation is not fictitious, and is mentioned in *The Historical Register of Remarkable Events (1833–1866),* by T. Fordyce.[2]

## A Visit to the Grotto

In *A Ramble to Marsden Rocks*[3], the author describes a visit he paid to the inn after Peter's death. Just before he left, one of Peter's daughters asked if he would sign the Visitors' Book. There is still a Visitor's Book in *The Grotto* today, and more than one of Peter's descendants has autographed it.

Back then the Visitors' Book was known as The Scrapbook, and the author duly obliged, 'scribbling an acrostic on Elizabeth Marsden Allan'.

One of Peter's sons was present. He is described as, 'a fresh, fair-looking young man' who 'bore a striking resemblance to his father, especially in the expression of the eyes, for there were the laughter-loving devils in their corners, so peculiar to the 'old man.'

Young Elizabeth is described thus:

> A dark-eyed maiden…dressed with great simplicity, wearing a Holland jacket that fitted tightly and displayed the graceful symmetry of her form. Her face is interesting, unassuming, and yet indicative of considerable mental activity; and we are told that her courage is of the "Darling" school, and without the slightest fear, she can heave on the stormy wave. She is also an admirable shot, and can provide a sparrow pie for her friends on the shortest notice.

Clay, meanwhile, was working on another plan to force the Allan family out of *The Grotto*. Around the time when legal proceedings were being instigated against Peter Allan, the farmhouse at Marsden Rock Farm had suddenly begun to sell refreshments to locals and tourists alike. Tea, scones and 'pop' were all readily available, and at remarkably decent prices. Neither Peter nor anyone else had any doubts what the motivation was behind this. Clay believed that if refreshments were available on the cliff top, customers would not bother going all the way down Blaster Jack's stairway to reach *The Grotto*. In short, Clay was trying to ruin the Allans' business and force them out. What he had not reckoned with was the incredible degree of local sympathy that Peter had attracted. He was a loveable character who could melt the stoniest heart, and Clay's efforts only served to turn people against him. Not easily dissuaded, however, Clay expanded the property and obtained a license to sell alcohol. That Clay had powerful associates helping him is obvious. In *Marsden Rock, or the True Story of Peter Allan and Marsden Marine Grotto*, we are told that 'the license … was granted before even the foundation stone was laid, such alacrity on the part of the justices contrasts somewhat invidiously with the pertinacious refusal that occurred in the case of 'poor Peter.'" [4]

The farmhouse was renamed *The Marsden Inn*, and the ales were supplied by the brewing company Deuchar Ltd. It never did rival *The Grotto* for popularity, and eventually the pub was demolished and relocated at a respectable distance away to the north. This building was in turn demolished, and the Marsden Inn was again rebuilt in 1935 at its present location. It is still there to this day, a well-run, friendly pub doing a thriving business. The old rivalries have been forgotten, and the folks of Marsden are happy to drink in either establishment, although each client undoubtedly has his or her preference between the two.

## Close To Disaster

In 1865 a near disaster occurred at *The Grotto*. The limestone cliff in which it is recessed is extremely soft and unstable. Quite regularly, large sections of the cliff will break away, landing on the sands below with a tremendous thud. Sometimes the pieces can be small: no bigger, say, than a grapefruit. But they are still big enough to kill you instantly if you happen to get in their way 'twixt cliff and sand.

One day, after a heavy rainstorm, Lizzie had risen early and was busy cooking breakfast for her family when she heard an extremely loud cracking noise. She ignored it. Then, as she dished out the porridge and bacon and eggs to her assembled offspring in the Upper Room, where the family traditionally ate, there was what seemed like an earthquake. Chunks of the vaulted ceiling came loose and careened off the springy floorboards below. There were screams and yells from the terrified Allans, but fortunately no one was hurt. When the 'earthquake' was over, the family ran downstairs to see what had happened. They left the bar and walked outside. They looked to the left, and stared incredulously at their 'cottage', or rather what was left of it. A huge chunk of cliff face weighing several tons had broken free and cut the house in two. The bedrooms and kitchen were flattened completely, as if they had never existed.

Lizzie Allan now had the job of rebuilding her home. True, there was plenty of room in *The Grotto* itself – a lot more room than most people realised, actually – but it wasn't her home. Lizzie had made the simple two-up/two-down beautiful. It was somewhere she could retire from *The Grotto* for some peace. Now, it would have to be built up again virtually from scratch.

Lizzie actually had little in the way of savings. True, Peter had sold a few antiquities in London and smelted down coins, but he hadn't yet stumbled upon the fortune, which he knew was still hidden in the cliffs. Consequently, when he died he left Lizzie comfortable – but not with the wherewithal to build – or rather rebuild – a house. Nevertheless, her family and friends helped. Even the smugglers helped. In fact, everyone who knew Lizzie helped. Within a few months her home had been rebuilt, and it was grander than ever.

Interestingly, huge retaining walls and buttresses were also built around the cliff wall behind and above *The Grotto* to prevent another calamity of this nature happening in the future. Who actually paid for this work to be done is a question we will return to presently. We can say clearly at this juncture, however, that Lizzie Allan did not pay for it. She just didn't have that sort of money.

What about John Clay? Well, Clay certainly had the motive. He wanted the Allans out of *The Grotto,* but there wasn't much point in inheriting the place if the cliff was ready at any time to bury it under tons of rock. Could Clay have financed the operation? At one time, yes, but not in 1865. At the risk of making a rather large digression, I will detail the reasons for this seemingly minor point in the next chapter. It is, in actual fact, of great importance.

## THE WRECK OF THE OSTRICH

On July 31 1866 a terrific storm blew up at Marsden and the surrounding areas. So bad was the tempest that ships were being blown around like corks. One ship, a barque named the *Ostrich*, had sailed down the Tyne earlier that day. Several of her crew were not with the ship for some reason, but had arranged to connect with her off the coast. The arrangement seems to have been that the *Ostrich* would anchor off the shore and the crewmembers would be ferried out to her.

Whilst the crewmembers were sailing in their dingy towards the ship the storm blew up, and they were lucky to get on board, although one document states that they were 'in a most unsatisfactory condition.'[5] The captain of the vessel, George Jackson of Church Way, North Shields, decided that it would be suicidal to put to sea in such atrocious conditions. Instead he anchored the boat at sea off Marsden Bay, deciding that it would be safer to travel the following day when the storm had subsided.

In the middle of the night the barque broke free of its anchor and was hurled towards the rocks at Marsden. The ship was torn to pieces, and of the fourteen-crew members on board only four survived.

## References

[1] Anon. *The History of Marsden Grotto*, (Vaux Breweries, date unknown) p 7.

[2] Fordyce, T: *The Historical Register of Remarkable Events (1833–1866)*, (published privately by the author, 1867), p. 341.

[3] Anon. *A Ramble to Marsden Rocks*, (publisher unknown), p. 6.

[4] Smith, Mr; *Marsden Rock; or the Story of Peter Allan, and Marsden Marine Grotto* (*The Sunderland & Durham County Herald*, 1848) p.16.

[5] Fordyce, T: *The Historical Register of Remarkable Events (1833–1866)*, (published privately by the author, 1867), p. 435.

# CHAPTER 32

# THE RISE AND FALL
# OF JOHN CLAY

John Clay was mockingly referred to by friends and enemies alike as 'the King o' South Shields'. In fact, despite his projected image of sophistication and breeding, Clay had very lowly origins. His father was a humble grocer who owned a corner shop in Nile Street, and although history now generally portrays Clay as purely a shipping magnate he was really nothing of the sort. Shipbuilding was only one of many business interests, and not necessarily the greatest. He also owned a brewery, shops, a marine insurance company and a substantial part of a bank.

John Clay was, as previously stated, an extremely wealthy man. He lived in a sumptuous house in East Boldon, although he also owned another residence in Cleadon Meadows, and his friends also shared a similar degree of affluence. J. Twizel Wawn, for example, had a quite ostentatious residence in West Boldon.

Clay mixed with the elite of South Shields society and had the money to keep up with them. On August 5th 1836 Clay and several others founded The North of England Marine Insurance Company. He already owned a thriving shipping business, Clay & Co., and in 1844 had amassed so much capital that he was spending it on lavish – and, it must be said – often successful projects. In 1844, for example, Clay's own firm allegedly built the Conside, the first steamship especially constructed for the carriage of coal, which used only her engines and no sails for propulsion.

John Clay's claims in this regard have not gone unchallenged, however Hodgson[1] claimed that Clay's shipyard was 'near the Mill Dam'. Others have claimed that the site was near the Middle Dock at South Shields some distance away. A map of the area from that time shows that the area where Clay claimed the ship was built, was actually littered with buildings connected with his sundry other business interests, including a bakery, a biscuit factory, two inns, a chandler's warehouse and many houses to name but a few.

When a journalist from *The South Shields Gazette* described Clay as the builder of the Conside he received a withering broadside from a Mr. R.J. Marshall in the letters column. The Conside, Marshall claimed, had not been built by Clay at all but by his own father, Mr. T.D. Marshall at Shadwell Street. Another local commentator also claimed that the vessel built by Clay had not been the Conside at all, but rather a barque named the Suffolk. Yet another stated that the Conside had certainly been built at Clay's premises, but by someone else. Those with an interest in shipping in the northeast still argue about this point today. It does seem that Clay's prowess as a shipbuilder was, however, overrated.

Amy Flagg, in her book *Notes on the History of Shipbuilding in South Shields, 1746 to 1946*, picked up on this historical curiosity, saying, 'It is strange that, considering the doubt cast on his career as a shipbuilder, he is consistently described as such rather than any other of his vocations. The whole question is a mystery and must be left at that.'[1]

Actually, it is no mystery at all, for John Clay had good reason to play up his rather anaemic interest in shipbuilding to mask one of his greatest interests; his passionate desire to get his hands on *The Marsden Grotto Inn* and the cave complex that lay both behind and beneath it.

Back in the 1830's friends of Clay had begun to make their own fortunes in banking. Of all his friends the most powerful were those of the Wawn Clan. Helped by Christopher Aikenhead Wawn the lawyer, E. Twizel Wawn – brother of John Twizel Wawn – had helped found The Newcastle Commercial Joint Stock Bank, of which he was a director. The bank was launched in June 1836 and, curiously, shared its offices for a while with those of Andrew Stoddart. As we shall see presently, this was unlikely to have been coincidental. In 1855, however, the bank made the disastrous mistake of taking on John Sadler as a director. Sadler was himself attempting to distance himself from an unsavoury financial scandal in which he played a crucial part, and which was known as the Tipperary Bank fraud. His involvement was like the kiss of death to the Newcastle and Commercial, and the bank folded the year after Sadler joined.

At exactly the same time that E. Twizel Wawn was opening his bank, his brother John was launching his own, The Sunderland, Durham, and North & South Shields District Bank (later abbreviated to The Northumberland and Durham District Bank). This venture was also launched on June 1st 1836, and had a capital of £500,000. Almost immediately after its inception, the bank took over the ailing Newcastle branch of Jonathan Backhouse & Co. Just one month later they also took over the firm's Sunderland and

South Shields branches. As soon as the South Shields branch was reopened as a branch of Wawn's new bank, Clay was installed as manager. This was a position he held for sixteen years.

Over the next few years the bank greatly expanded its interests, largely through making take-overs. In 1839 the Northumberland and Durham District Bank had taken over the Newcastle bankers Ridley & Co. In 1847 they increased the bank's capital from £600,000 to £1,200,000, and confidence in it soared.

For nearly a decade after the District Bank had absorbed the old Ridley & Co., Clay and his partners enjoyed unbridled success. But then, on Wednesday November 26, 1857, the bank suddenly suspended payment. To the horror of the 600-plus investors it was announced that the bank had liabilities of £3,255, 200, but assets valued at only £1, 190,318. What had gone wrong?

The failure of the bank was due to a disastrous decision to sink money into the Derwent Iron Company, which was collapsing under the weight of over £750,000 in debts. The bank's owners had figured that a quick injection of cash would turn things around and that the company would soon turn a profit. But it was not to be. The company was eventually wound up, and Clay and his colleagues were left in the middle of a financial nightmare from which he, at least, never fully recovered.

For these reasons one local historian told me what I already suspected; that, in 1865, it would have been "virtually impossible" for John Clay to have financed the building of the retaining walls and buttresses behind *The Grotto Inn*. The man was virtually broke. This means that someone else must have financed the work. We will discover just who that was presently.

At this juncture we need to divert from the dispute between the Allan family and John Clay and ask another and extremely pertinent question. Why would a respectable, wealthy businessman have been so obsessed with getting possession of *The Grotto*? Clay, before the crash of the District Bank, probably earned more in a day than the Allan family made in six months, and so the revenue from the inn's sales could hardly have been the motive. The truth, in fact, is nothing short of astonishing.

## References

1. Flagg, Amy; *Notes on the History of Shipbuilding in South Shields, 1746 to 1946* (South Tyneside Borough Council Library Service, 1979) p. 83 (ISBN: 0 9066 17 03 0).

# CHAPTER 33

# BARE AND TEMPEST RIVEN

*Within the limits of the tidal stream*
*A rock arises, bare and tempest riven;*
*Such a huge ruin might, as poets dream,*
*Be hurled by some proud giant against heaven.*
*Its base is scooped in many a rugged seam,*
*Through which the waves are by the wild winds driven,*
*And hollow arches, crusted o'er with shells,*
*Are filled or dry, as the sea ebbs or swells.*

*Under the beetling cliffs, right opposite,*
*Peter the Hermit lived of years some score,*
*Braving the brunt of many a stormy night,*
*With rude billows thundering at his door.*
*He was jolly but a worthy wight,*
*Who little cared for brevian lore;*
*A first rate shot – a poacher once, – some said,*
*A smuggler, – but a model host he made.*

*Out of the limestone he had dug such rooms,*
*As served for dining and for dancing halls,*
*And dormitories, like dark catacombs,*
*Of which the living rock composed the walls;*
*But seldom was there silence there, or gloom*
*For many were the rackets and the balls,*
*Held under Peter's quaint and sombre roof,*
*Which he had managed to make weather proof.*

*Gay crowds flocked to the place from far and near,*
*When summer smiled upon the velvet beds,*
*There to partake, for pay, of Peter's cheer,*
*While picnic parties had their modest spreads,*
*Some scaled the Rock, with less or more of fear,*
*By steps and ladders, apt to turn the heads*
*Of shy, coy damsels, who had sweethearts by them,*
*And oft shammed timidity to try them.*

The above lines were written in 1851 by William Brockie, editor of the *Shields Gazette* (1849–1852) after a visit to Marsden Bay. They also appear in Alan Robinson's book, *The Story of Marsden And Peter Allan*. The poem is unfinished, since Brockie died before he was able to complete it.

# CHAPTER 34

# THE TALE OF SIDNEY MILNES-HAWKES

As mentioned earlier, John Twizel Wawn very likely had connections with *The Grotto;* in all probability he drank there. My belief is that at some point he became aware of Peter's real reason for residing at Marsden, and heard tales about Roman treasure being hidden in the cliffs. Wawn did not keep this information to himself. He mentioned it, I believe, to a friend of his named Sidney Milnes-Hawkes. Hawkes himself was connected to a wider circle of influential friends, and they too would have been extremely interested to hear Wawn's tale.

This circle of friends may, on the surface, have appeared to the casual observer as a mere 'old boys' network'; a group of pals with similar financial interests who worked together to help each other out. But this wouldn't be a complete picture by a long shot. Clay, Stoddart, Wawn and the others were cemented together by more than financial bonds. They shared a common cause. That cause was an intention to radically alter the political face of Europe.

I have been critical of John Clay. The methods he used to remove the Allan family from *The Grotto* were underhand and morally repugnant. And yet, although the man had an irritating manner, and his actions towards the Allans were wrong in the extreme, he nevertheless had a decent side to him. He was an able and conscientious politician who basically had the best interests of the town of South Shields at heart. He was something of a philanthropist, too, and did nothing (at least nothing which I have been able to discover), which would lead me to believe that the man was inherently an out-and-out scoundrel, in fact quite the opposite. My belief is that Clay was not really happy, deep down, with his own actions. I think his conscience pricked him repeatedly. So why did he act so uncharacteristically when dealing with Peter Allan and his family? There can be only one reason. Clay's motives were not financial, so they must have been political. By getting Peter Allan out of *The Grotto* he believed that he could achieve something. There was a 'greater good' to be served in some way, which took precedent over the welfare of the Allan family. Like the pilot who regrets dropping bombs which he knows will kill civilians, but who carries on because unfortunately its necessary, John Clay persisted with his efforts to get the sitting tenants at *The Grotto* out. He didn't want to do it, but unfortunately it was necessary. The feelings of one publican and his family could not be allowed to influence the political map of Europe.

At this point we need to introduce in more detail a character who has largely stayed in the shadows; Sydney Milnes-Hawkes.

Sidney Milnes-Hawkes came from a wealthy Hertfordshire family. According to one source, from an early age he 'displayed a striking sympathy with the Continental patriots who were then struggling for their freedom.' [1]

This is highly relevant indeed, as we shall see.

In his early life he studied law and became a successful barrister. Hawkes married Emily Ashurst, the daughter of a prominent supporter of the Italian political reformer Giuseppe Mazzini, and Sir James Stansfeld, a leading radical who had supported many unconventional movements in his time, married her sister. Politically, Stansfeld and Milnes-Hawkes were soul brothers. Due to this they became good friends, and eventually set up in business together, Hawkes sinking a sizeable sum into Stansfeld's brewery. This was a disaster, and Hawkes went abroad to work for a while. Whilst on the continent he developed a passionate love of two things: Italy and gambling. At some point he was asked to return to England and serve at the Bar, which he did. However, he found that much of the fire had gone out of his belly insofar as law was concerned, and he no longer enjoyed the 'cut and thrust' of bamboozling juries and judges alike.

Nevertheless, he made a considerable fortune representing influential clients, and also received money from his family estate. The fortune he accrued enabled him to make choices not given to most of us, and he decided to retire from law and try his hand at journalism. He eventually ended up writing for the *Evening Chronicle* at Newcastle, although his talents as a wordsmith are debatable.

An uncontrollable gambler, Hawkes frittered much of his fortune away. Nevertheless, he still had a fair amount of it left when he purchased a row of three miners' cottages at Marsden. By this time Sidney and Emily had divorced, and Milnes-Hawkes had taken a second wife, also called Emily, surnamed Johnston. Some have expressed bewilderment at Hawkes' decision to live at Marsden, and it has to be admitted that there are certain peculiarities about it. Why Marsden? It was a considerable distance from Newcastle, which certainly wouldn't have helped in terms of his work. And why buy a row of cottages? They were hardly a fitting residence for a man of means. When Hawkes had purchased the cottages he converted them into one large residence. In fact, there were very few dwellings at Marsden to choose from in those days. Hawkes probably bought the only properties available.

One secondary reason why Hawkes moved to Marsden is that he was connected with people who lived either there or in South Shields. Many local historians are unaware, in fact, of the friendship that Hawkes enjoyed with the small network of people in the South Shields 'inner circle'. The reason for this is that, before his arrival on the scene at Marsden, there appears to be little or no record of his having any formal connection with South Shields. However, it seems that he did have connections, and they were quite important ones at that. It has been suggested to me that Hawkes had actually been a director of the Northumberland and Durham District Bank, and was also one of the founders of the bank, which briefly rose from the ashes of it after it collapsed – that of Hawks, Grey, Priestman & Co.

If this is true – and I must confess that I cannot be certain – then the reason why some researchers may have failed to notice the connection is because of the variant spelling; that is, Hawks as opposed to Hawkes. However, it could well be that Sidney Milnes-Hawkes made a habit of using various aliases, most of them simply slight variations on his proper name. These, I believe, included Sidney Milnes-Hawks and Sidney Milnes Hawke. As we delve deeper into Hawkes' background, we will see quite clearly why he may have done this.

Yet another variation of the name appears in the Sunderland Yearbook for 1906 where he is listed as Sidney Milnes *Hawks*. This proves that Hawkes may indeed have been using the *Hawks* variant as his surname.

Of course, all this may be very interesting, but it still does not tell us the *real* reason why Hawkes was moved to relocate himself to Marsden. This we will uncover presently.

## References

[1] From an undated and untitled newspaper cutting in the possession of the author.

# CHAPTER 35

# MARSDEN BAY

*Were I an artist I should paint this scene,*
*In many views and aspects. One by night –*
*The moon upon the waters, weirdly bright –*
*One lonely barque, with sails of silver sheen,*
*Filling the foreground. Outlined dark but keen*
*The rugged line of limestone cliffs should lie,*
*Athwart the fitful radiance of the sky.*
*Nearer – the great lone rock that guards the bay –*
*The shadowy stretch of sand, the shimmering spray.*
*That were the fairest scene. There should be more;*
*Views in the twilight, subtly soft and grey, –*
*Views sunlit – views of storm and flying cloud*
*Of cliff – fantastic – seagull haunted shore,*
*And weed-grown rock and cavern heavy browed.*
*No artist I, yet love thee none the less,*
*Child of the ocean in whose sun-kissed hands,*
*There lies a secret, but he understands,*
*All dimly, who can feel thy loveliness.*
*Oh, lovely, lonely spot, I'd keep thee so,*
*While cliff should threaten, – waters ebb and flo.*
*Not here should lie the worse than soulless throng,*
*Only the white-sailed ships should come and go;*
*And bear the memory to many distant lands.*
*The fair-haired sea-nymphs here should find retreat,*
*Or float in shining circles on the sands.*
*So should there be no fairer spot among*
*The spots that poets love to shrine in song.*

The above poem is attributed to one A.C. Nicholson, but we do not know the date of its composition.

# CHAPTER 36

# MEANWHILE IN ITALY...

Italy had been in a state of weakness for centuries. Under Napoleon Bonaparte the Italians had enjoyed a fleeting period of political pseudo-autonomy and stability. But then Bonaparte was defeated in 1814-15, and the old political order was restored to the dismay of a disenchanted populace.

The peninsula was divided into nine separate areas or states, most coming under the 'protection' of Austria. The two northern provinces of Venetia and Lombardy came under direct Austrian rule, their capitals being, respectively, the beautiful cities of Venice and Milan.

Sick and tired of being dominated by foreigners, the Italian people felt a surge of nationalism within their collective breast. Freedom and personal liberty became watchwords, and a resistance movement arose. Secret societies such as the *Carbonara* proliferated, all of them bound by an overwhelming desire to set Italy free.

Uprisings took place, the principle insurrections being at Naples in 1820 and Piedmont a year later. Although fought bravely, both revolts were crushed mercilessly by Austrian troops. One of the principle reasons for the failure was that the secret organisations, which coordinated the rebellion, were disjointed. Eventually a more sophisticated and cohesive resistance movement was formed, spearheaded by Giusseppe Mazzini (1805–1872). Mazzini founded the Young Italy movement in 1831, and for a while it was hoped that the rebellion it instigated would be more successful than those of the previous decade. Alas, it was not.

And then came another window of opportunity in the year 1848 – often referred to as the Year of European Revolutions. Beginning in 1846 Pope Pius IX had introduced a series of liberal reforms, which allowed the resistance movement to flourish once again. Austrian heavy-handedness was met with a tidal wave of anarchy, and the result was that a degree of constitutionalism was allowed to placate the people.

Whilst rumblings of discontent were once again stirring in Italy, Austria now found that it had similar problems to cope with at home. Uprisings took place in Vienna, and with the Austrian government being forced to contend with its domestic crises the Italian states of Lombardy and Venetia seized their chance. In March 1848, both states erupted in full-scale revolt. When the influential state of Piedmont also began to clamour for an end to Austrian interference, King Charles Albert was honour-bound to take to the field on behalf of the rebels.

But once again the rebellion was defeated. Somehow the Austrians managed to recover from their domestic crises and they quashed the Italian uprising in 1849. On the advice of Vatican officials the Pope fled Rome, and the people set up Mazzini as the king of a new Roman republic. Unfortunately, in an effort to curry favour with the French Catholics, Louis-Napoleon Bonaparte sent troops into Rome, and the newly formed republic was dismantled. By August the Austrians had retaken Lombardy and Venetia, and the uprising was effectively over.

Later, in May 1860, the rebel General Giuseppe Garibaldi launched a heroic attack against the enemy in Sicily. Further attacks – not all of them successful – chipped away at Austrian domination. In 1866 Italy joined forces with Prussia, and Austria was routed. By 1870, Italy – all of Italy – was free.

Curious though it may seem, the Italian rebels had some of their staunchest supporters amongst the working-class people of Tyneside in England. This was in no small measure due to the encouragement of Robert Ingham, the first Member of Parliament representing South Shields. Ingham was a Liberal who frequently spoke out in favour of Garibaldi. He was also deeply respected and admired by his constituents, and they demonstrated this in the most extraordinary way. Moved by Ingham's tales of how terribly the Italians were suffering under Austrian rule, many Tynesiders actually travelled to Italy to fight under Garibaldi's banner. Collectively they were known as the Tyneside Contingent.

In 1854, shortly after the failure of the Republic of Rome, Garibaldi actually visited Tyneside. His arrival on a ship that had been registered in Baltimore but which was now crewed entirely by Italian rebels in exile drew crowds to the mouth of the river.

A deputation agreed to meet Garibaldi – not that they would have taken much encouragement, as they saw him as a hero – and the members of it were indeed an interesting bunch. The leader was Joseph Cowen Jr, proprietor of the *Evening Chronicle* and a close friend of the paper's journalist Sidney Milnes-Hawkes. The remainder included Robert Sutherland, Richard Miller, Thomas Hudson and Solomon Sutherland. All from either South Shields or North Shields.

Thomas Hudson was a resident of North Shields, but owned two 'chemist's shops' in South Shields as well as a successful dental practice. Thomas himself ran the drug store at 23 Long Row, whilst his brother George operated the second dispensary at 76 West Holborn. Reasonably extensive biographies exist of Hudson, mainly in the form of lengthy obituaries. What is *not* generally known about Hudson – who, like his friends, also had a street named after him – was that he was a supporter, and possibly a member - of a peculiar organisation in North Tyneside called the Utopia Club.

The Utopia Club made no bones about its purpose. It was a recruiting post and organisational centre for Garibaldi's supporters in the northeast of England. Members loudly proclaimed their support for the Italian General, and yet deliberately obscured their meetings behind a thick veil of secrecy.

Garibaldi actually attended a meeting at the Utopia Club, which was at that time holding its gatherings in a rented room above a public house managed by one of his sympathisers. The location of the meeting room was not known even to the rank-and-file members, but only to a tight inner circle of senior believers. Aaron Watson comments [1]:'where the room was, nobody in North Shields, not a member of the club, or a frequent visitor, could have said. It was only to be found by habitues, though it was on the licensed premises of so well-known a man as George Shotton.'

Those who found the club would be astonished. It consisted of a single room, upon the walls of which hung portraits of Garibaldi and Mazzini. Here, ardent supporters of the Italian cause made plans, co-operating fully with their colleagues in South Shields.

Solomon Sutherland was actually the editor of the *Shields Advocate*, and did not hide his sympathies for the Italian cause. The others had also expressed similar views.

But many members of the delegation had another common denominator. They all happened to be members or supporters of an organisation called the Mechanics Institute, or – to give it its full title – the South Shields Literary, Mechanical and Scientific Institution. The Institute had been formed in 1825 and had originally held its meetings in the basement of the Independent Methodist Church in Cornwallis Street. According to Hodgson [2], the organisation 'formed classes for self-improvement in English grammar, Chemics,

Mathematics, French and Arithmetic.' Lectures were given by 'some of the most noted men of the day', and the organisation had an extensive library for the use of members.

Those who joined the Institute had to take their responsibilities seriously, and apparently obey some very peculiar rules. The President (a position which revolved on a monthly basis), for instance, was apparently fined the then substantial sum of one shilling if he 'took part in a debate.' If he went 'absent without leave' the fine rose to two shillings and sixpence, and woe betide anyone who 'submitted an essay without turning up to read it'. He would have to pay the princely sum of *five* shillings.

By 1834, the Institute was doing so well that the members decided to build their own purpose-built meeting hall. None other than Robert Ingham MP himself laid the foundation stone, and from that point onwards its support for the Italian rebels became pronounced.

When the delegation met with Garibaldi, they presented him with a beautiful sword and telescope. The sword was described as 'a handsome weapon with a gold hilt', on which this inscription was engraved, 'Presented to General Garibaldi by the Tyneside Friends of European Freedom'. Both had apparently been purchased by means of 'a penny subscription' levied from the workingmen of Tyneside. In fact, I suspect that the money – or at least part of it – actually came from the subscriptions and bizarre 'fines' meted out to the members of the Mechanics Institute. Many of the members were wealthy and did not mind in the least secretly donating money to the rebels. Some of the donations were simply called 'fines' as a cover.

Whereas the Utopians broadcast their propaganda at every opportunity whilst being incredibly discreet about their meeting places, the Mechanics Institute did exactly the opposite. The Institute had permanent and quite ostentatious premises, whilst simultaneously being more than a little discreet with regards to its political agenda. Both organisations served exactly the same masters; only their *modus operandi* was slightly different.

Although Garibaldi's visit to the Tyne took place in 1854, he had enjoyed support on Tyneside long before that. Garibaldi's campaign was a protracted one, seeing a succession of gains and losses until the victory was finally won. The crucial year, in the eyes of many historians, was 1848. It was in this year that Mazzini and his followers really felt that their time had come. Austria was in chaos because of domestic problems, Revolts against Austrian domination were taking place in Lombardy and Venetia, and Piedmont was about to throw in its hand with the other two states. Sensing victory (prematurely, we now know), a cry went out for support of any and every kind.

Foreign mercenaries were welcomed, and financial backing greeted with no
less verve.

And this is where Sidney Milnes-Hawkes entered the political stage with
impeccable timing.

Aaron Watson in his book *The Folk of Shields* [3] says:

> Hawkes ... a colleague and dear friend of mine in the early seventies of the last
> century, was one of the gentlest and most tender hearted of men, though he
> had committed some really desperate crimes in the cause of Italian liberty. He
> carried out to Paris the dagger and pistol, forged passports for Italian refugees;
> and frequently at the risk of his own life, he conveyed financial aid to both
> Mazzini and Garibaldi, dissipating his own fortune in a cause to which he was
> equally ready to surrender his own life.

Hawkes, then, was no mere intellectual supporter of the Italian rebels.
He was a derring-do activist, paymaster and gunrunner. Watson also says
of him:

> If Mazzini wished to entrust one of his friends with a more than commonly
> dangerous mission, it was Sidney Milnes-Hawkes who proffered himself. Most
> of his early life was spent in perilous flights between Italy and England. He
> might have been, and possibly was, the hero of Browning's, *The Englishman in
> Italy*. There were rumours that he had done even more dangerous things than
> Mazzini ever sanctioned, and there is no doubt that if he had been caught on
> some of his expeditions he would have been hung or shot.

It would certainly not be unreasonable to suggest that Watson may here be
hinting to us that Hawkes had actually carried out an assassination or two.
We do know that he was the 'courier' between Mazzini and his Tyneside
supporters, ferrying money to Italy that had been collected by the Mechanics
Institute and its members.

We know that Hawkes was connected to Robert Ingham, John Clay,
William Brockie and the other influential men of South Shields at that time.
All of them, we know, were supporters of Mazzini and Garibaldi. We also
know that they were closely associated with the Utopia Club and/or the
Mechanics Institute, and that both the Club and the Institute were certainly
used to generate funds for the Italian cause.

J. Twizel Wawn was also a close associate of the others, and we have some
circumstantial evidence that he used to drink in *The Grotto*. And it is at this

point that we can finally begin to piece together exactly what lay behind the desperate moves to evict the Allans from their dwelling in the cliff.

As stated previously, at some point Wawn must have become aware of Peter Allan's treasure-hunting activities at Marsden. He inevitably carried tales of Peter's excavations to his friends. My belief is that Hawkes, Ingham and the others saw here a golden opportunity to generate money for the Italian cause. If they could get Peter Allan and his family out of *The Grotto,* and install Hawkes as the new manager of the inn, they could find the Roman treasure for themselves and donate whatever money they made from it to Garibaldi. As we have already stated, Roman antiquities during this period commanded an extraordinary price both here and abroad.

But there was, perhaps, a deeper motive for their activities. Garibaldi and Mazzini had witnessed the setting up of the short-lived Republic of Rome in 1848–49. If Garibaldi could display treasures from the old Roman Empire, found and returned to their rightful owners by his own supporters, the galvanising power of such icons would be enormous. There is little doubt that such treasure would have had a value far beyond its material worth. Icons are extremely persuasive. The Christian cross, the Nazi swastika and the Egyptian solar orb are but three examples and proof positive that this is indeed the case. To present Garibaldi with an ancient goblet or *gladius,* which he could have held aloft before the cheering crowds, would have been seen by some as an almost prophetic witness to his destiny.

When the people of Tyneside presented Garibaldi with the gift of a sword, his supporters realised its symbolic significance. At the presentation, Joseph Cowan commented to Garibaldi:

> General, along with this address I have to ask you to receive this sword and telescope. The intrinsic value of these articles is but small, and to a Republican chieftain who is accustomed to animate his compatriots by deeds of personal prowess, such a sword may be more ornamental than useful. [4]

Garibaldi *understood exactly* what Cowan was saying. After receiving the sword he examined it carefully and replied, 'I thank you from my heart of hearts, and be confident of this; that whatever vicissitudes of fortune I may hereafter pass through, this sword shall never be drawn by me except in the cause of liberty.'

As things transpired, Garibaldi used his sword in numerous battles and dispatched many an enemy with it over the coming years, but this did not detract from the symbolic or 'ornamental' value. However, if the gift of a modern sword fashioned on the banks of the Tyne could move Garibaldi and his followers so deeply, what could be achieved if he gained possession of an authentic Roman icon hidden in the cliffs at Marsden?

But first his supporters had to get the Allan family out of *The Grotto*, and as we have seen they had been hitherto unsuccessful in this. By the time John Clay had exhausted every possibility in his efforts to get the Allan's evicted, it was, in a sense, too late. The urgency to supply financial help to Garibaldi had gone, and therefore he resigned himself to the fact that Lizzie and her children were going to be there for quite some time. Nevertheless, there was still hidden treasure buried in the caves for the finding. Clay, Hawkes and others still wanted to find it for obvious reasons. Now it would just take them longer.

It cannot be coincidental, surely, that at *exactly* the same time as the call went out for help to support Garibaldi's campaign, John Clay and Andrew Stoddart suddenly purchased the land around *The Grotto* and began their legal moves to have the Allans evicted as quickly as possible. They did it, as we now know, so that any money they could make from the uncovered artefacts could be donated to Garibaldi's 'Big Push' in 1848. But now they would have to wait. Or at least they would have to wait until they could explore the tunnels and caves behind *The Grotto*. But there was nothing, of course, to stop them exploring the multitude of other caves, large and small, scattered along the rest of the Bay area. Who knew what may be hidden there?

As we have seen, Marsden suddenly and curiously became the focus of attention in terms of geology and naturalism. Groups of people were now visiting the caves and exploring them. On June 24th 1859, a party of 'ladies and gentlemen' from both North and South Shields visited Marsden Bay as part of a 'scientific excursion'. Amongst the men present were, 'Dr. Dodd, Dr. Emmerson, Dr. Stevens, Rev. G.C. Abbs, J.B. Dale, esq J.W. Fenwick, esq E. Young, esq Messrs. L. Armstrong, G. Brady, E.C. Robson, W.H. Brown, Horatio Adamson, and F.R.N. Haswell, members of the Naturalists' Field Club.'

The women, it seems, were not important enough to mention!

The party visited Trow Rocks, the caves at Manhaven Bay, and other places of interest. They then had tea at - no surprise here – 'Mrs. Allan's' before adjourning to the Velvet Beds to hear 'a deeply interesting address by the Rev. G.C. Abbs, of Cleadon House, on the geology of the coast. The party [then] broke up after having spent a highly instructive and pleasing afternoon.'

In 1861, the Mechanics Institute created an offshoot called The South Shields Microscopical Society. The following year a second offshoot, The Geological Club, came into being. We should not be surprised to find William Brockie the naturalist, geologist and author involved in this organisation. What does surprise us is the fact that he only held the position of Vice-Chairman. The President of The Geological Club was one George Lyall. This is an even stranger choice, for Lyall's professional background seems to have been entirely in the Marine sector.

In 1844 Lyall was already serving as secretary of the South Shields A1 Freight and Outfit Club. On May 29 1845 he was elected secretary of the North and South Shields Auxiliary to the British and Foreign Sailors' Society, and on April 27 1849 he was also elected as secretary of the local Marine Board. As stated previously, the man's background was exclusively in shipping. Or perhaps I should say *almost* exclusively, for Lyall had one peculiar qualification which the Geological Club would have considered most advantageous when keeping in mind what its real motives may have been for coming into existence.

We need to bear in mind that in 1862, the Allans were still firmly ensconced in *The Grotto*. Since 1848 a group of influential figures in South Shields had believed that there was Roman treasure buried in the cliff face behind the inn. In 1862 they were still waiting for Peter's family to go so they could get their hands on it. Faced with the inevitability of the Allans living in *The Grotto* for some years to come, Garibaldi's supporters in South Shields decided to change tactics.

There had long been rumours circulating around South Shields that a Roman fort had once existed at an area of the town known as the Lawe Top. Pieces of Roman pottery – mostly Samian-ware – had been found, along with other artefacts. George Lyall had a fascination for such trinkets and became very interested in Roman history. In fact, he became something of an armchair expert in the subject. Considering that one of the primary motivating factors behind the setting up of the Geology Club was to find the hidden Roman treasure which the members now firmly believed was hidden in Marsden cliffs, Lyall's appointment is hardly surprising. His knowledge of antiquities would make him a valuable asset indeed when it came to assessing both the value of an artefact and the likely buyers who may wish to purchase it. That a club dedicated to the study of geology should elect as its president a man who apparently had little if any knowledge of geology and only an amateur interest in ancient history/archaeology informs us that scientific rigour may not have been its prime standard. This in itself tells a story.

The ruins of the Arbeia fort were not uncovered until 1874. By that time, Lyall had worked himself into a position where it was inevitable that, when the excavations began, he would truly be at the hub of things.

Several members of the Mechanics' Institute were in the habit of meeting at the home of a fellow member and river pilot by the name of Luke Mackay. Mackay was – again no surprise – also treasurer of the Geological Club. In December of 1865 the group decided to form a Life Brigade, similar to the one, which already existed at Tynemouth. A public meeting was held in the by now patently obvious venue of the Mechanics' Institute Hall on December 16. A deputation from the Borough explained to those gathered what the regulations and purpose of the Brigade would be. The deputation was led by none other than Thomas Salmon – an old friend of William Brockie, John Clay and Sidney Milnes-Hawkes, all of whom were supporters of Garibaldi.

On January 18 1866, a second meeting was held and it was unanimously decided that they should go ahead with the formation of the South Shields Life Brigade. Luke Mackay was one of the pilots appointed to the committee that would steer the Brigade into existence.

It must be obvious by now that the same names – Ingham, Clay, Salmon, Brockie, Wawn, Lyall, Mackay, Milnes-Hawkes *et al* keep turning up at different points in the political firmament of the Borough with monotonous yet astonishing regularity. This demonstrates the huge influence, which this small group of people possessed. We can also now see clearly how intimately George Lyall and Luke Mackay were acquainted with each other. But there's more. Lyall and Mackay were also good friends with Alderman John Broughton, the Mayor of the Borough and also the local agent for the Ecclesiastical Commissioners. For this reason the officers of the Life Brigade committee, who still met at Mackay's house to discuss more covert political topics under the guise of Life Brigade business, elected Lyall and Mackay to lobby Broughton to excavate the Arbeia site.

It can be seen, then, that during this entire period there was a powerful coterie of local businessmen and politicians who were extremely interested in a) gaining control of the land around *The Grotto Inn,* b) controlling the excavating activities at Arbeia, and c) organising and/or supervising any geological rambles or surveys at Marsden. This power was exercised either directly through the Mechanics Institute or indirectly through one of its offshoots, such as the Geological Club or the Microscopical Society. Other influence was gained even more covertly, utilising committees that had, ostensibly, nothing to do with Arbeia or geology at all, such as the committee of the Life Brigade.

During my research for this book I was heavily criticised by a college lecturer for suggesting that the Geological Club and the Microscopical Society were actually 'front' organisations whose real purpose was to help the Italian cause. This was, he told me, 'a ridiculous flight of fancy'. However, proof that I was right was soon to present itself, and will be detailed presently.

On March 2 1875, the excavation at Arbeia began, and four days later a supervisory committee was formed which had full control of the funds. Broughton himself was made President; Lyall was appointed Vice-Chairman and Mackay became Treasurer.

Lyall lost no time in attempting to find out whether the Arbeia site contained Roman artefacts of great value, and we know, because of a remarkable admission by Aaron Watson [5] that he was not too concerned about *how* the site was excavated, but purely about what may be buried there. When Watson recalled his first meeting with Lyall he said that he:

> ...Was then in his old age, a tall, straight, grizzled figure, exceedingly thin, remarkably erect for a man of his years, with some obliquity of vision, arising, it may be, from falling sight. Though he had been, and still was, connected with ship insurance societies, was a hero of the pilots, and had much to do, in many directions with those activities which promoted the growth and development of the town, he was also in a special way a representative of those intellectual energies and aspirations which were particularly active, especially among the working class, about the middle of the last century ... There was a Geological Society [undoubtedly the Geological Club] of which he was president. He was one of the promoters of the excavation of the Roman Remains at the Lawe, and it was mainly, I daresay, *through his influence that the pilots were wont to act to work in the evenings when the regular excavators had gone, and carry on the excavation gratuitously; so that the site was laid bare at less cost than now seems quite credible.* [Emphasis mine]

What Watson is admitting here is that, after the professional excavators had gone home, Lyall and his pilot friends from the river would go on to the site and do their own *private* excavating unsupervised! The Tyne Pilot's house was, in those days, only a stone's throw from the Arbeia site, allowing Lyall and his accomplices to quickly remove and hide any precious artefacts before morning.

We do not know for sure that Lyall and his colleagues found anything of value during their nocturnal unofficial excavations at Arbeia, although one archaeologist who does not wish to be named said he believed – and had actually been told, unofficially – that "basketfuls" of things had been spirited away under the cover of darkness. We must also remember that, by the time Arbeia was excavated, Garibaldi had drawn a successful conclusion to his campaign. If this was the case, why, five years later, were his supporters on Tyneside still trying to get their hands on the Roman antiquities, which they believed were buried both at the fort itself and at Marsden Bay? It is possible, of course, that they wanted the treasure for their own personal profit, but I doubt this. Despite their ruthlessness towards the Allan family in the cause of the Italian rebellion, there is no evidence that they took any pleasure in such actions, and I have seen nothing to suggest that they were simply money-grabbers. Perhaps they were still sending money to Garibaldi and his compatriots after the victory to ensure that the fledgling democracy did not falter during its first few years of power. It is also possible that the money was being diverted to charitable institutions in Italy to help relieve the suffering, which years of disruption had brought about.

Of course, it could be argued that there is no *conclusive* proof that the 'geological' outings, meetings of the 'Life Brigade Committee' and other activities were 'fronts' for anything. Maybe their ostensible purposes *were* the real ones.

Several things became apparent to me at this point. Firstly it was obvious that at some point the plotters had held meetings inside *The Grotto Inn*, and that such meetings must have been after the demise of Peter Allan. Secondly, it was obvious that Sidney Milnes-Hawkes himself was almost certainly unaware of the more brutish plans that had been hatched to see off Peter Allan and his family earlier. Had he known, despite his passion for the Italian cause he would not have stooped so low as to see a family evicted from their home. When court action was eventually launched against Peter it is interesting to note that Sidney Milnes-Hawkes' name is conspicuous by its absence. I suspect that if he did know what the others were planning for 'poor Peter' and his clan he wanted nothing to do with it.

So, why were the members of the 'South Shields Mafia' meeting up so regularly and under such a wide variety of different "fronts"? Of course, to the readers of this book the answer to that question will now be all too apparent. They were searching for Caesar's gold.

# References

[1] From the recollections of Aaron Watson published in an undated article, a copy of which is held at South Tyneside Local History Library.

[2] Hodgson, George B: *The Borough of South Shields* (South Tyneside Libraries, 1996) ISBN: 0 906617 25 1

[3] Watson, Aaron: *The Folks of Shields* (published privately by the author, date unknown). p.11.

[4] Bell, D; *Ships, Strikes and Garibaldi in Shields* (published privately by the author, date unknown).

[5] Watson, Aaron: *The Folks of Shields* (published privately by the author, date unknown). p.13.

# CHAPTER 37

# THE ERA OF THE HERMIT HOAR

It has been suggested that Sidney Milnes-Hawkes became the new 'landlord' of *The Grotto* in 1874, but other sources say 1871. The latter date is, I believe, correct.

Lizzie Allan died 'of old age' on May 7 1870, but there may be good reason to believe that life at *The Grotto* had already turned sour for her. Alec 'Archie' Allan is a retired schoolteacher. During one of my conversations with this descendant of Peter a tale was related to me, which has been passed down through the Allan family, although he admits to being a bit vague on the details.

Alec remembers being told as a youngster that something had happened to turn several members of the Allan family teetotal, and become passionately opposed to the drinking of alcohol. The incident involved someone apparently lying under a beer barrel or rum casket and allowing the alcoholic beverage to run into his or her mouth from the barrel tap. The person in question supposedly became drunk and choked on his or her own vomit. After this the family – or at least several members of it – 'turned against the drink'.

To have such a profound effect upon Lizzie and her children the death must have been that of a family member, almost certainly one of her children, but who? The first of her children to die was William, but he did not pass away until December 29, 1872, thus making his death too late to be the catalyst to either Lizzie's death in 1870 or the family's departure in 1871.

We may never know the truth about this incident or the effect it had on Lizzie Allan. After her death her children kept the pub going for several months, but their heart was not in it. *The Grotto* had lost its two greatest characters But whatever really transpired, the Allan dynasty ended in 1871 insofar as *The Grotto* was concerned. Almost immediately it was replaced by that of another family – that of Sidney Milnes-Hawkes.

By the time Sidney Milnes-Hawkes – nicknamed the 'Hermit Hoar' by friends – moved into the abandoned *Grotto*, the Allan family had stripped it of everything precious to them. The picture of Peter, which he had commissioned the artist John Reay to paint and which hung on a wall in the Upper Room, was spirited away, although I have managed to ascertain where it went. What happened to Ralphy and the display case that housed him I cannot say. It is possible that Lizzie could have left him in *The Grotto*, for we know from contemporary records that, when Hawkes took over, the Upper Room was still filled with display cases containing stuffed birds and animals. We do not know if Ralphy was amongst them, although I think not. I do not imagine that Lizzie would have allowed the remains of Peter's favourite animal companion to fall into the hands of his enemies.

To be fair to Sidney Milnes-Hawkes, he seems to have captured the essence of *The Grotto's* character and made every effort to maintain it. In fact, I suspect that he actually enhanced the charm and character, which Peter Allan had breathed into it. This is best illustrated by the following account, which describes the interior of *The Grotto* in 1875; just four years after Hawkes took over [1]:

The interior staircase leads to our sitting room, one side of which was entirely of this limestone and which we could only compare to a large and exquisitely coloured geological map. Nor was art wanting in our pretty suite of apartments, to which we had access by a rustic staircase without passing through the room already described. On the walls were some well-executed water colours, grateful souvenirs of artists that had come before us; an elegant piano in one corner; a soaf [sic] and easy state cabin chairs spoke of the luxury of repose; and some well chosen tomes – the more acceptable from being in reference to the localities of County Durham forms a select library.

Flowers adorned our windows and between their glorious bunches of blossom we obtained a view of the smiling or angry ocean. Ours however, was a week of peace on the far stretching sea; but this is indeed a most frightening coast in bad weather and the raging ocean has occasionally taken possession of the lower rooms, put out the kitchen fires, and driven the inmates to seek shelter in the upper parts of the dwelling.

The outer parts of *The Grotto* are constructed entirely of the debris of numerous wrecks, which testify by countless mementoes of dire calamities. Wreck, wreck is everywhere – it pervades the chambers, the kitchen and even the rifle yard in which was a store of floatabilities, each with its history, possibly, of some struggling wretch who had grasped it in a frenzied effort as rescue

from a fearful death, and, maybe, after all had gone down in sight of our snug
and cosy lodging. This impression was more and more pronounced as I carried
out explorations in out of the way recesses not usually entered by strangers
unless by a curious turn of mind.

Even in the dancing saloon, hewn out of the solid rock, measuring sev-
enty-five feet long and twenty-four feet broad, the flooring and orchestra are
portions of wrecks. Indeed the door is cut out of a ship's rudder and studded
thickly with ship's nails, while the heavy iron ring of an anchor serves as a
knocker.

I could not ascend a step without grasping portions of masts or clinging to
a porthole, while figureheads met me at every turn. Here was a carved bust of
Admiral Rodney; there one of Mercury and others with lettered titles. 'The
Saucy Sally', 'Constellation', 'Four Brothers', etc., all serving to individualise
and intensify the feeling of wreckage, a sentiment which during our slippery
wanderings for a mile or two, over labyrinths of fallen and weed-entangled
rocks, received additional strength from the numerous fragments of wrecks
half buried in the sand, or tossed about in the spray of the broken waves.

Hawkes, we know, excavated *The Grotto* further, taking up where the Allan
family left off. What we do not know is the direction or elevation he took.
The above description in *Chambers Journal* does, however, give us a very
strong clue. Notice that the writer says, first of all, that 'The interior staircase
*leads to our sitting room*, one side of which was entirely of this limestone
and which we could only compare to a large and exquisitely coloured geological map.' This tells us that the writer is, from his perspective, now on
Level 2 of the complex. But then he says, 'Nor was art wanting in our pretty
suite of apartments, to which we had access by a rustic staircase *without
passing through the room already described*.' This forces us to conclude that
there was a second stairwell, which he describes as 'rustic', which led from
Level 2 to his apartment. His apartment, therefore, must have been on a
*third* level of which we have hitherto been unaware, but the existence of
which I postulated in a previous chapter. This 'rustic stairwell' bypasses an
'entrance to the sitting room', which could only have been the room C5. If
there was such a stairwell, then it must have been superior to the first, which
could be found at the northern end of the Ballroom. Directly above the location of the first stairwell we find the southern wall C5. And here we have a
problem, for there is, apparently, no entrance to C5 at this location.

But all is not what it seems. My wife and I visited *The Grotto* on August
1 1999 and had another, closer look at C5 upstairs. At exactly the place

on the stone face where the entrance *should* have been the limestone has a rather odd look to it. On examination, Nick Garvey, Jackie and I suspected that there might have been an entrance there, but one that had later been blocked up and expertly hidden. As previously stated, directly opposite on the northern wall, the stone has a similarly peculiar appearance. Nick took out his pipe tamper and gently tapped the stonework. To our astonishment, there was a section of the wall that sounded distinctly hollow when tapped. The stone immediately around it was completely solid. Again, it appeared as if the hole had been blocked up and covered with a limestone paste to mask the fact that it had ever been there. Both of these hidden entrances could have given access to a third level of caves above, and we must conclude that it was this feature of the excavation which, although not begun by Sidney Milnes-Hawkes, was carried on by him. We will address the question of whether Hawkes actually found anything during his excavations presently.

Although Hawkes still wanted dearly to find the cache of treasure hidden in the caves, like Peter Allan before him his values seemed to alter to a degree when he actually moved into the place. This may have been due to his laid-back personality and easy-going nature. Aaron Watson [2] said of Hawkes:

> What Sidney Milnes-Hawkes bought was peace of mind. He had a most commanding natural indolence, though he could undergo great strain under emergencies. A more remarkable publican there can seldom have been. He himself was extremely abstemious except in the manner of cigars, and he had the manners of the highest type of old fashioned English gentleman. During Hawkes' time it became fashionable for eminent people visiting Newcastle to go down to Marsden for a sight of the landlord. He received them as a king might have done on some island of his own. Sometimes they returned in sad plight for, of course, they had to get to *The Grotto*, and the way there was a long path deep in mire. Mrs. Rousby, a very beautiful and famous actress of the day, came back without shoes on her feet - they had stuck inextricably in the tramped mud of the field.
>
> These visits enlivened the existence of the Hawkes family, no doubt. He himself was quite at home with visitors of every sort. In particular he seems to have had a talent for managing the miners. There were never any rows in his house. He was a master of the soft answer that turns away wrath; and the frequenters of *The Grotto* felt, no doubt, a strangely superior man. That quaint hostelry, hewn out of the rock, became a meeting place for kindred spirits interested in arts and literature and, oft times famous men from afar. They were always sure

of an intellectual treat, for the landlord himself was a fascinating conversationalist, and his life was crowded with romance and adventure.

Hawkes not only extended *The Grotto* into the cliff face, but also altered its interior by, as we have seen, creating strange apertures, recesses and interconnecting rooms from driftwood. The effect must have been startling and disorientating; giving the impression that one was exploring the interior of a huge ship. As the writer in Chambers' Journal stated, he 'could not ascend a step without grasping portions of masts or clinging to a port-hole, while figureheads met me at every turn.' It would, of course, have been very easy indeed to hide entrances and apertures in such a fairy-tale building.

But Sidney Milnes-Hawkes had a problem. Whereas Peter Allan had a natural energy that drove him forwards, ever achieving and ever making plans, Hawkes was lazy. Watson recalls[3]:

> As a businessman, I do not hesitate to state that he would have been a failure anywhere ... I once paid a fee to an eminent London medical man for a verdict on the condition of one of Hawkes' sons. "Your young friend," I was told, "has nothing the matter with him but laziness." It cost me a guinea for that opinion.

Like father like son, it seems. Although *The Grotto* seized Hawkes to a degree, it did not captivate him as it had his predecessor. After initially working on *The Grotto* with the help of local unemployed miners, and creating the most wonderful ambience which Peter Allan himself would have been proud of, Hawkes' enthusiasm began to wane ever so slightly. Watson also said of Hawkes[4], 'He was the actual journalist turned publican – not from any love of the thing that he dealt in either.'

Hawkes' inherent laziness, coupled with the fact that he was not a publican by nature, tells us that his efforts to keep *The Grotto* running as a lively business were motivated by outside factors. Sidney Milnes-Hawkes had simply wanted the treasure hidden in the cliffs. A sizeable amount for Mazzini and Garibaldi, and some for himself, of course.

Over the next few years, as well as excavating *The Grotto* further, Hawkes spent his time talking with the locals and 'putting the world to rights', as they say. The columnist 'Elfin', writing in *The Daily Chronicle*, described the way Hawkes idled his days[5]:

> I have very pleasant remembrances of many visits to the famous grotto [*sic*] during the time that Mr. Hawkes presided over it. Mr. Hawkes was, in his way,

just as famous and as widely respected as either of his predecessors [Blaster Jack and Peter Allan]. My first introduction to the genial and literary landlord was made through 'Jonathan Oldbuck' [the pen name of a fellow columnist, Weallands Robson] whose chief delight it was to drink a bottle of claret with the Hermit Hoar, as he styled Mr. Hawkes.

Elfin, Robson and Hawkes spent many happy hours together, both Robson and Hawkes entertaining the former with tales of Blaster Jack and Peter Allan.

We must remember that, by this time, Hawkes was not a wealthy man. His fortune had been dissipated by making huge donations to Garibaldi and by incessant gambling. He had divorced his first wife and remarried, and was, according to Watson, 'bringing up one of the largest families in the neighbourhood.'[6]

Watson also stated:

> He started life with means that would have kept him independent if he had not risked them in Mr. Stansfeld's business. Then some relative was always dying and leaving him money. The amount was never large; but it usually enabled him to have what he called a little flutter ... He had a scheme for breaking the bank – always a new scheme; and there was never one of the lot that enabled him to come home with money in his pocket.[7]

To be fair to Hawkes, he did have the odd stroke of luck that enabled him to win a few pounds, but this luck normally came in the fashion of betting tips given to him by his fellow gambler and wordsmith Weallands Robson.

Elfin also recalled how, whilst strolling along the beach at Marsden with Robson, the latter gave him a tip that a nag called Dutch Oven was a dead cert to win the St. Ledger that year. This conversation must have taken place early in 1882, for that was the only year in which Dutch Oven came first in that particular race.

Robson was altogether 'better at the horses' than Hawkes, and often made a tidy sum whilst Sidney just seemed to lose money hand over fist.

Hawkes' fortune was not just drained by his magnanimity towards Mazzini and Garibaldi, or because of his gambling. He was also, I believe, responsible for financing the building of the retaining walls and buttresses behind *The Grotto* to ensure that no further rock falls would seal off access to the treasure forever. At least one local historian has suggested to me that Hawkes was the 'likely' person to have funded the building project, and this would also explain why Hawkes' finances became so depleted.

But then, curiously, Hawkes' fortunes seem to have taken an upturn. In fact, there was a sudden and extraordinary change in his circumstances that is almost impossible to explain. In 1883, Hawkes suddenly decided to 'retire' to Bruges, where he said, "the gambling tables were not as far off as in England."

Aaron Watson [6] went to that city to visit him, and described Hawkes' surroundings as being, 'as agreeable as one could desire. He was the same, inexhaustibly pleasant companion as of old, full of anecdote, jest, reminiscence, and varied learning. No man could be more happy and contented.'

Suspicious, perhaps, of his old friend's sudden change of lifestyle, Watson queried Hawkes about his gambling habits. A snatch of the conversation is recorded in Watson's own book *The Folks Of Shields* [7]:

> Watson: "How is it that some men contrive to make a living out of the gaming tables?"
>
> Hawkes: "Oh that can be done with certainty if you are a cautious player, and if you have few needs, and a little capital to play with. I knew at Baden an old Colonel who lived on five francs a day, and always got his five francs from the gambling table. If you play on steadily there will always be some time of the day when you are the winner of five francs. Very well. When the Colonel had got his five francs he withdrew from the tables, running further risk. That required determination, of course; but it enabled him to live the life he loved, without exertion, in good surroundings, and always with pleasant interchange of society."

Hawkes was, of course, talking absolute and utter bunkum. A man who exists on five francs a day, and relies on having to make a profit of five francs every day at the gambling tables, only needs one bad day to wipe out his reserve. No gambler ever born has been lucky enough to come out on top every single day of his life. Even Hawkes conceded that such luck had to be enhanced by 'determination' and a degree of self-discipline, which would enable you to quit whilst you were ahead. The problem is that Hawkes, right throughout his life, never ever followed his own philosophy. He threw good money after bad and continually had to rely on inheritances from relations to survive. And further, what money he didn't gamble away he gave to Garibaldi and the Italian cause.

Wherever Hawkes gained his newfound wealth from, it was certainly not from gambling. So where did he get it? Personally I believe that during his excavations at *The Grotto*, he found what Peter Allan and others had searched for – the treasure (or a substantial part of it) hidden there by the Romans just before they fled from Arbeia. Of course, Hawkes wasn't the only one who had a stake in the excavations. We know that he had powerful allies such as Ingham, Wawn, Clay and Brockie. My suspicion is that Hawkes simply sold whatever he found and retired to Bruges on the proceeds, away from the prying eyes of his allies in South Shields. To my knowledge there is no direct documentary evidence to suggest that these friends of Hawkes were ever told whether he had discovered anything, and if so, what it was. However, I am not the first researcher to become suspicious of Sidney's sudden reversal of fortune.

On Friday, February 4 1966, David Jenkins published a full-page article in the *Shields Gazette* detailing the life of Milnes-Hawkes. In it he happened to make the following pertinent observation:

> A father of 14, his fortune was spent, and he drifted into journalism, preserving a keen interest both in the arts and education, and tried to provide the best for all his children. *This raises a strange contradiction*, for Mrs. James [Olive Emily James, Sidney's grand-daughter, who was still alive in 1966] tells me that her mother was sent to finishing school in France, to a Catholic establishment, when the Hawkes wealth had been expended in fighting the papal grip on a neighbouring country. [Emphasis mine]

Where on earth did Milnes-Hawkes suddenly get the money to send his daughter to finishing school and engage in other extravagances when the family was now almost penniless? Several other people also started to take an interest in Sidney's newfound wealth during his own lifetime. These were not his enemies, or even dispassionate researchers such as Jenkins and I. These people were his closest friends.

There is little doubt that the politicians in South Shields suspected something. Aaron Watson was certainly friendly with Hawkes and his associates. Indeed, he was probably Hawkes' closest companion. When Watson went to visit Hawkes in Bruges he was *really* on a mission do discover exactly where the retired money-courier, gunrunner and probable assassin had gained his new wealth from. Had Watson and the others suspected that Hawkes had cheated them, it is unlikely that they would have let the matter end there. As we know, however, Watson seems to have been convinced by the wily old journalist that Hawkes had indeed made his new fortune by altering his gambling techniques, and probably managed to convince the others of that as well.

In the latter years of his life Hawkes began to yearn for Britain. He eventually left his home in Bruges and went to live in Jersey. When he died, in July 1906, he left behind him a son, Mervyn, who was a reporter for a Wearside newspaper and a granddaughter who was a successful journalist in London.

## References

[1] *Chambers Journal*, September 1875.
[2] Watson, Aaron: *The Folks of Shields* (published privately by the author, date unknown). p. 5.
[3] *Ibid.* p. 6.
[4] *Ibid.* p. 6.
[5] *The Daily Chronicle, Tuesday 5 July 1887.*
[6] Watson, Aaron: *The Folks of Shields* (published privately by the author, date unknown). p. 11.
[7] *Ibid.* p. 12.

# CHAPTER 38

# THE SUCCESSORS OF SIDNEY MILNES-HAWKES

When Sidney Milnes-Hawkes retired to Bruges, he handed over *The Grotto* to one of his daughters. She was married to one Patrick 'Patsie' Gannon, a miner of Irish extraction who had helped Sidney excavate the inn further during his tenure there. The couple, it seems, kept the business going for a year or two and then sold it. It was during the 'reign' of Sidney Milnes-Hawkes that the entrances to the multitude of rooms and apertures were sealed, a situation that has not altered to this day. Sidney's daughter did not attempt to uncover them, so what does this tell us? The fact that Sidney Milnes-Hawkes covered up the 'secret' rooms of *The Grotto* and made them truly secret once again indicates that he had finished excavating in the cliff completely. This in itself indicates most strongly that he had found what he was searching for – the Roman treasure – and therefore stopped looking. Nevertheless, the fact is that the hidden rooms at *The Grotto* have been extremely well hidden, and finding them all, let alone exploring them, may not be an easy task.

In the succeeding years *The Grotto* passed through a succession of hands, few of which seem to have had any great competence. Watson tells us [1] that the splendid feasts of ham and eggs, singin' hinnies and cakes, which characterised *The Grotto* in earlier years were discontinued. They were, he relates, replaced by 'plain teas and pop'. One regular visitor to the inn, a miner by the name of Hann, remarked upon the "wild do's" and said that, "there was often *no limit* to the entertainment. People danced to the tune of the fiddle." [Emphasis mine]. One suspects that Hann was being discreet here, and we can only speculate on the reality behind his guarded words, although the late archaeologist Eve Waugh-Almond told me that during one period in the 1800s "*The Grotto* was little different to a brothel for a while."

Another local historian, who did not wish to be named, also commented: '*The Grotto* gained a terrible reputation for a while. They used to stand women on a wooden box at the end of the bar and auction them off to the highest bidder.'

By 1885, the lease had fallen to The Whitburn Coal Company. In 1891 the company got into difficulties, and a general meeting was called to discuss the situation on 23 June. Liquidators were appointed in the form of Lindsay Wood of Chester-le-Street and Robert Watson Cooper of Newcastle. After an extraordinary meeting of the directors, it was agreed to sell the business to the Harton Coal Company. The deal went through on July 1, 1891.

## WILLIAM "SEGAR" ROBINSON

By 1897 *The Grotto* was in dire straits. It had been allowed to degenerate to such a degree that in the winter months no one bothered visiting it and, once again, the inn was simply closed down until the summer returned. To try and rescue the situation, albeit belatedly, the Harton Coal Company installed a new manager in the person of James William Robinson. Robinson, incidentally, was the grandfather of Alan Robinson whose own work on Marsden Bay I have quoted from several times throughout this volume.

James Robinson was a tough stonemason who lived in the local area. He was born in 1859, the son of a foreman sinker who worked in a nearby pit. He was also an employee of the Harton Coal Company and well trusted. To his friends he was known as 'Segar', a nickname that apparently derived from the type of limestone he was an expert in working with. Like Peter Allan, the Robinsons were Scottish, having hailed from Dundee.

Robinson had a Herculean task ahead of him in trying to rescue the fortunes of *The Grotto*. Exactly to what degree he was successful we do not know, but we can state with confidence that he must have done something right, for just one year later the lease was purchased by Messrs. C. Vaux and Sons, Ltd., a local brewing company. They would not have done this unless Robinson had managed to turn the ailing pub around. At some point after this – we do not know exactly when – James Robinson and his family left *The Grotto* and the brewers put in their own manager.

But here we must draw attention to what seems to be an extraordinary coincidence. The reader will recall Catherine Cookson's aforementioned novel *Mrs. Flannagan's trumpet* [2], in which she mentioned a stonemason who lived at 'Rock End' the fictional house that really paralleled *The Grotto Inn*:

As I've said me grandfather was a stonemason, he could make two pieces of stone meet as if they'd never been split. He could make a stone swivel like an oiled hinge. They worked every spare minute they had on the house for three years. People came out and had a look at it. "What thick walls you are building!" they said, "But you'll need them with the sea at your door." "What's those long narrow rooms on the end for?" they said. "Oh, they're going to be a couple of storerooms and a water closet."

We have already discussed the fact that the hidden rooms at Rock End actually parallel *The Grotto*, but what of the stonemason? Was he purely an invention of Catherine Cookson's creative genius, or did she base him on a real-life character? It is curious that the grandfather, who gains only scant mention in the novel, is explicitly stated to have been able to 'make a stone swivel like an oiled hinge'. What on earth could Dame Catherine have meant? She was obviously talking about a hinged door of some kind, which was made of stone and yet easy to move. I believe that there is a distinct possibility that this fictional moving stone door had a real-life counterpart, and that the writer of Ramble to Marsden Rocks mentioned the real door:

Leaving the bar, we penetrated a side-door to an inner room, in which a large, limestone slab was shown, measuring, as we supposed, about five feet long by three feet broad, and five inches thick. The upper surface has been polished, and exhibits wavy lines like watered silk: The under part is in its native state, and very smooth: the edges being cellular, and resembling open lace work. As a thick pillar interrupts the light from the outer room, you should examine this curious production of nature by a candle.

This aforementioned limestone slab was, I believe, the one that was found in the 'Inner Room' which itself could be accessed in the centre of C2.

But what of the man who constructed it? I believe that the stonemason who maintained the *real* limestone door, which led to the ancient tunnel complex –or at least 'made it swivel', was none other than the young James Robinson himself. I further believe that Catherine Cookson based her stonemason character in *Mrs. Flannagan's Trumpet* on no other personage than James Robinson.

Robinson was 'an expert stonemason and cutter', and we know that, from a young age, he actually drank at *The Grotto*. But there's more. Segar Robinson was installed as a manager at the inn to 'turn it around' and make it into a decent hostelry once again, but the owners of *The Marsden Grotto* also wanted Segar Robinson to take over the inn because of his legendary abilities as a stonemason. They wanted him in to expand *The Grotto* and to enlarge the already complex network of caverns.

As if *The Grotto* wasn't big enough, then, the Harton Coal Company, which owned it, apparently wanted to make it bigger! My suspicion is that the Harton Coal Company may well have known what was hidden in the caves at Marsden, and installed the expert stonecutter Robinson as manager to find it. There may be an indication here that Jack the Blaster, Peter Allan and Sidney Milnes-Hawkes may not have found all of the Roman treasure hoards at all. Some of it may still have been there in 'Segar' Robinson's time, and may still be hidden in the cliffs to this day.

## Roll Out the Barrels

One of the bizarre aspects to life at *The Grotto* was that a veritable mountain of beer and brandy barrels was slowly crowding out the tenants and visitors. Brewers were quite happy to deliver their wares to *The Grotto*, but couldn't be bothered to pick up the empty containers as getting them from the inn to the cliff top was just too much hard work. When Vaux and Co. took over the pub in 1898 they found literally thousands of barrels stored in piles along the beach in amongst the wrecks and in the caves. As previously mentioned, Alan Robinson told me how, as a boy, he and his brother had found a cave filled with barrels which had been covered over with boulders.

Vaux solved the problem by employing some labourers to collect all the 'empties' and place them on the beach near the water's edge. They then simply floated them out on an ebb tide and watched them disappear. Herbert Iverson, a resident of Marsden at the time, remarked. "It was the strangest thing I ever did see. There were barrels, barrels, barrels as far as your eye could see. The whole sea just looked like it was made of barrels."

## Smugglers Cave Claims Another Victim

In 1912 a curious incident occurred [3] that indicates that other parties were possibly interested in appropriating treasure hidden in the caves. A man – whose name I have not been able to discover – apparently tried to lower himself down the vertical shaft which led from the cliff top to the Hairy Man's Cave at Velvet Beds. The rope snapped, seemingly, causing the man to fall to his death in the cave below.

Why on earth anyone would wish to attempt such a dangerous exercise without good cause is a mystery. Of course, the unfortunate explorer may well have had good cause. Perhaps he was looking for interconnecting horizontal passages, which led off from the vertical one. *Perhaps he was looking for something hidden in the cliff.*

## WATCH OUT FOR THE HUNS

During the 1914–18 war, the authorities decided that the steps which had been cut into the cliff by Blaster Jack were dangerous, in as much as they would provide easy access for 'the Hun' from the beach to the cliff top should he ever invade England. Subsequently they were removed, and not replaced till after the war was over. How access was gained to *The Grotto* during this period is a mystery that I have not been able to solve, unless visitors descended to the shore at Velvet Beds to the north and walked along to the inn by way of the beach.

## SUICIDES AND SHIPWRECKS

By the 1920s a disturbing trend had manifested itself at Marsden Bay. A steady rise in the number of people committing suicide by jumping over the cliffs was causing great consternation. This, coupled with the regular number of bodies still being washed ashore – they were usually the unfortunate victims of shipwrecks or boating accidents – necessitated that the managers of *The Grotto* during that time did an early morning 'body check' along the coastline. Extraordinarily, a makeshift mortuary was erected on the sands next to the inn and in front of the Ballroom. On a regular basis the corpses of these unfortunates were placed in the mortuary (known as 'Black Hut') until the authorities could retrieve them.

One evening in 1923, one of the regular drinkers in the pub – 59 year-old Jack Bellas – had imbibed to slight excess and decided that the ascent up Blaster Jack's stairs was too much to face. Jack had drunk at *The Grotto* for over forty years, and was well loved by all who knew him. Finding a doorway adjacent to the pub he crept inside and found what seemed to be a bed. There he lay, in pitch darkness, contentedly sleeping off the effects of the alcohol.

The following morning Jack awoke, and was somewhat surprised to find that another drinker had apparently had the same idea. Unbeknown to Jack he'd actually shared his 'bed' with the other chap during the night. Surprise turned to terror, however, when Jack took a closer look at his 'fellow drinker' and discovered that he had actually spent the night sleeping beside the corpse of a 6' 2" Norwegian sailor who had apparently perished in a marine accident the day before.

One Vaux publication [4] states that there were 'dozens of sailors' bodies constantly being washed up on the beach'. The same publication also mentions the roaring trade that the undertakers did at that time.

During the early 1930s the inn was managed by a lady whose name was Broomfield. Only vague oral legends survive regarding her tenure at *The Grotto*, all of which suggest that she was extremely likeable and "something of a character". Some of her descendants still reside in Sunderland, and one related to me how, when she died, his father and other relatives had to carry her coffin up Blaster Jack's stairs to the cliff top for transportation to the church. "They were exhausted by the time they got to the top", he told me.

In 1938 Vaux and Co. bought *The Grotto* outright. The following year they bought the land at the top of the cliff. The company then spent the (then) colossal sum of £12,000 in refurbishing the entire premises. The main alteration was the addition of the Copenhagen Room or Front Bar, which extended the front of *The Grotto* towards the coast by a further twenty feet. Above the new frontage another room was added, this becoming the new restaurant. Although Peter Allan would have been delighted, no doubt, at the extension and enlargement of *The Grotto* to its present size, I cannot think he would have been happy with the architectural style. The extension reeked of 1930s modernism, and it would take a creative genius to remodel it externally so that it regained something of the character of the old inn. Nevertheless, the fortunes of the pub steadily revived. My aunt and uncle, Valerie and Ian Robinson, held their wedding reception in *The Grotto* in the 1950's, and eventually it became *the* place to dine and socialise.

Periodically, Vaux and Co. would release booklets promoting *The Grotto* and its mysterious past. The company repeatedly emphasised how they had made every effort to retain the original spirit and character of the inn. Much as I appreciate the help that Vaux gave me in my research, I am afraid I must take issue with them on this point.

During the period 1960–1996 the brewery refitted *The Grotto* several times. The restaurant was 'updated' to cater for a more youthful clientele, and a toilet adapted for people with disabilities was installed on the ground floor. During the period of renovation the natural stone walls of the inn were covered with heavy tarpaulins and facing boards to prevent damage.

*Where do the shadows brighter sleep,*
*Than on thy calm unruffled deep,*
*When each sail stretched to catch the breeze,*
*Unnumbered vessels stud thy seas?*

*Sweet Marsden! Near thee let me stray,*
*With heart light as thy wild waves spray;*
*Or seated in thy sheltering caves,*
*List to the murmur of thy waves.*
*And let me muse as I gaze around,*
*And think that numbers have tread this ground;*
*Numbers, that Time with ruthless sway,*
*Has like the ephemera swept away.*

*Many who gaily pac'd this shore,*
*Sleep now alas! To wake no more;*
*Yet still each year fresh guests are seen,*
*To frolic in this charming scene.*

*So mortals, flourish and decline,*
*Whilst thou, bold rock, still mocks at Time!*
*Unchanged – thou still remains to me,*
*An emblem of Eternity.*

The above poem was written in 1813. The author, obviously a resident of the South Tyneside area, is unknown to us.

# CHAPTER 40

# TREASURE TROVE

Many, many generations ago the Roman legionnaires were forced to leave Arbeia. They were faced with a stark choice; take their valuables with them and run the risk of the indigenous inhabitants stealing them, or hide them in a place where they could be retrieved later. It is my firm belief that they plumped for the later option. Sadly, they never did come back.

For the better part of two millennia, whatever the Romans deposited in the cave network at Marsden Bay lay undisturbed. A succession of individuals, including Blaster Jack, Peter Allan, Sidney Milnes-Hawkes and even the enigmatic Hairy Man, all searched for Caesar's gold. Some found nothing, others a little, and some may have found much indeed.

From time to time reports come in of precious artefacts being found in the caves. A gold goblet was reputedly found in a cavern at Marsden called Faeries' Cave. According to legend it now resides in a locked cabinet at Durham Cathedral. It is likely that, hidden deep in the cliff face, more treasure still waits to be found. Alas, the dangerous and unstable condition of the cliffs make searching for it an extremely hazardous task indeed. No one should explore the caves at Marsden Bay without expert guidance and proper permission.

A vast network of caves and tunnels lies both behind and beneath the inn known as *The Marsden Grotto*. Within that complex of apertures lie undiscovered secrets.

The true story of the treasure hidden at Marsden Bay is not yet over. Between our ignorance and the staggering truth is a quaint old pub built into a cliff beside the sea.

Welcome to the twilit world of the treasure hunter.

Welcome to the house that Jack built.